The Supreme Court in American Politics

((The Supreme Court in American Politics))

New Institutionalist Interpretations

Editors

Howard Gillman
Cornell Clayton

University Press of Kansas

The Supreme Court in
American politics

© 1999 by the University Press of Kansas

Published by the University Press of Kansas (Lawrence, Kansas 66049), which was
organized by the Kansas Board of Regents and is operated and funded by Emporia
State University, Fort Hays State University, Kansas State University, Pittsburg State
University, the University of Kansas, and Wichita State University

Library of Congress Cataloging-in-Publication Data

The Supreme Court in American politics : new institutionalist
    interpretations / edited by Howard Gillman, Cornell Clayton.
        p.   cm.
    Includes bibliographical references and index.
      ISBN 0-7006-0975-X (cloth : alk. paper). —ISBN 0-7006-0976-8
    (pbk. : alk. paper)
        1. United States. Supreme Court—Decision making.   2. Judicial
    review—United States.   3. Law and politics.   I. Gillman, Howard.
    II. Clayton, Cornell W., 1960–   .
    KF8748.S879   1999
    347.73'26—dc21   99-21885

British Library Cataloguing in Publication Data is available.

Printed in the United States of America

10 9 8 7 6 5 4 3 2 1

The paper used in this publication meets the minimum requirements of
the American National Standard for Permanence of Paper for Printed Library
Materials Z39.48-1984.

CONTENTS

ACKNOWLEDGMENTS

First, we must acknowledge the wonderful work of our contributing authors, as well as their conscientiousness and good cheer, as we worked to bring this book to fruition. As a group we represent a variety of competing methodological and theoretical perspectives, but we hold in common a belief that there are important things to study about the Supreme Court other than the voting behavior of the justices.

Over the years our commitment to this principle has been inspired and fortified by some friends and colleagues who did not contribute to this volume but who have otherwise contributed to our collective understanding of the Supreme Court. We have benefited enormously from the work of Sue Davis, Steve Griffin, Christine Harrington, Sandy Levinson, David O'Brien, H. W. Perry, Rogers Smith, and Keith Whittington. Some of our other intellectual debts should be evident in the essays we wrote for this book.

Michael Briggs, from the University Press of Kansas, has been a terrific editor, and we are grateful for his support at each stage of the process. Melinda Wirkus kept things moving efficiently through the production process, and we appreciate all her help. We also benefited from the thoughtful and careful advice offered by the reviewers of the manuscript.

We appreciate the institutional support we received from the chairs of our departments, Sheldon Kamieniecki (USC) and Lance LeLoup (WSU). Lisa Janowski (at WSU) and Randa Issa (at USC) provided invaluable assistance in assembling and completing the various pieces of the manuscript.

Finally, Cornell extends his deepest gratitude to his wonderful children, Katherine and Nicholas, who more than once saved his sanity with sweet distractions. Howard is most grateful for the love and support of wife Ellen and his children Arielle and Danny, who (as he writes this) are waiting for dad to finish, killing time by conjuring up exciting tall tales about almost everything except the Supreme Court.

The Supreme Court in American Politics

Chapter 1

Introduction

Cornell Clayton
Howard Gillman

Beyond Judicial Decision Making

For many political scientists, studying the Supreme Court means studying judicial behavior. This level of inquiry tends to focus on the backgrounds, attitudes, and ideological preferences of individual justices rather than on the nature of the Court as an institution and its significance for the political system. The exemplar of this approach, the so-called "attitudinal model," posits that the Court's decisions reflect the individual attitudes or worldviews of the justices who inhabit it at any given time. This approach to judicial politics, pioneered by the work of C. Herman Pritchett (1948) and developed in the writings of scholars such as Glendon Schubert, Herbert Jacob, David Danelski, Sidney Ulmer, and most recently in the work of Jeffrey Segal and Harold Spaeth (1993), tends to treat courts in general, and the Supreme Court in particular, as little more than organizational shells within which judges act according to their individual, predetermined preferences. The goal of such research is to demonstrate that justices with different values vote differently and that changes in the Court's decisions can be traced to changes in its personnel.

Despite the success that behavioral scholarship has achieved in modeling decisional outcomes in the Supreme Court, it is clear that there are important questions left unanswered by narrowly focusing on how particular justices vote in discrete cases and Guttman-type scaling of judicial attitudes. Among these is the question of *why*, and not just *how*, justices vote the way they do. Even if it is true that justices' votes in particular cases correspond with their ideological preferences, one cannot conclude from this that they are simply behaving like other political actors. For example, justices who vote to strike down state laws restricting abortions may do so because they believe that as a matter of sound policy or partisan loyalty women should be able to obtain abortion services; or alternatively they may do so because they actually believe the Constitution or some other fundamental principle of law requires the protection of a woman's individual right. While the latter would be consistent (at least in the mind of the justice) with traditional conceptions of the rule of law, the former would not. In either case, it is only with reference to the goals and motivations of the justices, not just to their votes, that we can explore some of the characteristics of the Court as an institution and its relationship to larger political structures.

Scholars seeking to explore the broader cultural and political contexts of judicial decision making are thus examining how judicial attitudes are themselves constituted and structured by the Court *as an institution* and by its relationship to other institutions in the political system at particular points in history. This more "interpretive" approach to studying the Supreme Court, relying on historical and ethnographic analyses, is not only useful in examining judicial decision making, but it can also be used to examine the impact that the Court has on other political and social structures. In this sense, social scientists may find themselves in a much better position to understand the full range of "judicial politics" if they move beyond the question of how individual justices promote their preferences and toward an exploration of the role that the Court plays in maintaining or disrupting major political, social, and economic structures and processes.

Supreme Court Politics and the New Institutionalism

Many of these larger questions were routinely considered by prebehavioralist scholars of Supreme Court politics, such as Edward S. Corwin (1934), Charles Grove Haines (1922), Robert E. Cushman (1925), and Thomas Reed Powell (1918). Among other aspects, these scholars were interested in examining how judicial commitments and attachments to doctrinal norms shaped judicial decision making and how those norms were themselves sensitive to larger political contexts such as class relations, ideological conflict, and state development. In the words of Cushman, "The Supreme Court does not do its work in a vacuum. Its decisions on important constitutional questions can be understood in their full significance only when viewed against the background of history, politics, economics, and personality surrounding them and out of which they grew" (1925, 2).

Even in the midst of the behavioral revolution sweeping the discipline after the 1950s, political scientists such as Robert McCloskey and William

Beaney continued to focus their research on doctrinal development and legal forms in order to explain how judges reached particular decisions. Prominent scholars such as Robert Dahl and Martin Shapiro also continued to show how Court doctrines were related to historically conditional features of American politics, including partisan control of Congress and the presidency and the agendas and institutions associated with the New Deal regime (Dahl 1957; M. Shapiro 1968). More recently, political scientists studying comparative judicial politics have also begun focusing on the role that courts play in the way power is organized and exercised in particular political systems, as well as on the relationship between judicial power and larger elements of political culture (Kommers 1989; Stone 1992; Stetson 1982).

Still, the behavioralist emphasis on decision making continues to shape research agendas in the field. Even a cursory review of the mainstream journals in political science demonstrates the continuing dominance of the behavioral paradigm in the published research, and even scholars who do not choose to use behavioralist methods will often focus on the constituent elements of judicial decision making rather than on questions associated with a broader conception of judicial politics. There is of course truth to the frequently repeated sentiment that scholarship in the field represents a commitment to "a healthy pluralism" (Sarat 1983) or to "let a hundred flowers bloom" (Pritchett 1968; Stumpf 1983). Nevertheless, there continues to be a latent hostility to new modes of research and an instinctive suspicion that deviation from behavioral methods and questions represents, in the words of Martin Shapiro, a return to the bad old days of "old-fashioned constitutional law among political scientists—that mixture of doctrinal manipulation, literary criticism, selective history and seat of the pants policy analysis" (Shapiro 1983).

It is hardly novel to suggest that in scholarship, as in other human endeavors, change transpires from one generation to the next, as each new generation of scholars seeks to define themselves against the dominant views and attitudes of their predecessors. This may explain why in recent years we have seen in the social sciences generally a renewed interest in studying how political behavior is influenced by institutional arrangements and relationships (March and Olsen 1989; Powell and DiMaggio 1991; Steinmo, Thelen, and Longstreth 1992; Robertson 1993; Koelble 1995). This research has recently begun to make its mark on public law scholarship as well (Clayton and Gillman 1999, R. Smith 1988).

Like traditional, prebehavioral legal studies, the new work takes seriously the effects on judicial decision making of judicial norms and legal traditions and also attempts to situate the Court in larger political and social contexts. In this sense, the work rejects the assumption made by both attitudinal and rational choice approaches that judicial behavior is motivated primarily by the justices' policy preferences. The new work instead seeks to understand legal and judicial institutions as independent variables that both constitute and constrain judicial attitudes and motivations. Furthermore, this new research resists the behavioral tendency to reduce courts to individual, quantifiable units of analysis and instead seeks to emphasize the cognitive structures that attach courts and judges in general to culture and society.

None of this departs radically from more traditional institutional analyses of law and courts, and much can be lost by obscuring the continuity of the "new" with the "old." Nevertheless, the "new institutionalism" does proceed in some innovative ways and adopts slightly different analytic emphases from earlier institutional approaches. To begin with, much of the new work tends to focus on modes and forms of justification and legitimization as a driving force behind judicial activity. In this sense, legitimization is viewed as an organizational imperative for courts, serving both as a source of judicial inertia and a requirement for justification of particular judicial decisions and practices. Justification in turn compels courts to be highly sensitive and adaptive to their professional, cultural, economic, and social contexts. To this extent, new institutionalists tend to see doctrinal innovation as a product of more organic and structural political processes rather than as the function of formal institutional mechanisms such as the judicial selection process or political acts of noncompliance alone.

Related to this view is the tendency in much of the new research to focus less on formal offices, doctrines, and structures, as was the preoccupation with traditional legal scholarship, and more on informal norms, practices, attitudes, and myths. In this sense the formal institutional structures that constitute courts, that is to say their "official" procedures and legal doctrines, are themselves understood as created within a framework of culture and constraint. The research is sensitive to the fact that the interaction between courts and culture is always mediated by the socially constructed mind; and thus judicial activity is not merely influenced by, but is inseparable from, the web of social patterns of cognition and evaluation (including race, class, and gender) that situates all political activity.

Like their traditional counterparts, those scholars engaged in this new work are also less fastidious about maintaining barriers between normative and empirical inquiry, a pattern that was a hallmark of much behavioral research. At its core, the process of institutionalization is the infusion of certain processes, functions, and forms with value beyond what is technically required by the task at hand (Selznick 1996). Because this research approaches the topic of Supreme Court politics as "if politics matters" (R. Smith 1992), it often doubles as both a description and a critique of norms and traditions that are believed to have either fortunate or unfortunate consequences for judicial behavior. Here it parallels the direction of much of the work in normative jurisprudence by faculty in law schools, work that increasingly conceptualizes legal doctrines either as a form of normative political philosophy (Fiss 1982; Tribe 1987; Dworkin 1986) or in a critical fashion as political ideology that rationalizes unequal power relations (Kairys 1982). Moreover, by broadening the scope of inquiry to include features of judicial activity besides votes on cases, this scholarship holds out the promise of making research more relevant to the issues commonly addressed in the classroom and thus may help close the gap that has emerged between teaching and research in the field of public law.

In this book we hope to provide a collection of some of the best work written by ethnographic and historical scholars who are interested in focusing attention on how the distinct institutional characteristics of the Supreme Court, and their relationship to other features of the political system and to social and cultural structures generally, are essential to an adequate understanding of Supreme Court politics. The essays are ethnographic in that their primary concern is the role that institutional structures play in motivating and giving direction to judicial behavior through conditioning the judicial mind to a sense of what is appropriate for a judge, proper for a court, or normatively justifiable as a matter of law. They are historical in the sense that they recognize the contingent nature of these structures and attempt to explain their development over time.

We begin in Part I with authors who examine the origin and development of institutional norms specific to the Supreme Court, such as its procedures for selecting and deciding cases, and the Court's relationship to distinctive rights and polity-based doctrines, such as the doctrine of judicial review. The emphasis in these chapters is how the law interacts with distinctive habits of the judicial mind in order to shape judicial behavior and decisions.

To begin, John Brigham in chapter 2 examines the very idea of "judicial" norms and the way they constitute the Court. Brigham argues that what makes something recognizable as a court, as opposed to another institution such as the presidency, is the existence of a set of distinctive norms and characteristics that gives its members unique goals and motivations. But he argues that *how* we know institutions, not just *what* we know about them, is definitive. There are many different ways of knowing the Supreme Court; for example, one might know it through its physical attributes, like the architecture of its building, or one might know it by studying the attitudes of the justices or the political struggles inside the Court, or one might analyze the cases it has decided, or rules it has promulgated. But the Court, Brigham argues, is not simply robes and marble or codes and documents; rather, it is best described as a common set of practices, each of which has socially constructed meaning. In this sense, the Supreme Court is constituted by the interpretive community that is familiar with its practices and their commonly accepted meaning. Brigham describes this "community in law" and how it animates and gives life to the Court's institutional norms and practices.

In chapter 3, Mark Graber examines the origin and development of a specific legal institution: judicial review. Graber argues that contemporary debate over the Court's exercise of judicial review often ignores the historical context that conditioned the origin and development of that practice. In particular, he explores how that contemporary doctrine, which implies not just the authority to interpret the Constitution but also the supremacy of judicial interpretation, became institutionalized after *Marbury* (1803). He argues that the Court put the doctrine on a more concrete political foundation only after 1809, when its decisions began to serve important interests of the dominant political regime. In this sense, the power of judicial review was from the beginning neither the countermajoritarian check on regime power discussed in contemporary constitutional theory (i.e., Bickel 1962), nor was it simply a means for extending regime power as suggested by writing in political science (Dahl 1957; M. Shapiro 1981).

In the final chapter of Part I, Ronald Kahn examines one of the most perplexing questions for institutional scholarship: explaining institutional change. If legal institutions such as rights and polity principles shape and constrain judicial attitudes and behavior, how is it that legal principles or doctrines change over time? Kahn argues that doctrinal change takes place when existing legal norms or value structures are examined in light of new social facts. For example, the "separate but equal doctrine" enunciated in *Plessy v. Ferguson* (1896) was discarded by the Court in *Brown v. Board of Education* (1954) when the justices evaluated the constitutional commitment to equality in light of new data about the social-psychological consequences of state-enforced segregation. Kahn emphasizes that the mere existence of new empirical facts or data about social relations is not enough in itself to lead to doctrinal change; rather, the justices must be convinced that such facts are relevant to existing normative frameworks that give them legal meaning or precedential value. Once the justices are so convinced, however, social facts have the ability to alter the legal structures and frameworks themselves. The Court is therefore always at the center of the symbiotic relationship between legal institutions and broader social and cultural changes.

In Part II we turn from the question of the Court's relationship to various legal and judicial institutions to the question of how the Court is situated within the broader political system and its relationship to politics. The justices' sense of their power, authority, and responsibility is certainly different today from what it was in the 1790s, and much of this difference is linked to an evolving conception of the role and power of the state generally. Likewise, the Court's adherence to, and application of, particular doctrines or principles will have varying effects over time and in different political contexts (for example, the application of a particular view of presidential authority has different ramifications during periods of divided government than when the two branches are unified). Thus, the authors in this section seek to situate and contextualize the Court, its role, functions, and decisions within the historical development of other institutions and movements that constitute American political life.

Michael McCann begins this discussion with an expansive and thoughtful chapter on how the Court matters to politics. Like other contributors to this book, McCann recognizes that the Court impacts politics both in "strategic" and "constitutive" ways. Considered from a strategic perspective, the Court's actions and decisions communicate discrete signals about institutional opportunities, resources, and constraints to political actors. From a constitutive perspective, the Court's "policing" of official legal meanings, practices, and symbols contributes to the construction of shared cultural understandings about how society is organized and what are appropriate or inappropriate goals and expectations for political action. Using historical examples of the Court's involvement in issues ranging from abortion and racial equality to government regulation of economic activity, McCann examines the ways in which these two "political" roles for the Court interact and are inherently connected in actual social practice. He concludes the chapter by calling for more efforts to integrate and synthesize both strategic and constitutive dimensions of analysis as well as for greater attention to the question of the Court's role in sustaining systemic hegemony through its constitutive power in our culture.

In chapter 6, John Gates explores the relationship between the Court and the political party system in the United States. He argues that in addition to provoking and contravening partisan change during historical periods of electoral realignment, the Court plays an important role in the party system during more conventional or less transformational periods. In particular, Gates suggests that the Court's recent decisions involving abortion acted to diffuse partisan conflict and thus may have helped blunt a major political realignment.

Kevin McGuire examines the Supreme Court's relationship to the lawyers and counsel who practice before it. Unlike Congress and the executive, each of which is enabled to fulfill their missions with the assistance of large bureaucracies, the Court has only a modest staff and is institutionally dependent upon outsiders to provide it with information and analysis to support its policy making. McGuire argues that the Supreme Court has historically relied on the Washington bar community to provide it with reliable information and the legal frameworks and justifications for its decisions. From the office of the solicitor general, who represents the federal government in litigation before the High Court, to boutique-style private law firms that specialize in Supreme Court litigation, the elite bar enjoys high levels of success before the Supreme Court, not only because of the importance of the interests they represent but also because of the Court's institutional dependency on them.

In chapter 8, Mark Silverstein examines how changes in the American political system since the 1960s have transformed the process for selecting justices. Political polarization, divided control of the legislative and executive branches, the emergence of a more fragmented Senate, and the intervention of a growing number of interest groups in the confirmation process have combined to transform the appointment of justices to the Supreme Court. Considered from an institutional and historical perspective, the modern confirmation process leaves presidents with little room for appointing to the Court nominees with national stature or broad political experience. What was once a presidential asset, the power to appoint justices, has increasingly become a political liability. The consequence, Silverstein argues, will be a less activist and less political Supreme Court, as presidents are forced to appoint cautious, centrist jurists who accept a limited role for the federal judiciary.

In Part III we examine Supreme Court agenda setting and decision making in context. After all, the Court arose from a particular cultural and political milieu, and both by design and accident it will make a particular kind of contribution to the community of which it is part. The authors of this section seek to explain how the Court's decision making in particular areas of law or periods of time is both influenced by, and influences, the complex web of political attachments and social relations within which it is embedded, including the general patterns of conflict and consensus generated by specific political alignments and cultural, professional, or class frameworks; the relationship between the Court's decisions in particular areas of law and the beliefs and interests of key constituencies or classes; and the ability or inability of key opposition groups or classes to develop the motivation or power to oppose the Court.

Cornell Clayton begins this discussion with an analysis of the constitutional decision making of the Rehnquist Court. Clayton argues that two historical developments, one legal and the other political, have altered the norms that govern decision making by the modern Court. First, the destabilization of the party system and the changing confirmation process over the past thirty years have produced three distinct ideological blocs on the Court and made it virtually impossible for contemporary presidents to alter radically its direction. At the same time, these ideological blocs are further crosscut by jurisprudential cleavages whose roots are found in the legal realism of the 1930s and the collapse of a consensual approach to constitutional interpretation. The result, Clayton argues, is a Court that is simultaneously more fragmented and more pragmatic. The Rehnquist Court has been unable either to expand boldly or abandon established constitutional rights and doctrines, and its retrenchment of constitutional law has been marked by a dramatic rise in splintered opinions and an unwillingness to discuss substantive values or to articulate defining principles.

In chapter 10, Leslie Friedman Goldstein examines the strategic role that the Court played in shaping gender policy between 1974 and 1994. She begins by charting the Court's constitutionalization of the right to reproductive freedom between 1965 and 1977 and the eventual cessation of dramatic policy innovations in this area after the late 1970s. By contrast, the Court's agenda in gender equity included a similar period of constitutionalization of rights between 1971 and 1982 but then moved into a second phase of development with the Court using a dynamic approach to statutory interpretation. Goldstein explains the difference between these two areas in the Court's policy-making agenda by examining a number of institutional factors, including the flow of litigation, the Court's interaction with Congress, judicial beliefs about the proper judicial role, and judicially produced legal doctrines.

Susan Burgess's thought-provoking chapter explores the possibilities for developing a "queer new institutional" approach to understanding the Court and constitutional theory. After discussing the common claims of queer theory and new institutionalism, she suggests a hybrid approach. Using the Court's decision in *Griswold v. Connecticut* (1965) and Herbert Wechsler's famous theory of "neutral principles" as case studies, Burgess suggests that such a hybrid approach holds great promise for understanding the structure and limitations of mainstream constitutional theory and constitutional law, particularly regarding the central problem of finding an "objective" standard of constitutional interpretation upon which the Court can ground and justify its exercise of judicial review.

In chapter 12, Keith Bybee examines the broader frameworks of race and representation that situate the Court's decisions involving legislative redistricting. In particular, Bybee considers the theory of representation that undergirds the Court's decisions in the line of cases leading to, and following, *Shaw v. Reno* (1993). He argues that the Court's opposition to majority-minority districts depends upon a particular conception of political identity that is closely tied to interest-group pluralism. After contrasting this theory with representational alternatives that the Court rejected, he concludes by evaluating this theory against the representative role that the judiciary plays in the American political system.

In chapter 13 Howard Gillman encourages new institutionalist scholars to examine the ways in which modern Supreme Court politics is related to the historical development of American capitalism. He notes that although it is commonplace for scholars to specify links between the Court and capitalism in the periods before the New Deal, it is also widely assumed that as the Court shifted its agenda away from issues of economic liberty and market regulation, the relevance of capitalism as an explanatory variable decreased. Gillman urges a reconsideration of this assumption by discussing some of the ways in which contemporary capitalism shapes or constitutes post–New Deal Supreme Court decision making in a number of areas, including those that may seem only distantly related to capitalism, such as modern civil rights and civil liberties jurisprudence.

Gillman ends his discussion of the Court's relationship to capitalism by noting that "the question of what features of the Court's context deserve to be placed in the foreground of an analysis depends ultimately on the ability of researchers to demonstrate that we are in a better position to understand certain aspects of Supreme Court politics if we pay more attention to heretofore neglected or underappreciated structural variables." Each of the chapters in this book is premised on the assumption that there is still much to be learned by paying attention to the various contexts within which the justices exercise their power, whether those contexts are law and legal doctrine; the structures of power that make up the political regime or the state; or social structures such as race, class, and gender. Progress is already being made with the rise of new institutionalist studies of the Court, and it is our hope that this book helps expand the range of contexts and methods considered useful, persuasive, illuminating, or provocative in understanding Supreme Court politics.

Part I

Legal Norms and the Historical Development
of Supreme Court Politics

Chapter 2

The Constitution of the Supreme Court

John Brigham

Constituting the Court

In America, the Supreme Court's Marble Temple behind the Capitol sym-bolizes finality in the law.[1] When robed men and women announce opin-ions from this building, those opinions have authority derived from the Court and the place of that institution in public life. Like Justice Potter Stewart's response in another context, Americans feel they know the Su-preme Court when they see it, but we have trouble when we try to say what this institution is. Institutions, ignored for a time by social scientists, are receiving more reflective attention than scholars had been giving them a decade ago.

Though many Americans would recognize the Court if they were shown a picture of the building in Washington, DC, few would be able to distin-guish the building from similar neoclassical temples in the United States, like the New York Stock Exchange. Similarly, although their place in a jurisprudence of the First Amendment is little known, phrases such as "clear and present danger" are quite familiar. Knowledge of this sort constitutes the institution in the culture.

Today, much Court commentary claims insider access, and the views of insiders can be instructive. I once had occasion to talk with an intern at the Court about the value of access. We discussed what might be gained from being on the inside and, conversely, what one risked losing. In a spirited defense of the insider perspective, this young woman claimed that the advantage in getting behind the scenes was that one could never teach con-stitutional law with a "straight face" again. She argued that the reality of the chief justice wearing his slippers inside the Court demystified the Constitu-tion. Insiders present the Supreme Court through the perspective of realism as if this were a new discovery. But a political view of judging has become the orthodoxy, and the authoritative foundation of law has shifted. This new orthodoxy, is an institutional reality. On the inside, and to an increasing extent on the outside, political explanations have become a nearly sufficient basis for the authority of the Supreme Court. The surprise is not that the Court is political but that we appear to accept politics as an adequate basis for the Court's authority. The story of this institution is more than a synthesis of personality traits and individual interests.

The challenge is to provide insight into the Supreme Court through a perspective that transcends investigative journalism and resists excessive identification with the institution. The Court as a political institution dominates commentary on it that has ranged from muckraking exposé, like *The Brethren*, to fawning iconography, like Fred Friendly's *The Constitution: That Delicate Balance*. The authors of *The Brethren*, Bob Woodward and Scott Armstrong, produced a vivid picture, yet they merely intensified a view of judges as political actors. The glimpse inside not only sold millions of copies of their book, but it eventually left the inside even more guarded, as Chief Justice Warren Burger reacted against the "intrusion" of journalists. Friendly, a self-described "salesman for the Constitution," developed his book from material produced for television. It settled some nerves jarred by *The Brethren* in its engaging portrayal of what the Supreme Court does while its attention to detail did not intrude on the protected inner space behind the Purple Curtain. Both books contribute to the cult surrounding the institution and both depend on it.

For more than one academic generation, or for over thirty years, social research on courts and law has been grounded in political jurisprudence (M. Shapiro 1964). Whether the subject has been judicial interpretation, doctrinal developments, or policy impact, this frame has given priority to interests. This research was diverse. It included the game theoretic models of Walter Murphy (1964), the attitude studies of Glendon Schubert (1965; 1974), the impact work of Kenneth Dolbeare (1967), and even some attention to the Supreme Court as an institution (Schmidhauser 1960). The political view emerged from legal realism in law schools and became implanted through the work of behavioralists in political science departments. The bloc analysis pioneered by C. Herman Pritchett (1948) made the nature of judging definitively political. Since the mid-1970s, that work has taken stock of institutional behavior (Tate and Handberg 1986; Segal and Spaeth 1993). Yet the research and the method remain political in the "realist" sense, because their insight is drawn from disagreement and the "storms" of political controversy (O'Brien 1996). The conventional wisdom is that the judge can do whatever he wants and that only in some unenlightened prior age did people believe the law really mattered. We hear that the justices decide as they wish and write the opinion as a rationalization.

Elements of political reality in court are so widespread today that they have lost their critical edge. Both politics and disputes have broadened our knowledge of the bench and increased familiarity with courthouse corridors, judicial chambers, and law offices.[2] Yet for some time the lack of serious attention to the legal terrain and the diversion of interest from the traditional subjects—law and legal thought—have been a problem. An institutional investigation would abandon the preoccupation with disagreement and struggle and move toward a study of social practices.

Beyond Politics

The "cult of the robe," a highly formal belief in law and the scholarship of judges that was the basis for legal authority fifty years ago, no longer functions as it once did. A realism in law that includes a critique of formalism as part of its narrative keeps the cult of the robe alive. This realism, as it applies to the authority of courts, particularly the Supreme Court, I have called the "cult of the judge." Similarly, a "cult of the Court" has replaced the formalism of mechanical jurisprudence. The way we view the Court today depends less on robes and forms than it does on hierarchies, the image of justice represented by the building, and the special place of the Supreme Court in the law. Pursuing these "cults" can be scary, but viewing the institution at this level promises some resistance to the pull of authorized material or official opinion from the bench. Moreover, the effort to portray the cult around the institution provides a framework for interpreting a variety of Court-related materials. Opinions, history, and commentary on the institution are keys to institutional politics.

Over a decade ago, political scientists began turning away from the politics of interests and behavior to shared practices in legislatures (Ethridge 1985), in international political economy (J. Goldstein 1986), and to public opinion (Bennett 1980). Some even described a "new institutionalism" (R. Smith 1988; March and Olsen 1984), which became contested terrain itself and in many of its manifestations lost much of the cultural perspective at the forefront of academic debate over the last decade. The turn from more traditional political inquiry and necessarily from dissents and disputes in the following material is a natural one for public law scholarship that never totally lost its connection to the stuff of tradition (Harris 1982; O'Neill 1981). That stuff, law and courts, doctrine and rhetoric, is being brought back to social research through explicit attention to institutions (Brisbin 1993; Gillman 1993).

The modern Court functions through a dynamic between politics and law, human interest and institutional practice. It stands apart from individual action most of the time. That is why *The Brethren,* with its portrayal of scheming and self-interest, received so much attention. There is politics on the Court and there is a politics in the way we know the institution. The second kind is newer. We began to see this kind of politics in the debate over the Supreme Court and the Constitution. Attorney General Edwin Meese stimulated the debate in speeches from 1985 to 1986, holding that we should repeal the doctrine of incorporation applying the Bill of Rights to the states. He also argued that the Supreme Court was not the last word on the Constitution. The legal community promptly condemned this position, leaving some to wonder how the understandings Meese challenged had become so ingrained. In this approach, I have been less interested in what very few people know and more in what most people take for granted. Expectations that we learn, as we learn what something like the Supreme Court is, set limits on action.

The implications of going "beyond" politics means less attention to cases. Like individual political choices, cases are illustrative. *Marbury v. Madison* and *U.S. v. Nixon* are integral to the shifting ideologies of authority. *Regents of the University of California v. Bakke* is one of my favorite cases for showing how doctrinal material transforms practices into action. As with other instances of choice, the focus should be on the whole, the tradition in terms of which cases are seen, rather than on outcomes. The cases resemble other aspects of institutional life such as statutes, like the Judges Bill of 1925; with commentary like *The Federalist Papers* or *The Brethren;* personality, like John Marshall's; and places, like the building constructed for the Court in 1936. Just as the message of both discourse analysis and sociolegal studies is that law is more than the opinions, the institution is more than its cases.

Conventional Practices

One quality of a social institution is that we take it for granted. Institutions like the Supreme Court and parts of it, like the majority opinion, are ways of doing things that provide the background for law. Disputes take place with reference to them, and politics is in, around, and about them. Before any cases are decided, we want to know how they will come out. Once they are decided, the attention shifts only marginally to the impact of a decision. Ordinary political understanding of institutions presents a challenge simply because the understanding is ordinary. We tend not to want to talk about what we know. We might debate the actions of a Supreme Court, but we find it harder to investigate the fact that the Supreme Court in Washington is the end of the line in law. These practices, though historically contingent, constitute limits on action.

The ways we know institutions indicate what they are made of. One way of knowing is through physical manifestations. In law, the bench, the robes, and the marbled walls signal that the activity is important. Although it is no secret that the Court had makeshift quarters until only fifty years ago, we lose track of that fact. After Chief Justice William Howard Taft acquired a new building for the Supreme Court, his successor referred to the black-robed justices as "Beetles in the Temple of Karnak." The new building was more than many of the justices believed appropriate for the Court.

Institutions, if they are to be taken on their own terms as meaningful social phenomena, present a challenge to social scientists because they have a range of significations and a variety of uses. Sometimes an institution is quite animated, as when a voice on the other end of the telephone says, "Supreme Court, may I help you?" An institution is often represented by the people who work in it (see Vining 1986, 110–32). A justice may speak for "the Court" or the chief justice may lend his name to the institution, as in the Marshall, the Taney, the Warren, or the Burger Courts. These names suggest a human quality, and they are more common today than they were in the past.

Institutions are able to transcend changes in membership. This characteristic suggested to Aristotle the analogy of rivers that have a "constant identity" even as the flow changes the composition of the thing (Barker 1962, 99). In classical philosophy this quality accords an institution a "Naturalness." In this sense, an institution is identifiable across time in ways that rivers are. The Supreme Court is said to have decided *Brown v. Board of Education* (1954) and *Adarand Constructors, Inc. v. Pena* (1995). Here, the institution mediates policy shifts in the meaning and relevant context for interpreting another "continuous" institution, the Constitution of the United States.

Portrayal of an institution requires a leap from the commonsense concreteness evident in buildings and from the social-scientific concreteness evident in the voting patterns of the justices to the shared perceptions that tell us what these things mean in the broader context of American politics and society. New Dealers saw "nine old men." Their efforts to transform the institution were met by "Lions under the Throne" (Curtis 1947). The Warren Court was a trumpet, or at least responded to the calls of convicts like Clarence Earl Gideon. *The Brethren,* as a title, is an allusion to collegiality that turns out to be paradoxical since the book plays on discordant personalities and judicial disregard of tradition. Such characterizations are not simply rhetorical flourish; they reflect a public perception.

The relative disinterest of social scientists in what it means to be all these things has been due, in part, to professional effort to create a distinct language based on the scientific model. That project found interests (politics) and conflicts (disputing) to be appropriate foundations. Students of the Supreme Court and the Constitution have generally been more resistant to the drift away from the formal institutions of social life than most social scientists. Although this has often meant an insensitivity to the enterprise of social research, it has sometimes led to self-consciousness about the objects and methods of study. Judicial behavioralists, in their prime from the early 1950s until the late 1960s, charted judicial attitudes in their research and taught case law in their classrooms. Though the frame has been political, discourse and teaching about Court and Constitution have been largely doctrinal. Institutional materials remain important for Court scholars to a degree unimaginable to students of voting behavior. Official discourses also remain in the picture even while their significance is undercut. This makes it difficult for public law to produce a model of their subject susceptible to rigorous investigation.

In the present context, the challenge to providing a sociological account of convention is to be met by looking at the ordinary or folkways of knowing.[3] Law and office become institutions when there is agreement, expressed or implied, that they exist. An institution may be as internally complex as "the Pentagon" or "the Catholic Church" or as simple as a squad of soldiers or a prayer. Institutions share a capacity to order social life because people act as if they exist, as if they matter. They are isolates of human experience and can be examined with reference to the authority in social life to which they contribute (Goodrich 1984, 1986; McCann 1994). The result is a framework for studying legal institutions as constitutive (Klare 1979; Brigham 1987b; Harrington 1988).

Often institutional conventions are at the center of political controversy.

In a letter to the *New York Times* on September 9, 1986, Prof. Christopher Pyle of Mt. Holyoke College drew attention to Rehnquist's deciding vote in *Laird v. Tatum* in 1972. Pyle describes Rehnquist, a former Justice Department official, as a custodian of the records in the case he later decided. In the main, however, social scientists leave the given quality of the institution unexplored. Traditional treatments do little more than describe the conventions, reinforcing the perception that the institution is simply there. When Stephen Wasby discussed judicial review (1984, 59–64), he lost his critical instinct, announcing that "judicial review has become fully established" (1984, 64). Larry Baum on judicial review (1985) indicated that John Marshall *asserted* the power in 1803, that it survived the contest over slavery fifty years later, and that it has been employed on the average once every two years. We see historical moments in the institutional life of judicial review, but not enough about how the institution has changed with that monumental development. We are not given a basis for understanding the grounds on which that institutional power rests.

Institutional studies can rely on common perceptions or conventional understandings, called *practices* here. Practices capture the cultural significance of representations without losing track of the social relations that maintain our culture. They are the ways of doing things that make up institutions. Institutions are not simply robes and marble, nor are they contained in codes or documents. By convention people know the appropriate institutional meaning to give to action. Practices are understood in terms of place, like the steps of the Court that give meaning to a lawyer and client ascending or a newscaster reporting, and of performance, where signing a name gains special significance from the practices that associate a judicial signature with an opinion.

Practices may be distinguished from the particular actions, like votes and signatures, where we see them. A vote is an intentional action, "the vote" a democratic institution. In the Supreme Court, the meaning of each vote comes from the practices in that setting. In the *Bakke* case, Justice Powell's holding that an aspiring white person should be admitted to medical school is steeped in the traditions of constitutional discourse. Powell's contribution, which opened the doors to Alan Bakke and allowed race to be taken into account in admissions decisions, is a consequence of its institutional status as a holding of the Court. Nobody joined him entirely, but the opinion captured the Court. Its status for the country has not been assessed.

In some respects, the institutional approach is similar to that professed by early behavioralists. Practices, like behavior, shift attention from words to something more "real," and the perspective holds out the promise of insight beyond ordinary discourse. Yet the institutional approach differs from positive frameworks like behavioralism. As opposed to a focus on maneuvers abstracted from action, like attitudes, an institutional investigation relies on the actual parameters within which action takes place, the "intersubjective" dimensions of the legal environment that some behavioralists all but lost track of in their focus on dissent, disagreement, and divergence from the norm.

Institutional practices are evident even where politics is the focus, as in *The Brethren*. This treatment relies on expectations and institutional practices to tell its story. Justices of the Supreme Court are selected and evaluated with reference to an institutional understanding about what a justice should be. Warren Burger pursuing an appointment went against the expectation of institutional passivity. Similarly, the influence-peddling described in *The Brethren* would not have been worth mentioning had the book been about most other institutions in Washington. However political the process is, there may still be distinctive institutional expectations.

Kinds of Practices

There are various kinds of practices in an institutional setting that can be distinguished as strategies and maxims, conventions, and constitutive or "institutional" practices, depending on their relationship with the institution. On one extreme, there are *strategies and maxims* adopted by the people who operate within the institution. These suggest how to "take advantage of the institution for particular purposes" (Rawls 1971, 56). A strategy would not be essential to the very nature of the institution. For example, issuing opinions on various days or circulating drafts of opinions are strategies that are part of the political life in the Supreme Court, but they do not determine the nature of the institution (W. Murphy 1964). Whether the Court issues most of its opinions on Monday matters a great deal to individuals who cover the institution, giving that day some media significance, but the Court does not depend on that practice for its existence.

Over time, an opinion supported by the majority of the justices came to be understood, as a matter of *convention,* as the Court's opinion. Conventions are ways of doing things that we associate with the institution more completely than strategic choices. With this status in the life of the institution, conventions are not simply ways to get something done. The majority opinion has become an expectation that gives meaning to individual opinions. Practices of this sort are the terrain on which political strategies are played out. With dissents common again, the institution may be returning to the practice of seriatim opinions. But with a long tradition of opinion by the majority, individual holdings are conventionally seen in terms of the majority. Conventions, however, do not determine what an institution is.

Practices that become "constitutive" of the institution we call *institutional practices.* Politics has become constitutive in recent years and has been associated with the Court as a matter of institutional practice. Ever since C. Herman Pritchett introduced the analysis of dissents and constructed a "bloc" of judges in *The Roosevelt Court,* the culture has moved toward an incorporation of politics into its picture of the Court. Every day a political institution is represented in articles like "Farewell to the Old Order: The Right Goes Activist and the Center is a Void," by Linda Greenhouse (*New York Times,* July 2, 1995). These stories take their spirit from politics—at the end of the term in 1995 it was the decisions of Rehnquist, Scalia, and Thomas—and they present the Court in terms of political messages, such as the relative weakness of the traditional swing votes in cases decided during that term. Without the practice of seeing politics in the institution, it would certainly still exist but it would not be the body as we understand it today. The link between the Court and the legal profession, evident in the practice of appointing lawyers to the bench, appears to have become constitutive over the same period. And among the most important constitutive practices is the institutional authority to interpret the Constitution.

Distinguishing among kinds of practices is difficult, and the extent to which a practice constitutes the Court will be a matter of interpretation. For instance, the assertion of judicial review by John Marshall in *Marbury v. Madison* (1803) reiterated a possibility that had been mentioned by others, most notably by Hamilton in *Federalist* 78 and 81, but it was certainly not conventional, much less constitutive of the institution at that time.[4] Marshall articulated the possibility for the Supreme Court, introducing it into the institutional setting. The basis for such a claim was in Blackstone's *Commentaries, The Federalist Papers,* and in the fact of a written constitution (Corwin 1928). By the late nineteenth century, Americans knew judicial review as something the Supreme Court did.

In the struggle over authority to interpret the Constitution precipitated by the split between the majority on the Court and the political majority held by the New Deal, the authority of the Court over the Constitution was a matter of debate. The publication in 1938 of Edward Corwin's *Court Over Constitution* is a benchmark indicating the shift from the then "outmoded" doctrine of formal or static constitutionalism to the living constitutionalism of political jurisprudence or legal realism. From this statement we see the emergence of a new myth of judicial power. This is the view of the Supreme Court that treats even the failure of Roosevelt's plan to pack the Court as due to the "switch in time that saved nine" or to the political savvy of Justice Owen Roberts (O'Brien 1996, 82). With a judicial review grounded in political jurisprudence as constitutive of the Supreme Court, the consequence is not only a political court but a political constitution. Marshall's suggestion that justices draw authority from the Constitution has been turned on its head. Now it is conventional to know the Constitution through the Supreme Court.

Social Foundations

Practices are socially constructed ways of acting (Winch 1958; Flathman 1976). They are evident in folkways from praying to litigating, and they exist because actors in a social setting take them into account. It does not matter whether they are formally stipulated. Conversely, a text, a theory, a law on the books is not a practice without more. When two states present a dispute to the Supreme Court, this is understood within the Court's "original jurisdiction." In original jurisdiction cases, the justices will appoint a "master" to hear evidence as a matter of institutional practice. This is a normal Court procedure, an expected form of action. Presidential appointment of justices and oral arguments are Supreme Court practices, and judicial review over acts by Congress and the president also has become an institutional practice.

Institutions as bodies of practices existing in a society mean that there are communities who understand the practices and operate according to them. An institution like the Supreme Court is constituted by the communities familiar with it, which means knowledgeable groups or even entire societies where the practices are accepted. Traditionally these groups know something others don't. We say of a text, in the case of law, or a court, in the case of office, that its social foundation is the group or community that can interpret the text or understand the court. Legal doctrine has been seen for some time as an ideological activity, but its social foundations have been ignored while courts have been so completely understood in terms of action that their ideological qualities have been missed. The special sociological contribution of an investigation into the practices making up an institution comes from identifying the ways of operating and the social relations behind them that give the elements of law and office their significance. The social base makes practices a foundation for a legitimate science of society (Husserl 1965, 189).

This interest in law's social foundations originates in traditions of literary criticism, which are heavily indebted to language philosophy and hermeneutics. The practices of these disciplines have been introduced into the legal community from a number of quarters, but nowhere more provocatively than by Owen Fiss in his article "Objectivity and Interpretation" (1982). Fiss portrays the interpretive work of the appellate judge as "neither a wholly discretionary nor a wholly mechanical activity" (1982, 739) but as an interactive process that takes place within an "interpretive community" (1982, 746).[5] The notion of such communities brings in the reality of a professional life. These are the social relations that underlie and maintain legal activity.

The community in law is very well defined, in comparison with other communities, such as those of literary criticism, and consequently it acts as a constraint upon individual lawyers and judges. But its participants are a large group engaged in a variety of tasks, and their place in the community is less clear than the official theories of law would have us believe. Law professors like the late Robert Cover are participants in the legal community, and they approach its universes of meanings in a different fashion from the social scientist. Cover exhorted his colleagues to tell tales, spin yarns, and create a legal order grounded in new practices. This is his job. We expect that the great law teacher will send his students out to break through the paradigms or, to appropriate an epistemological issue, intentionally to confuse "is" and "ought." Cover's call is "to stop circumscribing the nomos . . . to invite new worlds." This is more difficult for those of us who operate outside the great law schools or who do not have access to the appellate bench. The community of law professors makes their yarns particularly important. Thus, when we say here that there are social foundations to law and office, we mean that the nomos is not completely up for grabs.

The failure to recognize the boundaries of interpretive communities surrounding the Supreme Court and the Constitution is evident in a treatment by Lief Carter in his book *Contemporary Constitutional Lawmaking* (1985). Carter offers a view of constitutional interpretation he calls "aesthetic" and suggests that the way a justice looks at the Constitution resembles the way a gallery visitor views a work of art. This comparison is offered as a helpful corrective to those who see law as rules and its significance and signification in orders backed by threats, or as Carter puts it, "*stare decisis,* consistency with canons of legal reasoning, discovery of the intent of those who adopt legal rules, judicial self-restraint, and so forth" (1985, 1). While poetic license in a work such as Carter's must be freely given, it is excessive to say that the Supreme Court has never paid much attention to stare decisis. This is the perspective that legal realism has brought into fashion. In deconstructing the confidence of the uncritical in the law field, interpretive practitioners, like the realists with whom they ally themselves, elevate other standards such as the aesthetic and the political over the traditional legal forms.

Interpretation in this formulation becomes a matter of individual choice. As with the interpretivists in law school, the work plays down the sociological dimensions of community and misses the communities that give some people greater access than others. Settings like Yale, and of course others in the "higher circles," have a special place, and their aesthetic assumes a priority status in comparison with contributions from other institutions and locales where people have something to say about the Constitution. The Supreme Court, at the apex of this configuration of American legal authority, is subject to the way the authority is organized. The aesthetic perspective, though it restates an important epistemological caveat, is naive sociology.

Social relations and group life enforce the dictates of sensible communication. These social forces are often missed by interpretivists. One of the interesting things about the often discussed case of *INS v. Chada* (1983), in which the Supreme Court declared the "legislative veto" unconstitutional, was that the Court's decision on the Constitution had relatively little effect on congressional practice. Congress, operating from its own institutional setting, continued to rely on veto provisions in its legislation (Fisher 1985), suggesting that the Court's view on what the Constitution means may be less significant than constitutional lawyers believe. Ultimately, neither the text nor judicial logic determines the social meaning of the fundamental law. Instead, it is institutional practice and its interpretation by people who matter.

Notes

1. This chapter is adapted from the author's book *The Cult of the Court* (Brigham 1987a).

2. Social scientists have been avoiding the positivist label for a decade now, although the pejorative edge is sharper when quantitative work is criticized from this perspective than when the critique is applied to theoretical discussions

3. According to Stanley Cavell (1984), an early disseminator of interpretive approaches in the social sciences, the study of convention encompasses "the common, the familiar, the everyday, the low, the near."

4. There are a number of scholarly treatments of this point, although it has dropped from general view. See Ellis (1971) and Corwin (1938), also Mark Graber's chapter in this volume.

5. This idea comes from Stanley Fish (1980).

Chapter 3

The Problematic Establishment
of Judicial Review

Mark A. Graber

The standard constitutional law course, text, or history begins with *Marbury v. Madison* (1803), the first case in which the Supreme Court explicitly declared a federal law unconstitutional and explained why the Constitution vested the federal judiciary with that authority.[1] The course, text, or book then focuses on the judicial power to declare state laws unconstitutional. That discussion starts with Justice Story's opinion in *Martin v. Hunter's Lessee* (1816) and finishes with *Cohens v. Virginia* (1821), the first case in which John Marshall defended the judicial power to void local laws. Conventional wisdom concludes that this line of decisions from Marbury to Cohens "*firmly established* the power of federal courts to exert judicial review over national and state action" (Epstein and Walker 1995, 73) (emphasis added). The rest of the course, text, or book explores how the judiciary has exercised that power from 1821 until the present.

These confident assertions of judicial power are puzzling. Power is often conceptualized as the capacity to "get [someone] to do something that [he] would otherwise not do" (Dahl 1969, 80).[2] The cases conventionally used to illustrate the establishment of judicial power, however, better illustrate the relative impotence of the federal judiciary during the first decades of the constitutional order. Neither *Marbury* nor *Cohens* ordered elected officials to abandon cherished practices. Both decisions were strategic judicial retreats in the face of threats by executive or state power. The Marshall Court in *Marbury* declared an obscure jurisdictional measure unconstitutional in order to avoid issuing a writ of mandamus that President Jefferson probably would have disobeyed. The first half of Marshall's *Cohens* opinion declared that courts have the power to strike down state laws, but the second half held, on dubious grounds, that Virginia could legally ban a federal lottery (Graber

1995). Interpreted politically, *Marbury* and *Cohens* merely established the judicial power to utter such declaratory sentences as "it is emphatically the province and duty of the judicial department to say what the law is" (5 U.S., at 177), a power possessed by anyone with a minimal knowledge of English.

Judicial review had to be established both legally and politically. Supreme Court justices could influence the course of American politics only when influential members of the incumbent regime supported judicial review. This political support depended in the long run on the extent to which judicial decisions advanced policies that influential members of the political regime favored. John Marshall's opinions played a central role in the process by which the federal judiciary acquired and solidified the legal and political power to declare laws unconstitutional. Still, scholars must pay equally close attention to the political forces that threatened, tolerated, and sometimes facilitated Marshall's institutional pretensions. The status of judicial review in 1789, 1801, 1835, or 1998 can be determined only by examining beliefs and behaviors throughout the American political system, and not solely by reference to selected judicial writings.

This "political systems" approach to the Marshall Court recognizes that the judicial power to declare laws unconstitutional was from the beginning neither the countermajoritarian check on regime power discussed in contemporary legal lore (i.e., Bickel 1962) nor, as political science writing suggests (Dahl 1957; M. Shapiro 1981), a mere means for extending regime power. Judicial review is a political instrument used by factions that *partly* control the elected branches of the national government. The Supreme Court is "a part of the dominant national alliance" (Dahl 1957, 293) and often functions as an "institution by which central political regimes consolidate their control over the countryside" (M. Shapiro 1981, viii), but the federal judiciary has also been an important site for struggles between the various winners of American politics. Events from 1789 to 1809 demonstrated that the federal judiciary would rarely check regime power. Federalist justices during the Washington and Adams administrations avidly supported administration policy. Marshall from 1801 to 1809 recognized that any effort to frustrate a united Jeffersonian coalition would fail. The judiciary Marshall led became a relatively autonomous institution in American politics after Jefferson left office by exploiting divisions within the dominant national coalition. *Marbury,* the case commonly cited as providing a crucial legal precedent for judicial review, is actually better conceptualized as the case that merely preserved existing, but abstract, political support for that practice. The Marshall Court placed judicial review on more concrete legal and political foundations only after 1809, when its decisions served important interests of the more nationalistic wing of the incumbent Jeffersonian regime.

In this chapter I explore how, and the extent to which, a politically consequential power of judicial review was established in the United States during the first fifty years of the American constitutional regime. In the first section I explain and expand the narrow legal and political conceptions responsible for the conventional claim that *Marbury* established judicial review and document the limited sense in which the Supreme Court exercised judicial power when John Marshall was chief justice. Next I suggest how broader legal and political understandings of judicial power might modify conventional understandings of *Marbury*. Then I consider how, in the aftermath of *Marbury*, judicial power gradually developed firmer foundations. The claims are suggestive rather than conclusive and await further development elsewhere (Graber 1995, 1998a, 1998b). Still, I have illustrated various ways in which the interaction of law and politics structured judicial decision making during the early years of the American republic and may still structure the present political regime.

The analysis reflects certain themes common to the new institutionalism or historical institutionalist scholarship, although the affinities frequently reflect temperament rather than conscious methodological choices. The crucial point may simply be that the "historical" in "historical institutionalism" needs as much emphasis as the "institutional." Judicial decisions cannot be adequately explained or assessed in the absence of fairly thick descriptions of the legal arguments, political constraints, and strategic maneuvers open to judicial actors at particular historical times. Moreover, rather than conceive attitudinal, strategic, and legal models as distinctive explanations of judicial behavior, the experience of the Marshall Court suggests that the strategic and policy choices justices make are largely but not fully constrained by the legal arguments that can plausibly be made at a given time. As Quentin Skinner (1974) among others has noted, persons can only do what they can say. At the very least, detailing the interactions between legal, strategic, and attitudinal influences on the Supreme Court is likely to prove a more fruitful approach than academic competitions aimed at proving which single variable explains the most judicial behavior.

Establishing Judicial Review

The Supreme Court in *Marbury v. Madison* established the power of judicial review in a narrow legal sense. Judicial decisions in common law countries are sources of law. Hence, federal justices in the United States could acquire the legal right to declare laws unconstitutional by uttering the declaratory sentence, "It is emphatically the province and duty of the judicial department to say what law is," whenever that proposition was necessary to the outcome of a case before the Court. *Marbury* established judicial review in this limited sense. The Marshall Court declared that the federal judiciary had the power to declare laws unconstitutional, and that declaration was necessary to the Court's ruling that the justices lacked the jurisdiction to issue a writ of mandamus on behalf of William Marbury. *Marbury* did not establish the legal right to receive a judicial commission that was signed and sealed by the president because that part of Marshall's opinion was dicta, not necessary to the outcome of the case.

Marbury also established judicial review in a narrow political sense. Courts lack meaningful judicial power when justices consistently suffer severe political and personal consequences after uttering such declaratory sentences as "it is emphatically the province and duty of the judicial department to say what law is." Had Jeffersonians responded to *Marbury* by torturing the justices until they recanted their institutional pretensions, no one would now claim that American courts in 1803 established any power to declare laws unconstitutional. In fact, most Jeffersonians exhibited little interest in the actual holding of that case. Thus, *Marbury* demonstrated that federal courts in the early nineteenth century could assert a judicial power to declare laws unconstitutional and to declare politically inconsequential laws unconstitutional without political reprisal.

Marbury seems less influential when judged by broader legal and political criteria for judicial power. Legal precedents are firmly established only when they are not likely to be overruled or significantly narrowed in the foreseeable future. A general consensus must exist that the original decision was correctly decided, morally just, or too embedded in the present constitutional order to be abandoned. This consensus must be significantly widespread as to make almost inconceivable the possibility that the present judicial majority or any five justices who might be appointed in the foreseeable future would hand down a contrary decision. *Brown v. Board of*

Education (1954) held that separate but equal schools were unconstitutional. That egalitarian principle, however, was firmly established in American law only during the late 1960s when no realistic possibility existed that the Supreme Court would overrule *Brown* within a generation (Ackerman 1991, 110). *Roe v. Wade* (1973) established a constitutional right to an abortion, but that liberty to terminate a pregnancy is still not firmly established in the United States.

Marbury v. Madison did not establish the judicial power to declare laws unconstitutional in this legal sense. That decision failed to secure the widespread legal and political support necessary to guarantee that judicial review would not be abandoned in the foreseeable future. No former Anti-Federalist or prominent Jeffersonian endorsed judicial review after reading the relatively unoriginal arguments for that power in Marshall's opinion. Jeffersonian attacks on the federal judiciary remained sufficiently threatening that, one year after *Marbury* was decided, Marshall (1990, 347) privately expressed his willingness to abandon judicial review of federal legislation should that step forestall Jeffersonian efforts to impeach Federalist justices. Opposition to judicial review of state legislation remained strong throughout Marshall's tenure on the bench. Throughout the 1820s, Congress repeatedly considered and almost passed legislation prohibiting federal justices from hearing appeals from state courts (see Warren 1925; Rosenberg 1992, 387). The chief justice's last letters frequently bemoaned the limited authority of American judicial institutions. "I yield slowly and reluctantly," Marshall confessed shortly before he died, "to the conviction that our constitution cannot last" (Warren 1947, 769).

Marbury also did little to improve the political power of the federal judiciary or to establish the Supreme Court as an influential policymaker. Courts lack significant political power when, although elected officials tolerate justices who assert in the abstract a judicial power to declare laws unconstitutional, those officials ignore or punish justices who attempt to exercise that power. Debates exist over the extent to which judicial decisions actually influence public policy (Rosenberg 1991; McCann 1994) and over whether judicial review entails judicial supremacy (Murphy 1986).[3] Still, the power of judicial review must entail some willingness on the part of some officials to make some policy adjustments in response to some judicial decisions, at least to the extent of obeying some judicial orders in particular cases.

Supreme Court decisions during the first third of the nineteenth century often failed this political test of judicial power. Many Marshall Court efforts to exercise judicial power were ignored by local officials. Georgia refused to enforce *Worcester v. Georgia* (1832), Kentucky refused to enforce *Green v. Biddle* (1821; 1823), and New Jersey refused to enforce *New Jersey v. Wilson* (1812) (Jessup 1987, 159, 221–31, 363–64). Leslie Goldstein (1997, 156–66) counts thirty-two antebellum instances where states "reject[ed] [the] authority of federal courts to interpret law," and twenty where states "defi[ed] . . . a federal court order." Early nineteenth century politicians failed to comply with federal court orders so frequently that an Ohio legislature committed to taxing the national bank asked how, in light of the general disrespect for judicial rulings at the time, their state could "be condemned because she did not abandon her solemn legislative acts as a dead letter upon the promulgation of an opinion of that tribunal?" (Annals of Congress, 16th Cong. 2d sess., 1697).

The Marshall Court prevented noncompliance in other cases by manipulating law and fact to avoid handing down decisions that state or federal officials could ignore. The justices in *Marbury* refused to issue a writ of mandamus that the Jefferson administration probably would have disobeyed (McCloskey 1994, 26). They subsequently found various excuses to avoid declaring unconstitutional the 1802 Repeal of the Judiciary Act of 1801.[4] The Court in *United States v. Schooner Peggy* (1801) responded to potentially strong political opposition in a similar way. Jeffersonians had previously condemned the Supreme Court for supporting Federalist party positions in admiralty cases decided before the election of 1800. An influential Jeffersonian journal even threatened impeachment should the justices not adopt a more pro-French position. Marshall in this highly charged political environment defused looming executive challenges to judicial authority by ordering the ship in controversy returned to its French owners. As in *Marbury,* his *Schooner Peggy* opinion reached a politically convenient conclusion by twisting the law in question in ways that even Jefferson's attorney general regarded as legal nonsense.[5]

Cohens v. Virginia (1821) is another instance where the Marshall Court ducked controversy by misconstruing a law. Virginia's ban on out-of-state lotteries seems nearly identical to the Maryland tax on out-of-state banks that the justices declared unconstitutional in *McCulloch v. Maryland* (1824). Prominent early-nineteenth-century lawyers recognized this parallel and assumed that the cases would be adjudicated in the same way. Marshall, however, concluded that Congress did not intend to prohibit state bans on federal lotteries, even though Virginia's ban effectively prevented the Grand

National Lottery from making a profit. The difference between the bank and lottery cases may be that Maryland agreed before *McCulloch* to respect the eventual judicial verdict, but Virginia seemed committed to resistance.[6] Marshall was well aware of the risks involved in challenging Virginia's pretensions. A year after he handed down *Cohens,* the Chief Justice found a statutory excuse to avoid voiding Virginia's ban on the entry of free blacks. "As I am not fond of butting against a wall in sport," he informed Story, "I escaped on the construction of the act" (Warren 1947, 626).

Marshall Court decisions influenced some important policies. Maryland stopped taxing the national bank after *McCulloch, Gibbons v. Ogden* (1824) effectively ended the Fulton steamship monopoly, and *Dartmouth College v. Woodward* (1819) prevented Dartmouth College from becoming Dartmouth University. These successful interventions suggest that the Marshall Court wielded the same degree of judicial power as its descendants, at least after 1809 (Graber 1998b). Judicial decisions are frequently disobeyed, and many courts retreat when faced with strong political opposition. Certainly, by 1835 the Court enjoyed far more prestige and respect than was the case when Marshall took office in 1801. Still, this increase in judicial status did not occur by judicial fiat but through various interactions between judicial decisions and political struggles. *Marbury* played a key role in the eventual establishment of judicial review, but that role is somewhat different from what scholars have thought.

Marbury Revisited

Marbury v. Madison was an ingenious solution to the political crisis the federal judiciary was bound to face whenever prominent politicians first anticipated that the justices might declare a major piece of legislation unconstitutional. Judicial review did not need to be legally established in 1803. Federal court precedents for that practice already existed, and the Supreme Court's failure to cite *Marbury* as justifying judicial review before 1887 (Clinton 1989, 120)[7] suggests that additional legal buttresses for that power were unnecessary. Rather, *Marbury* played a crucial role in preserving the political support necessary for the long-term survival of judicial review at a time when the federal judiciary was identified with a discredited vision of the American political order.

Marbury highlights the theoretical and practical relationships between support for particular judicial decisions and support for judicial review as a practice. Arguments for judicial review rely heavily on analyses of past judicial decisions and predictions about the course of future decision making. Persons who claim that judicial review protects minority rights, for example, point to past cases where the justices protected minority rights and explain why justices are likely to protect minority rights in the future. A judiciary that consistently protected the "wrong" rights and failed to protect the "right" rights would, for this reason, practically refute claims that the judiciary is institutionally structured to protect the "right" rights. Thus, legal and political support for judicial review will remain strong only when politically influential persons believe that the Supreme Court has been correctly interpreting the Constitution or is likely to correct its more serious constitutional mistakes in the near future.

Supreme Court justices during the early 1790s benefited from a consensus among political elites that federal courts possessed the power to declare laws unconstitutional (Rakove 1997, 1040–41; Marcus 1996). Prominent Jeffersonians and Federalists agreed in principle that judicial review was a desirable feature of the American constitutional system. The Judiciary Act of 1789 recognized and facilitated judicial power to declare federal and state laws unconstitutional (Marcus 1996, 26–27). During the last decade of the eighteenth century, the justices established without controversy several legal precedents for that practice (Marcus 1996, 28, 35–44). No storm arose when in the course of sustaining some statutes Supreme Court justices indicated that they had the power to declare laws unconstitutional. No political crisis occurred when the justices in *United States v. Yale Todd* indicated that constitutional norms would not permit them to adjudicate certain veterans' claims left over from the Revolution.[8]

Late-eighteenth-century Americans supported judicial review in principle partly because no national tribunal, American or foreign, had ever declared a major government policy unconstitutional.[9] In the absence of any substantial experience with judicial review, each faction in American politics could and did regard the federal judiciary as an ally in their struggles. Federalists anticipated an institution that would protect minority rights against factious majorities. Jeffersonians anticipated an institution that would protect the people when government officials violated their constitutional obligations. Put differently and only slightly tongue-in-cheek, Federalists assumed that courts would sustain constitutional Federalist policies and strike down unconstitutional Jeffersonian policies; Jeffersonians assumed that courts would sustain constitutional Jeffersonian policies and

strike down unconstitutional Federalist policies. These differing expectations meant that the broad, generalized support for judicial review that
existed during the Washington administration was likely to dissipate the first
time the Supreme Court handed down a ruling on the constitutionality of
some hotly contested public policy. Whatever decision the Court made, some
politically influential persons would conclude that the justices had made a
mistake. Should the justices persist in making that and similar mistakes,
many politically influential citizens were likely to conclude that the real mistake was judicial review.

Judicial review faced this political crisis during the first years of the nineteenth century. Jeffersonians in firm control of the elected branches of government had been and increasingly expected to be extremely disappointed
with the course of judicial decision making. The unswerving allegiance of
the Jay and Ellsworth Courts to Federalist policies had already inspired Jeffersonians to rethink the place of the federal judiciary in the American constitutional regime. The judicial refusal to declare the Alien and Sedition Acts
unconstitutional demonstrated to many Democratic-Republicans that the
Supreme Court could not be trusted to protect democratic liberties under
attack from politically remote elites. Worse, the Court in 1803 seemed poised
to defeat the will of the people as expressed in the election of 1800. Jeffersonians had particular reason to fear future Marshall Court decisions, given
overt Federalist efforts to ensure that the justices would obstruct Jeffersonian policy initiatives.

John Marshall, in *Marbury* and other potentially controversial cases decided during the Jefferson administration, defused this crisis and preserved
political support for judicial power by constructing opinions that tem-
porarily separated the issue of judicial review from other contested constitutional and political issues. The Marshall Court did so by vigorously
asserting judicial power in theory while declining to exercise it in practice.
This tactic enabled Marshall to maintain the fragile existing consensus that
existed even among Jeffersonians in favor of the judicial power to declare
laws unconstitutional. By not interfering with popular Jeffersonian measures, Marshall made judicial review safe for Jeffersonians, thus enabling
future federal justices working under friendlier political conditions to reap
the benefit of the generalized support for judicial review that the Chief Justice had inherited.

Marbury and other early Marshall Court cases were defensive measures
aimed at maintaining in a potentially hostile political environment exist-

ing support for judicial review, not ambitious efforts to strengthen the legal foundations of judicial power in the United States. Indeed, *Marbury* is best conceptualized as a trial balloon. Some Jeffersonians had launched the first serious national attack on judicial review during the debates over repealing the Judiciary Act of 1801. What was not clear at the time was the extent to which these attacks were based on a democratic antipathy to judicial power or on a Jeffersonian antipathy to a Federalist judiciary. Marshall's *Marbury* opinion clarified matters. By divorcing issues of judicial review from other constitutional differences between Jeffersonians and Federalists, Marshall isolated democratic opponents of judicial review from more moderate Jeffersonians who merely objected to the federal judiciary becoming an auxiliary of the Federalist party. This tactic effectively prevented a strong antijudicial-review coalition from forming and radically altering judicial institutions. As the nonreaction to *Marbury* and the failed Chase impeachment demonstrated, substantial political support for judicial review existed during Jefferson's presidency as long as that practice did not obstruct Jeffersonian goals. Little was gained in *Marbury*, except perhaps the firmer establishment of a judicial power to declare politically inconsequential laws unconstitutional. Of more significance, little was lost. The nature of early support for judicial review made crisis nearly inevitable, but Marshall managed to avoid using the power of judicial review in ways that antagonized crucial political supporters of that practice. By not exercising power when power could not be exercised successfully, the Marshall Court maintained the political backing necessary to exercise power in more hospitable political conditions.

Exercising Judicial Power

The federal judiciary could and did establish a fair degree of political power after 1809 by siding with the more nationalistic wing of the Jeffersonian coalition on those issues that divided Old and Young Republicans. The window of judicial opportunity first opened when James Madison, a very moderate Jeffersonian, became chief executive (J. Smith 1996, 374; Jessup 1987, 58, 412).[10] The fourth president had barely settled into the White House when the justices handed down two major decisions, *United States v. Peters* (1809) and *Fletcher v. Peck* (1810). Both furthered policies favored by the national executive and influenced public affairs. *Peters* played a crucial role in settling an admiralty dispute that dated back to the American Revolution.

Fletcher, while having no immediate impact, strengthened the bargaining power of those nationalistic Republicans who favored compensating the Yazoo landholders.

Marshall Court policy making accelerated when in the years following 1815 many Democratic-Republicans endorsed broad exercises of national power and more limitations on the states (Haskins and Johnson 1981, 649). *McCulloch v. Maryland* highlighted the increasingly supportive relationship between the judicial and the elected branches of government. Virtually all influential national politicians in 1819 agreed that the Democratic-Republican chartered Bank of the United States was constitutional and not subject to discriminatory state taxation. While *McCulloch* was pending, Congress defeated by a large margin an effort to shut down the bank, and the official organ of the Monroe administration immediately endorsed the Marshall Court's decision (Warren 1947, 509–10; J. Smith 1996, 446). Marshall took advantage of this administrative backing by writing an opinion that provided a strong precedential basis for even broader exercises of national power. Madison grumbled about some passages in *McCulloch,* but satisfied with the result in that case, he and other Republican nationalists maintained their staunch support for judicial review.

The other two major cases handed down during the Supreme Court's remarkable 1819 term, *Dartmouth College v. Woodward* and *Sturges v. Crowninshield* (1819), demonstrated the Marshall Court's capacity to influence public affairs when no national consensus on appropriate policy existed. *Dartmouth College* had significant repercussions in American history (Beveridge 1919, 276–77), but during the Era of Good Feelings the judicial decision that corporate charters were subject to contracts clause restrictions attracted little public attention (Stites 1972, 101–64). Bankruptcy attracted a good deal of attention during the 1810s, but no majority formed on any policy question. State legislators insisted that the national legislature pass a uniform bankruptcy law, national legislators thought state legislatures should pass local bankruptcy laws, and legislators who agreed that their legislature should make bankruptcy policy could not agree on any specific law (Coleman 1974, 18, 21–22, 34–36). As a result, the Marshall Court could rule without significant political risk that state bankruptcy laws did not govern contracts made previous to the legislative enactment. *Sturges* did not "thwart the representatives of the people of the here and now" (Bickel 1962, 16) because the statute the justices declared unconstitutional had been repealed six years earlier by the New York legislature (Coleman 1974, 127).[11]

The Marshall Court was able to exercise significant power after 1809 because its rulings either enjoyed broad political support or did not arouse substantial opposition. Federal judicial power increased as judicial decisions both established legal precedents for further exercises of judicial review and swelled (or at least did not diminish) the ranks of influential politicians who favored that power. Congress demonstrated their appreciation by increasing judicial salaries and perks of office (3 U.S. Stat. 106, 110). The main organ of the Madison administration described the Supreme Court as "a branch of Government which it is important to hold in due veneration" (*Daily National Intelligencer* 1814). James Monroe and John Quincy Adams continued Madison's strong support for federal judicial power. Monroe (1896, 260–61) even proposed a judicial reorganization bill similar to the Judiciary Act of 1801.[12] Marshall did have some constitutional differences with both Madison and Monroe concerning federal power over internal improvements, but "institutional rivalry between the Court and the executive branch" during the Madison, Monroe and Adams administrations, Dwight Jessup notes, "was virtually non-existent" (1987, 410).

Important pockets of resistance remained, particularly among Old Republicans. When resistance was too great, Marshall either avoided handing down hostile decisions, or judicial decisions were ignored. Significantly, however, in most cases where one state issued a broad challenge to federal judicial power, other states banded together to defend judicial action (L. Goldstein 1997, 185). Which camp a state joined depended on the issue (L. Goldstein 1997, 155–56). Thus, at a time when the dominant national coalition was splintered, the Marshall Court was able to tilt the balance of power toward more nationalistic Jeffersonians and to resolve important policy questions when no national consensus existed.

The Rise of Judicial Review

The Supreme Court's identification with moderate Jeffersonian policies belies the common claim that the Marshall Court established judicial review by separating law from politics. Marshall did refuse to side with Federalists in their politically doomed struggles against Jeffersonians. The tribunal he led, however, gained power and crucial political support by consistently siding with nationalistic Republicans in their struggles against the Old Republican branch of the Jeffersonian coalition. Judicial power increased in the years between 1808 and 1828 because the exercise of the power advanced policies preferred by important members of the dominant national coalition, not because the Court remained above the political fray. Federalist fears that the judiciary was too weak to challenge elected officials (Rakove 1997, 1060) were both prescient and mistaken. The justices were unwilling to challenge united political regimes but frequently could find enough political support to sustain a fair degree of political influence.

Subsequent antebellum developments further solidified political support for judicial review. Marshall pulled in the judicial reins after the election of Andrew Jackson and the installation of a hostile Democratic party regime in the national government. Virtually all the major decisions in which his tribunal ruled in favor of a state against either a claim of individual right or national preemption were handed down during Jackson's presidency (Jessup 1987, 284, 326, 405–6, 433–35). Still, Jacksonians soon found uses for judicial power. In the wake of the nullification crisis, Jackson proposed and Congress passed a bill that gave federal courts increased authority to strike down unconstitutional state policies (4 U.S. Stat. 632). Fifteen years later, Jacksonians from all regions of the country sought to end a bitter intraparty dispute by agreeing that the Supreme Court was the only national institution constitutionally authorized to determine the status of slavery in the territories. Lincolnian Republicans who objected to *Dred Scott* did not move to destroy judicial review. Following in Jackson's footsteps, they first gained sufficient control of the national government to force a judicial retreat and then began to reconstruct the judiciary in their own image (Lasser 1988, 56–57).

As other political coalitions imitated both Jackson and Lincoln, judicial contests became struggles between different constitutional visions rather than disputes over what role the judiciary should play in ongoing attempts to define the American constitutional regime. Elected officials frequently failed to comply with unpopular judicial decisions, and justices frequently avoided decisions that might antagonize too many elected officials. Still, by the end of the Civil War, if not by the end of Marshall's tenure, the Supreme Court did not face severe threats that their decisions might create a backlash strong enough to destroy permanently the judicial authority to declare laws unconstitutional. Judicial review was firmly established, legally and politically.

This political explanation of judicial review complements theories that focus on the ideas expressed in and precedents established by Marshall Court opinions. Judicial review survived in part because a general consensus existed among elites in favor of that practice. This abstract consensus, however, might break down should the justices actually declare a popular law uncon-stitutional. John Marshall's achievement (aided and abetted by numerous colleagues, successors, state justices, and elected officials) was to exercise judicial power in such a way as to influence government policy significantly without antagonizing sufficient political opposition to bring down the Court. The Supreme Court has never been free to roam willfully through the con-stitutional woods, but the fragmented American political system provides more opportunities for justices to participate in policy making than much theory recognizes.

The establishment of judicial review also sheds light on recent debates over strategic voting by justices (Epstein and Knight 1997; Gillman 1996, 1999). Marshall often voted strategically. He sustained laws he thought unconstitutional when more aggressive judicial action would damage the political foundations for judicial review. Still, Marshall Court justices tended to employ legal strategies and to pursue legal goals. They were concerned with institutional powers, not specific policies. Marshall sought to establish federal judicial authority to declare laws unconstitutional and national authority to interpret constitutional powers broadly. He was less interested in promoting any particular exercise of national power. Moreover, the Mar-shall Court sought to establish institutional authority through traditional legal means: the manipulation of legal doctrine and modalities of legal argu-ment. The period from 1801 to 1835 witnessed a marked reduction in judi-cial employment of other political strategies, most notably political speeches to grand juries (Whittington 1995).[13] Thus, while helping to establish judicial review, the Marshall Court played an important role in structuring the goals that future justices would seek and the strategies that they would employ when seeking those goals.

Notes

1. The justices apparently declared a federal law unconstitutional in *Yale Todd v. United States* (1794), but opinions in that case were either not delivered or recorded. See *United States v. Ferreira,* 54 U.S. 40, 53 (1851).

2. Other conceptions of power exist in the social science literature, but this simple definition best captures conventional understandings of judicial power.

3. How judicial decisions influence public policy is also a matter of debate. Some com-mentators claim that the Supreme Court is a "republican schoolmaster" that most often influences public policy by persuading citizens to alter preexisting constitutional per-spectives. See Lerner (1987, 91–136), and Eisgruber (1992).

4. *Stuart v. Laird,* 5 U.S. 299 (1803); *United States v. More,* 7 U.S. 159 (1805). See O'Fallon 1992, 1993. Ruth Wedgewood (1997, 268–69) has uncovered a letter from Marshall to Henry Clay clearly stating that the former believed the 1802 Repeal Act was unconstitutional.

5. These claims are discussed at length in Graber (1998a).

6. These claims are discussed at length in Graber (1995).

7. The case was *Mugler v. Kansas,* 123 U.S. 623, 661 (1887).

8. Questions were raised about judicial review during the early 1790s, but the practice did not seem particularly threatened until the first decade of the 1800s.

9. Several state courts had declared laws unconstitutional. These decisions do not seem to have significantly influenced expectations concerning the course of national judicial decision making.

10. For Madison's defense of judicial review, see Madison (1910, 66, 140–43, 388–98).

11. Justice Washington on circuit in 1814 struck down a similar law that had also been repealed by the state legislature. See *Golden v. Prince,* 10 F. Cas. 542 (D. Pennsylvania, 1814). See Coleman (1974, 153). The editorial on *Sturges* in the *Daily National* indicates probable administrative support for that decision (*Daily National Intelligencer* 1819).

12. Madison (1896, 577) had proposed similar legislation.

13. Though as Justice Story's lobbying efforts on behalf of bankruptcy legislation demonstrate, Marshall Court justices did not confine themselves exclusively to legal strategies.

Chapter 4

Institutional Norms and the Historical Development of Supreme Court Politics: Changing "Social Facts" and Doctrinal Development

Ronald Kahn

Except for die-hard originalists, most Supreme Court justices assume that constitutional doctrine must take into account changing social circumstances, considered by some people as "social facts" or "beliefs about social reality." My central concern here is how the Supreme Court brings the realities of the outside world into its decision making. In order effectively to protect important constitutional values the Supreme Court must occasionally reconsider whether these values are sufficiently protected in light of the changing social, political, and economic realities. As a result of this process it is possible that judicial doctrines change, not simply when different justices develop different values, but also when the Court adjusts to new social facts. Understanding this process is crucial if we are to apprehend what it means for the Constitution to be viewed as a "living Constitution" (Gillman 1997). It is also crucial to an understanding of the relation between the Court and the large social context within which it is embedded.

Relating Beliefs About Social Reality to Doctrinal Change

Howard Gillman and Michael McCann argue that simply acknowledging social facts will not provide a predictable shape for or direction to constitutional interpretation, nor will they make constitutional interpretation more sensitive to the plight of marginalized groups and classes (Gillman 1995, 7). "Facts . . . only become conspicuous and relevant within particular, con-

testable theoretical frameworks [and] we should not automatically assume
that 'our' beliefs about social facts will be the beliefs accepted by others"
(Gillman 1995, 7–8). Michael McCann (1995, 9) supports this view:

> New facts sometimes can pose an awkward dilemma for particular policy argu-
> ments of normative positions. . . . Yet more often, "inconvenient" facts are sim-
> ply ignored, discounted, countered by other facts, or interpreted differently by
> our adversaries. Again the key point is that facts have no meaning apart from
> the interpretive frames themselves—the beliefs, values, knowledges—in which
> they are understood; facts cannot resolve interpretive disagreements.

McCann laments that all the studies and social facts made no difference as
conservative judges and justices came to federal courts in the 1980s: "Once
'invited facts' and welcomed causal stories about systemic discrimination
were rejected and discarded to the dustbin of judicial irrelevance" (McCann
1995, 10).

How do "beliefs about social reality," or changing conceptions of social
facts, lead to changes in doctrine? To put it another way, in what sense is
doctrine often inextricably related to assumptions about social reality?
H. N. Hirsch, in his pathbreaking book *A Theory of Liberty: The Constitution and Minorities,* seeks to emphasize "the centrality of social facts to constitutional decision making . . . and the inevitable 'embeddedness' of
constitutional doctrine in social and political reality" (1992, 2). For Hirsch,
Brown turned on a change in social facts—what we knew to be the negative effects of segregation on a child's education and self-esteem. Conversely,
Roe v. Wade turned on what we could not know about the fetus as person
(Hirsch 1992, 92).

Unlike Hirsch, however, I wish to leave open the possibility that at times
the employment of new social facts may lead constitutional law to be less

While I accept Gillman's and McCann's views on the relationship of
beliefs about social reality or social facts and the "interpretive frames themselves—the beliefs, values, knowledges—in which they are understood"
(McCann 1995, 9), at the same time I hold out the possibility that new circumstances might actually put pressure on existing beliefs. For example,
understanding beliefs about social reality may help us better explain why the
Supreme Court chose to overrule the central holdings of such landmark
cases as *Lochner v. New York* (1905) and *Plessy v. Ferguson* (1896) and its
refusal to overturn *Roe v. Wade* (1973).

supportive of the needs of subordinated groups. For example, the Supreme Court in *Adkins v. Children's Hospital* (1923) invalidated a law establishing minimum wages for children, after validating an hours law for women in *Muller v. Oregon* (1908). The Court wrote (at 543):

> But the ancient inequality of the sexes, otherwise physical, [has] continued "with diminishing intensity." In the view of the great [changes] which have taken place since [*Muller*], in the contractual, political, and civil status of women, culminating in the Nineteenth Amendment, it is not unreasonable to say that these differences have now come almost, if not quite to a vanishing point.

To further explore this relationship between social facts and the Court's doctrinal change I will first consider examples of justices' incorporating their beliefs about social reality in certain paired landmark decisions: *Lochner v. New York* (1905) and post-*Lochner* cases; *Plessy v. Ferguson* (1896) and *Brown v. Board of Education* (1954); and *Bradwell v. Illinois* (1872), *Roe v. Wade* (1973), and *Planned Parenthood of Southeastern Pennsylvania v. Casey* (1992). I then shall consider the place of social facts in a line of cases in the doctrinal area of capital punishment. One objective is to understand the conditions under which beliefs about social reality gain acceptance in law and become important to judicial decision making. Another is to explore the relationship between the judicial recognition of certain social facts or beliefs about concrete social contexts and the concern that rule of law requires adherence to abstract principles embedded in precedent. In so doing, we can better appreciate a major premise of the new institutional approach to understanding judicial decision making: that institutional norms, not simple policy preferences, inform the decisions made by justices. I then conclude by suggesting how studying the role of beliefs about social reality in Supreme Court decision making will yield a more complete understanding of the conditions under which constitutional decision making is transformative with specific regard to the redefinition of the rights of subordinated groups.

In such an analysis it is helpful to view Supreme Court decision making as a two-stage process. The first stage is the identification of the presence and nature of constitutional principles at issue in a particular case. The second stage then asks how the recognition and definition of political, economic, and social facts change over time and how changes in the definition of social facts inform changes in constitutional law or doctrine.

Beliefs About Social Realities in Paired Landmark Cases

Scholars have differed over what the central problem of the *Lochner* era was. What is clear is that justices' beliefs about the social realities of the times played an important role in their decisions. One could not explain the decisions of that era without considering justices' beliefs about social reality, especially given the fact that the Court supported the constitutionality of many state and federal laws that were passed to benefit the health and safety of citizens but struck down others on the ground that they violated the liberty to contract (see Gillman 1993).

In *Lochner v. New York* (1905) the Court found unconstitutional a law that would have limited the hours that a baker could work each day and week. Members of the Supreme Court employed their beliefs about social reality in two ways to consider whether the right of employer and employee to contract freely for labor under the due process clause of the Fourteenth Amendment had been violated by the New York law. First, the *Lochner* Court spoke about the social realities of the baking industry: "As to the trade there is no danger to the employee in a first class bakery and so far as unsanitary conditions are concerned the employee is protected by other sections of the law" (*Lochner,* 49). Second, the Court then argued that the law was not passed to rectify the social reality of poor working conditions or employee health: "The statute in question was never intended as a health provision but was purely a labor law" (*Lochner,* 50). In this sense, the Court opted to view the law as regulating labor relations and contracting rather than as state protection of public health and safety. The Court notes that both the company employing a baker and the individual baker were equally free to buy or sell labor, if the liberty of contract is to be protected. Having found the working conditions of bakers not as intolerable as those of miners, the Court decided that the right to contract trumped the need for the state to regulate the hours for workers. For the majority the facts were clear: working in a bakery was not a risk to health, and employers and employees in this industry were perfectly capable of using their freedom of contract to protect themselves.

The central holdings of the *Lochner* case were challenged in a number of rulings that ultimately culminated in *West Coast Hotel v. Parrish* (1937), a case that upheld a state minimum-wage law. What is significant about *West Coast* is that it eviscerated many of the central premises or assumptions about social facts held by the *Lochner* Court. These included the notion that employers and employees had equal bargaining power and could thus take care of their own interests by exercising their contractual freedom. In *West Coast,* the Court wrote, "The exploitation of a class of workers who are in an unequal position with respect to bargaining power and are thus relatively defenseless against the denial of a living wage is not only detrimental to their health and well being but cast a direct burden for their support upon the community" (399).

Another familiar example of how beliefs about social reality affect Supreme Court decision making comes to light in comparing *Plessy v. Ferguson* (1896) to *Brown v. Board of Education* (1954). The belief about social reality in *Plessy,* where the Court upheld racial segregation and enunciated the "separate but equal" doctrine, is one in which there is an extraordinary unwillingness to acknowledge the social consequences of segregation, an unwillingness so stubborn that it led the Court to claim (in essence) that the evils of segregation existed merely in the minds of blacks. The Court wrote: "We consider the underlying fallacy in the plaintiff's argument to consist in the assumption that the enforced separation of the two races stamps the colored race with a badge of inferiority. If this be so, it is not by reason of anything found in the act, *but solely because the colored race chooses to put that construction upon it*" (emphasis added).

Brown, on the other hand, is animated not merely by change in doctrine but primarily by a change in the justices' beliefs about the social reality of segregation. In *Plessy,* the stigma, or imputation of inferiority, caused by the state's separating whites and African Americans by race in railroad cars was viewed as personal and social, not induced by state action in separating the races. In *Brown,* the Court views such stigma as caused not by simple individual perceptions of inequality but as created by law as it interacts with human psychology. Quoting the trial court judge, the *Brown* Court (at 494) wrote:

> Segregation of white and colored children in public schools has a detrimental effect upon the colored children. The impact is greater when it has the sanction of law; for the policy of separating the races is usually interpreted as denoting the inferiority of the negro group. A sense of inferiority affects the motivation of a child to learn. Segregation with the sanction of law, therefore, has a tendency to [retard] the educational and mental development of Negro children and to deprive them of some of the benefits they would receive in a racial[ly] integrated school system.

The Court further noted that "whatever may have been the extent of psychological knowledge at the time of *Plessy v. Ferguson,* this finding is amply
supported by modern authority." Thus the Court's change in doctrine
hinges on its recognition of a new social reality about legally enforced segregation and its impact on individual self-esteem and self-respect. However, it is important to note that the Court's beliefs about social reality in
Brown are drawn from two separate sources: the justices' conception of
rights or legal principles in the Constitution, and their recognition of particular social, economic, and political inequalities or particular empirical
facts. The moral force of *Brown* does not come from the empirical facts
alone—psychological experiments with dolls or the fact of measured differences in levels of self-esteem between black and white children—but
from their relationship to a particular conception of equality that the justices think required by the equal protection clause. Hence, there is a distinction between sociological or political facts as simple statements of
empirical data and beliefs about social reality that tie such facts to a conception of legal principle. The former is simply a description of empirical
reality, but the latter is a statement about socially constructed reality, carrying with it normative implications that become embedded in doctrine,
with important precedential value.

   This process of the Court's bringing empirical facts to bear on socially
constructed and contingent values or frames of understanding can be seen in
a second set of cases. In *Bradwell v. Illinois* (1872), the Supreme Court refused to overturn an Illinois law that denied the right of women to be
licensed as lawyers. In a concurring opinion (*Bradwell,* 141), Justice Bradley
wrote:

> The civil law, as well as nature herself, has always recognized a wide difference
> in the respective spheres and destinies of man and woman. Man is, or should
> be, women's protector and defender. The natural and proper timidity and del-
> icacy which belongs to the female sex evidently unfits it for many of the occu-
> pations of civil life. The constitution of the family organization, which is
> founded on divine ordinance, as well as in the nature of things, indicates the
> domestic sphere as that which properly belongs to the domain and functions
> of womanhood. The harmony, not to say the identity, of interest and views
> which belong, or should belong, to the family institution is repugnant to the
> idea of a woman adopting a distinct and independent career from that of her
> husband.

One hundred years after *Bradwell,* the Supreme Court established the right of abortion choice for women in *Roe v. Wade* (1973). In *Planned Parenthood of Southeastern Pennsylvania v. Casey* (1992) the central question was whether the right of abortion choice that was established in *Roe* should be maintained. The justices' beliefs about social reality and the part it plays in deciding whether a right has become a settled expectation was central to *Casey.* The Court found that the role of women in the economic, social, and political system had expanded to such a degree that the right of abortion choice in 1992 was almost more important than it had been in 1973. Moreover, beliefs about social reality also supported the conclusion that women should not be required to notify a husband of an abortion. Given current knowledge of domestic abuse and contemporary social norms, such a restriction, the Court concluded, would pose an "undue burden" on a woman's liberty. The point is not whether the evidence shows there is more physical abuse of women today or just more reported physical abuse. A majority of the Court was placing within the precedents on privacy and abortion rights a belief about social reality, which added to the moral force of the women's liberty interest at stake in the case.

As we have seen then, beliefs about social reality are built into the development of an area of case law or doctrine as precedents. What is contestable and for the Court to decide in new cases is whether the justices' beliefs about social reality in a case before it are congruent with the beliefs about social reality in past cases so that they can determine whether a particular right or legal principle should be extended in the new case. In making this determination, the Court may reinvigorate, or change, the belief about social reality, so as to make it congruent with changes in the nation's economic, political, or social life—and thus continue to protect the principles in the Constitution.

From these paired cases we can begin to understand the benefits derived by studying beliefs about social realities. First, we can begin to gain a better understanding of why landmark cases may be overturned. Once beliefs about social facts become embedded in precedents, they inform the nature of future definitions of rights. Beliefs about social realities in precedents can become foundational to the definition of future rights. This also creates the possibility of potentially anachronistic beliefs about social realities, as was the case in *Lochner.* As beliefs about social reality change, the justices are forced to ask what is similar and different in society as a basis for considering new notions of rights or legal principles in new situations.

Beliefs About Social Realities and Doctrinal Change in an Unsettled Area of the Law: Capital Punishment

We have explored the presence of beliefs about social realities in landmark cases in order to define the term and to suggest that beliefs about social reality have been present throughout the history of the Court and are central to the development of constitutional law. This approach has also helped us to understand how the Supreme Court has defined some of the most important political and social issues facing the United States and to gain insights into how it relates its decision making to important tensions in our nation's social fabric. We now turn to consider the role of beliefs about social realities in the unsettled doctrinal area of capital punishment. In doctrinal areas in which beliefs about social reality are unclear or not fully developed, there is the possibility that the impact of changing social, political, and economic facts on the development of constitutional law will be greater.

In *McGautha v. California* (1971) a 6-to-3 Court held that states need not specify in statute the factors that juries must consider before imposing death sentences. Writing for the Court, Justice Harlan argued that such a requirement would not only be an unwelcome judicial intrusion on the power of the legislative branch but that it would also be an impossible one for state legislatures to meet: "To identify before the fact those characteristics of criminal homicides and their perpetrators which call for the death penalty, and to express these characteristics in language which can be fairly understood and applied by the sentencing authority, appear to be tasks which are beyond present human ability" (*McGautha,* 204). Instead, the Court emphasized the need for the nation to place its trust in the jury system for making decisions about capital sentencing. According to Harlan (at 208, 221):

> The States are entitled to assume that jurors confronted with the truly awesome responsibility of decreeing death for a fellow human will act with due regard for the consequences of their decision and will consider a variety of factors, many of which will have been suggested by the evidence or by the arguments of defense counsel. . . . The Constitution requires no more than that trials be fairly conducted and that guaranteed rights of defendants be scrupulously respected.

The *McGautha* Court thus emphasized the need for the nation to place its trust in the jury as the appropriate organ to reflect the community's values, act as an agent of mercy, and exercise discretion when deciding the fate of a convicted criminal. In the Court's view, forcing standards upon the legislative branch would be inconsistent with history and the constitutionally assigned roles of the two branches of government. Moreover, the Court noted that justices throughout history had feared that a lack of jury discretion would create rigid guidelines that would force many prisoners to be put to death.[1] Justice Cardozo wrote in *McGautha* (194): "What we have is merely a privilege offered to the jury to find the lesser degree when the suddenness of the intent, the vehemence of the passion, seems to call irresistibly for the exercise of mercy. I have no objection to giving them this dispensing power, but it should be given to them directly and not in a mystifying cloud of words." *McGautha* also quotes Chief Justice Warren, writing in *Witherspoon v. Illinois* (1968), that juries "do little more—and must do nothing less—than express the conscience of the community on the ultimate question of life or death" (*McGautha*, 202). Finally, the lack of fixed standards in jury sentencing does not violate the rule of law principles, the *McGautha* Court argued, because the jury system itself has become part of the rule of law: the jury with its discretionary role is thoroughly ingrained in our Constitution.

Just one year later, however, in *Furman v. Georgia* (1972), the Court struck down the application of a jury-imposed death sentence and unsettled this formulation of the role of juries, legislatures, and courts in the capital sentencing process, leaving the fate of capital punishment in limbo. The Court's shift in *Furman* was caused in part by the turnover of personnel; Justices Harlan and Black were replaced by Rehnquist and Powell. The *Furman* majority consisted of Justices Douglas, Brennan, Stewart, White, and Marshall, and each issued a separate opinion. The *Furman* dissent consisted of Chief Justice Burger and Justices Blackmun, Powell, and Rehnquist. Only two justices, Brennan and Marshall, voted to overturn the death penalty in its entirety. The four dissenting justices left the death penalty in its then-current state, but Justices Douglas, Stewart, and White disliked the inconsistent nature in which they felt the death penalty was applied by juries that had no legislatively imposed standards or restrictions (*Furman*, 310).

Consequently, *Furman* did not create a new view of where the nation should place its trust in making decisions about capital punishment. Not only did the Court fail to present a majority opinion, but only two of the five in the plurality—Justices Marshall and Brennan—called for the outright abolition of the death penalty as inconsistent with the Eighth Amendment's ban on "cruel and unusual punishments" and other constitutional principles that protect "human dignity." The remaining three members of the majority argued that the penalty would be constitutional if properly applied by juries. Justice Douglas based his opinion upon his beliefs that "there is increasing recognition of the fact that the basic theme of equal protection is implicit in 'cruel and unusual' punishments" and that the poor are disproportionately put to death. This empirical fact, which Douglas gleaned from the President's Commission on Law Enforcement and Administration of Justice, led him to conclude that equal protection required some controls on the disproportionate jury sentencing of the poor and minorities (*Furman*, 249). Justice Stewart also expressed concerns over how inconsistently the penalty was applied and argued that states must ensure that it is not "wantonly and freakishly" imposed by juries. Justice White thought that the death penalty was not being imposed with enough frequency and consistency to render it a deterrent of crime, an important justification for its constitutionality.

The dissent held the view that determinations of the effectiveness and morality of a crime are powers delegated to the legislative branch. A punishment is cruel if the society characterizing the punishment believes it to be cruel, but the standard itself does not change. Thus, the legislature is entrusted with the task of responding to the will of the people, and the people speak to their elected representatives in terms of what they believe to be moral. If the dissent believed the decision was beyond the power of the Court, the majority obviously did not. At the time *Furman* was decided, forty states and the District of Columbia allowed the death penalty, and despite Justice Brennan's contention that "legislative authorization, of course, does not establish acceptance" (*Furman*, 279), to say otherwise would allow for untrammeled Court power.

The lack of a clear view about the social reality of the death penalty and what constitutes cruel and unusual punishment necessarily complicated the role that "social facts" could play in the Court's decision. For what legitimate social condition informed change, what legal principles influenced possible "social facts," and what compelled Justices Stewart and White to alter their views so drastically that *McGautha* was overruled a year after its decision? Justice Blackmun wrote, "The argument [against the death penalty], plausible and high-sounding as it may be, is not persuasive, for it is only one year since *McGautha*, only eight and one-half years since *Rudolph*, fourteen years since *Trop*, and twenty-five years since *Francis*, and we have been presented with nothing that demonstrates a significant movement of any kind in these brief periods. The Court has just decided that it is time to strike down the death penalty" (*Furman*, 408). Justice Blackmun, like the rest of the dissent, feared that the death penalty would be imposed far more frequently if standardized jury discretion were mandated (*Furman*, 413). The overarching issue for Blackmun was the lack of a principled basis for change from trusting juries in *McGautha*: social conditions, the application of the sentencing scheme, the structure of government, public support for capital punishment, or a specific constitutional principle. Justice Blackmun was raising the issue of instrumentalism by these assertions, and one cannot help but question whether the Court truly acted as a policy-making body. Justice Blackmun even wrote that "the temptations to cross that policy line are very great. In fact, as today's decision reveals, they are almost irresistible." In closing, Justice Blackmun wrote, "I fear the Court has overstepped. It has sought and has achieved an end"(*Furman*, 414).

Furman is best read as a rejection of unmitigated jury discretion and a call for guided jury discretion, but not as a fiat to abolish the death penalty, for only two of nine justices viewed such action as compelled by the Constitution. Significantly, the history of the futile attempts to classify crimes for application of the death penalty, which figured so prominently in Harlan's opinion in *McGautha*, was glossed over entirely by the plurality in *Furman*. In fact, none of the five majority opinions even discuss *McGautha* in any detail. In this sense, the nature of the death penalty, the conception of cruel and unusual punishment, and the role of the jury in capital sentencing remained unclear in *Furman*. Thus, one should not view *Furman* as merely the debate in the Court on the contemporary meaning of the cruel and unusual punishment clause. *Furman* was problematic because it did not consider the belief about the social reality of the death penalty and the inability of legislatures to offer practicable guidance to juries in *McGautha*. Four years later, in *Gregg v. Georgia* (1976), beliefs about social realities for capital punishment cases were finally solidified.

Gregg was convicted of killing a travel companion, and in order for the jury to give the death penalty, the state required that three aggravating circumstances be met. "One—The offense of murder was committed while the offender was engaged in the commission of two other capital felonies, to-wit the armed robbery. . . . Two—The offender committed the offense of murder for the purpose of receiving money and the automobile described in the indictment. Three—The offense of murder was outrageously and wantonly vile, horrible and inhuman, in that it involved the depravity of the mind of the defendant" (*Gregg v. Georgia,* 161). The jury found that the first two circumstances were met and sentenced Gregg to death.

The Court held that "the punishment of death does not invariably violate the Constitution" (*Gregg,* 169). In so doing, *Gregg* confirms that the Court did not resolve the issue of the death penalty in *Furman;* that is, the death penalty is not unconstitutional on its face and Georgia now had adequate safeguards. The opinion of Justices Stewart, Powell, and Stevens held that "the [Eighth] Amendment has been interpreted in a flexible and dynamic manner. The Court early recognized that 'a principle to be vital must be capable of wider application than the mischief which gave it birth.' . . . The Amendment must draw its meaning from the evolving standards of decency that mark the progress of a maturing society" (*Gregg,* 173).

Gregg effectively replaces *Furman* in the capital punishment doctrinal area by viewing it as an unsettled case. First, the Court's plurality of Justices Stewart, Powell, and Stevens settled the issue of the extent of state legislative and judicial power over sentencing and the question of whether capital punishment is in nature cruel and unusual: "We may not require the legislature to select the least severe penalty possible so long as the penalty selected is not cruelly inhumane or disproportionate to the crime involved. And a heavy burden rests on those who would attack the judgment of the representatives of the people. . . . The deference we owe to the decisions of the state legislatures under our federal system is enhanced where the specification of punishments is concerned, for 'these are peculiarly questions of legislative policy' " (*Gregg,* 176). The three justices also found that it is outside the Court's scope to determine the legitimacy or effectiveness of the motives of deterrence or retribution, for such a determination is for the legislature and is an expression of "the community's belief that certain crimes are themselves so grievous an affront to humanity that the only adequate response may be the penalty of death" (*Gregg,* 184). Following *Gregg,* the legislatures of at least thirty-five states enacted new statutes that provide for the death penalty for some types of crimes that result in the death of another person. Thus, the acceptability of capital punishment as a form of punishment under the cruel and unusual punishments clause has been resolved.

Next the Court tackled the question of jury discretion. To begin with, they point out that "the relative infrequency of jury verdicts imposing the death sentence does not indicate rejection of capital punishment per se.

Rather, the reluctance of juries in many cases to impose the sentence may well reflect the humane feeling that this most irrevocable of sanctions should be reserved for a small number of extreme cases" (*Gregg*, 182). The conception of the jury is settled and is quite similar to the one found in *McGautha*, albeit slightly modified, as we shall see. The Court is here concerned only with the imposition of the death penalty in the case of murder, and the Georgia legislature modified their rules so as to fit with *Furman*'s ruling against unmitigated jury discretion. Indeed, the Court interpreted *Furman* as reading that "where discretion is afforded a sentencing body on a matter so grave as the determination of whether a human life should be taken or spared, that discretion must be suitably directed and limited so as to minimize the risk of wholly arbitrary and capricious action" (*Gregg*, 189). The problems of prejudice in sentencing are thus solved by Georgia's bifurcated process of sentencing, the limiting of the death penalty to certain cases, and guidance by the presiding judge, whose instructions to the jury contained the three mitigating circumstances.

The most important change from *McGautha* with respect to the role of the jury is the belief that definite standards can be set to guide jury discretion. In *Gregg* (193–95) the three justices write:

> While such standards are by necessity somewhat general, they do provide guidance to the sentencing authority and thereby reduce the likelihood that it will impose a sentence that fairly can be called capricious or arbitrary. . . . The concerns expressed in *Furman* that the penalty of death not be imposed in an arbitrary or capricious manner can be met by a carefully drafted statute that ensures that the sentencing authority is given adequate information and guidance.

Finally, the Court settled the concerns raised in *Furman* relating to the use of the death penalty compared to the granting of mercy by a jury. According to Justices Stewart, Powell, and Stevens, "The isolated decision of a jury to afford mercy does not render unconstitutional death sentences imposed on defendants who were sentenced under a system that does not create a substantial risk of arbitrariness or caprice" (*Gregg*, 203).

In *McGautha* the Court said the jury system is an integral part of the constitutional order. *Furman* also said the jury system is integral but that it must be modified to the point of guiding the discretion of the jury to ensure that some measure of equal punishment for equal acts be secured. In *Gregg* the Court approved Georgia's design for jury discretion. Thereby, the Court has chosen to stay with a belief about social realities that emphasizes the principle of trust in juries to make decisions, even death sentences, as long as each jury has clear guidelines as to what type of actions might result in a death penalty.

Eleven years later, in *McCleskey v. Kemp* (1987), the Court reinforced the place of the jury system as an integral part of our system of justice, as indicated by the belief about social reality solidified in *Gregg*. *McCleskey* clarifies the difference between social facts about the specific party in a case and social facts as they are related to the bigger picture—development of the rights of subordinated groups. It also demonstrates how stubborn justices can be about accepting social facts that they view as not being linked to the rights or legal principles they strongly believe are controlling in a case.

McCleskey considers whether the race of the defendant and victim is an important factor in whether a defendant receives a death penalty. The *McCleskey* majority refused to consider social science data that demonstrated the death penalty was disproportionately applied to racial minorities. Rather, they continued to place their faith in juries acting under proper state guidance. According to Justice Powell, "It is the jury's function to make the difficult and uniquely human judgments that defy codification. . . . Where the discretion that is fundamental to our criminal process is involved, we decline to assume that what is unexplained is invidious" (*McCleskey*, 311–13). The plurality then says that the issue is better presented to the legislature, for it is not "the responsibility—or indeed even the right—of this court to determine the appropriate punishment for particular crimes" (*McCleskey*, 319).

The belief about social realities in the death penalty area emphasizes the polity principles of trust in juries and deference to states in the determination of criminal penalties. The belief rejects as important the sociological facts as to race and the disproportionate imposition of the death penalty because it would undercut the polity principles of prior cases, trusting states and juries. Moreover, while the data on race and death penalties could raise questions of equal protection of the law, the belief about the social realities of respecting polity principles is so clear that consideration of the data on race and the death penalty is cursory at best, even though the evidence about the correlations is dramatic. Instead, the Court relies on the principle of stare decisis to reject the equal protection claim. Justice Powell has written, "To prevail under the Equal Protection Clause, *McCleskey* must prove that the decision makers in his case acted with discriminatory purpose" (*McCleskey*, 292). *McCleskey* offered none. Consequently, the failure of the Court in prior capital punishment cases to look at defendants by race as a suspect class or at the effect of race on jury decisions to impose the death penalty makes it difficult to do so in *McCleskey*. Nor is there a normative predicate for looking at such data in terms of an equal protection violation, absent a showing of specific evidence of patterns of discriminatory purpose.

The only way a change in doctrine in this area can occur is if social facts as linked to constitutional theory are introduced into the Court's thinking. That is, the empirical facts on race and the imposition of the death penalty must be viewed as relevant to the question of whether the death penalty is itself constitutional and not from the viewpoint of whether a particular defendant has been denied equal protection. To make this change means developing a constitutional theory that links such facts to the structural conditions of jury operations, thus undercutting the faith in the jury system and deference to states. In this same way, the social facts about segregation in schools in 1954 looked very different from segregation on railcars in 1896. The linkage of social facts to normative polity and rights principles is required if the belief about social reality is to change.

This brief discussion of the role of the justices' beliefs about social reality in the Court's decisions regarding the death penalty illustrates how focusing on those beliefs helps us understand linkages between political culture and Supreme Court decision making. Examining the justices' beliefs about social reality forces us to conceptualize constitutional law in ways that simply considering legal principles and arguments in a case does not. If the Supreme Court does not engage in mechanical doctrinalism or simply reflect the social and economic power in society, as I argue elsewhere, then we must gain a better sense of why the Court defines new rights, offers more complex notions of the political system's malfunction, and presents new definitions of what constitutes important constitutional questions over time.[2]

What is clear is that except for perhaps the most extreme originalists, beliefs about social realities inform most judicial decisions, whether the judge be conservative, moderate, or liberal. By analyzing what beliefs about social reality are embedded in different areas of doctrine, we can determine whether the role of beliefs about social realities differs within and between doctrinal areas. As the abortion rights cases demonstrate, beliefs about social realities are central to the analysis of what constitutes "ordered liberty," under the Fourteenth Amendment's due process clause. However, beliefs about social reality may be less central to, say, First Amendment speech issues because of the importance of the premise of content neutrality, as seen in cases in which the Rehnquist Court has approved flag burning and banned content-based hate-speech laws.[3] Also, beliefs about social reality may be less central to environmental law cases because each case involves complex factual and scientific issues and procedural questions, so that set beliefs about social reality in precedent may be less prevalent. Therefore, the role of social, economic, and political facts in doctrinal change requires careful evaluation and comparison of different doctrinal areas.

Beliefs About Social Realities and the History and Politics Paradigm—Explaining How the Outside World Gets into Supreme Court Decision Making

Over the years our nation has reinvigorated its constitutional ideals, including its conceptions of liberty, due process of law, and equal protection. It has done so while upholding the rule of law, polity and rights principles, and the legitimacy of the Court. In order for the Court to continue to play a progressive role in expanding protections for subordinated groups, the reformation of constitutional values in the future must be predicated on the inclusion of the experiences of all groups and individuals in our nation.

Social facts that become embedded in legal precedents play a substantial role in the evolution of constitutional values. The consideration of such facts is possible only if one views Court decision making in constitutive terms, meaning that as a body it is viewed as respecting precedent, applying polity and rights principles, and cognizant of the dialectical nature of American political culture and the importance of the historical relationship of political institutions to each other. Because most scholars have considered social facts only as sociological facts, as simple facts, rather than as beliefs about social reality as outlined here, too few have dealt with social facts as related to constitutional precedent and theory. Therefore, they have understated the possibilities for their role in informing new conceptions of constitutional values and transforming American legal and political culture.[4]

Studying justices' beliefs about social realities in the context of their relationship to social facts in precedents and constitutional theory is a way to understand how facts about the outside world become part of constitutional law. Moreover, beliefs about social reality in precedents aid the justices in determining whether there has been significant change within a doctrinal area, as well as in determining the strength of a polity or rights principle within a case or doctrinal area, as we saw in the comparison of *Plessy* to *Brown*.

The capital punishment cases demonstrate that beliefs about social reality can inform constitutional norms that are built on views about the polity or political structure, such as deference to state courts and juries. When this occurs we can expect that beliefs about social realities in the larger sense, in this case the relationship between race and capital punishment, will be less central. Future research must identify and compare patterns of beliefs about social realities in doctrinal areas. Only in this way can we fully understand the nature of Supreme Court decision making, the social context in which such decisions are made, and how the rights of subordinated groups might be redefined in the future.

Acknowledgments

I want to thank the editors of this volume as well as Steven Manthe, research assistant, and Susan Dennehy, McNair Summer Research Intern, for their very able assistance. I also want to thank Oberlin College for financial support from the James Monroe Chair Research Fund and the McNair Summer Student Research Program.

Notes

1. See Chief Justice Burger's opinion, *Furman v. Georgia* (1972), starting at 375.

2. See Greenstone (1988) for the concept of a liberal political culture with conflicting strands. See Kahn (1996) for a discussion of Greenstone's vision of liberalism as applied to Supreme Court decision making.

3. See *Texas v. Johnson* (1989) and *Lee v. Weisman* (1992). Studies must be undertaken to see to what degree beliefs about social, economic, and political facts play a role in different areas of constitutional law.

4. By drawing upon the republican, reformed humanist, and reformed liberal strands of American liberalism, though, one can see various elements of a liberal tradition that allow one to discern more accurately the proper use and role of present social conditions and structures that affect the life chances of citizens. These areas of American liberalism allow one to bring the outside world into Court decision making in that they align social facts in a hierarchy of American political culture and place them within a framework that respects constitutional principles and precedents.

Part II

The Supreme Court in Political Context

Chapter 5

How the Supreme Court Matters
in American Politics:
New Institutionalist Perspectives

Michael McCann

Scholarly perspectives regarding how and how much the U.S. Supreme Court matters in the nation's public life have varied widely over recent decades. By and large, assessments have shifted in response to broader political currents.

It was common from the late 1950s through the 1970s for intellectuals—and especially those with liberal commitments—to portray the Court as a significant democratizing force in post–New Deal American politics. This understanding responded to and largely heralded the Warren Court's activism in areas of equal protection, due process, and free speech. Many social scientists found in this activity new evidence of the dynamic political "pluralism" that characterized American politics. In this view, the federal judiciary established itself not only as one of many significant actors in the political landscape but also as a unique source of institutional "access" for those citizens disenfranchised or ineffective in gaining voice elsewhere in the system. Other intellectuals emphasized instead the distinctive moral authority of the Court as a defender of individual rights and liberties. In the most idealistic version—popularized in books like Anthony Lewis's *Gideon's Trumpet,* Jack Peltason's *Fifty-eight Lonely Men,* and Richard Kluger's *Simple Justice*—the High Court was portrayed as a heroic band of White Knights who courageously wielded their swords of principled legal reason to slay monstrous injustices long afflicting our nation. Although these accounts varied in focus and tone, each tended to assume that winning in court was the key indicator of political success and that the Court's actions were inherently consequential in addressing the social problems at stake.

Scholarly assessments of judicial importance grew more circumspect as the political context changed, liberal hopes faded, and the judicial legacy was subjected to new modes of analysis beginning in the 1970s, however.[1] Behavioral social scientists, relying on a positivist epistemology and sophisticated research methods, were among the first to question earlier expectations. On the one hand, such studies attempted to show that the Court rarely acts boldly or independently. Rather, it has followed the lead of the dominant political coalition or lawmaking majority most of the time (Dahl 1957; Funston 1975). On the other hand, behavioral scholars demonstrated as well that the actual "impacts" of heralded landmark judicial decisions on established social practices have been far less significant than often assumed.[2] For example, a host of studies found that local government evasion was widespread among police responding to historic Court decisions mandating fair investigative and interrogation practices as well as among education administrators in the aftermath of rulings barring religious practices in public schools (Horowitz 1977; Dolbeare and Hammond 1971). More recently, Gerald Rosenberg's trenchant treatise, *The Hollow Hope* (1991), identified similar patterns of noncompliance for a variety of landmark decisions in postwar America. Perhaps most important, he demonstrated how the Court's high-profile order of school desegregation at "all deliberate speed" in *Brown v. Board of Education* (1954) met with widespread evasion and open defiance throughout the South. Only when the president intervened with armed force and Congress later took statutory action backed by financial sanctions did significant desegregation commence. In sum, behavioral impact studies have tended to conclude that the Court rarely challenges the prevailing currents of national politics and that its capacity to command compliance in resistant institutional settings distant from the nation's capital is weak. As such, these studies dramatize the great gap between the promises of liberal court action and its actual impact on social practice (Becker and Feeley 1973). For many scholars, these findings have underlined a basic insight of "legal realism"—that judicially constructed law is mostly epiphenomenal and derivative of, rather than an independent force shaping, social and economic life.

Other scholarly approaches recently identified with new institutionalism have refined or revised the skeptical conclusions of such behavioral impact studies. Much of this scholarship has endeavored to demonstrate that the Supreme Court matters rather more than most behavioral gap studies suggest, although such influence is highly complex and contingent in character as well as normatively ambiguous in its implications for the advancement of social justice. In this chapter I shall briefly outline two specific dimensions—one focusing on "strategic interaction" among political actors, the other focusing on law's "constitutive" power—of recent institutional analysis regarding the many roles of courts, and especially of the Supreme Court, in American society.[3] Each of these orientations differs in its core questions, its foundational assumptions, its basic units of analysis, and its standards of assessing judicial "influence." So far, only limited effort has been made to integrate insights of both approaches into a single, comprehensive, multidimensional framework for understanding how legal institutions matter in public life. However, I shall argue that the recent development of the new institutionalism as an intellectual movement provides both opportunity and motivation for the development of just such linkages between different but potentially complementary analytical modes.

Politics in the Shadow of the Court: The Strategic Interaction Approach

The Court and Strategic Politics

The first dimension of institutional analysis that we shall review has focused on the strategic interaction of courts with other political actors. Studies focusing on strategic interaction have emanated from a wide variety of scholarly traditions, including traditional behavioral science studies of the Court's roles in national government (Dahl 1957; Casper 1976; Funston 1975); more qualitatively oriented, quasi-positivist historical studies of judicial roles in particular policy processes (Melnick 1983; Johnson and Canon 1984; Graber 1993; Rodgers and Bullock 1972; Burgess 1992); interpretive studies of civil disputing and legal mobilization (Scheingold 1974; Zemans 1983; Olson 1984; Milner 1986; McCann 1994; H. Silverstein 1996); and, most recently, more formalized models derived from rational choice and game theory frameworks (Epstein and Walker 1995; Knight and Epstein 1996; Farber and Frickey 1991; Eskridge 1991).[4] Although all of these types of studies have contributed to contemporary scholarship on the Court, the last two—interpretive and game theory frameworks—have been most commonly identified specifically with the new institutionalism (R. Smith 1988). The common focus of such studies regards how the deliberations and actions of various social agents—including individuals, groups, and institutions both in and beyond the state—are shaped by understandings about settled norms articulated by courts as well as by expectations of likely court action in unsettled areas of law. Such interaction among political agents is considered to be "strategic" to the extent that it is consciously deliberative, oriented toward instrumental "effectiveness" in advancing particular goals, and hence loosely understood as "rational" (see Epstein and Knight 1997; Gillman 1999).[5]

Understood in these terms, the strategic approach departs from core assumptions of traditional institutional accounts of behavioral impact studies in some important ways. For one thing, the two approaches differ somewhat in how they view the legal products of judicial activity. Behavioral impact studies tend to view judicially constructed law in narrow terms of relatively discrete and determinate rules or commands. This is important, for this model of law establishes clear standards for evaluating compliance by targeted groups. Scholars who address judicial influence in terms of strategic interaction, by contrast, tend to view judicial actions as more variable and open-textured in character. As Marc Galanter puts it, the law articulated by courts is better understood as complex signals rather than as "a set of operative controls. It affects us primarily through communication of symbols—by providing threats, promises, models, persuasion, legitimacy, stigma, and so on"(1983, 127). As such, judicial constructions of law are understood to be inherently indeterminate and subject to multiple interpretations by differently situated actors.[6]

It follows that most studies of strategic interaction likewise assess judicial influence itself in somewhat different terms from those of impact models. Traditional behavioral approaches to institutions tend to conceptualize judicial impact in quite mechanical terms of "causality." The logic is well captured in political scientist Robert Dahl's classic formulation: "A has the power over B to the extent that he can get B to do something B would not otherwise do" (1961, 12). Adapted to the institution in question, the Supreme Court is viewed as the legal agent whose impact is measured by its effectiveness in altering specific behaviors of various targeted officials and citizens in prescribed ways. This influence of legal directives, to the extent it exists, is viewed generally as unidirectional, linear, and direct. Moreover, in many schemes, the intended behavioral change must occur relatively quickly and affect a wide scope of targeted subjects to count as significant.[7] Finally, only responses that are in compliance, or at least are consistent, with Supreme Court mandates count as noteworthy. Again, the assumption that law is manifest in clear, determinate directives is essential to measuring impact in these causal terms.

Social scientists interested in strategic politics generally concede the central insight of behavioral gap studies alleging that federal courts alone rarely "cause" significant social change in predetermined directions. But most contemporary scholars interested in strategic action find such a claim hardly remarkable. After all, no single institution in our mixed governmental system possesses sufficient power to unilaterally cause widespread, significant social change. Moreover, our courts were designed as the "least dangerous branch" of our governmental scheme; they generally possess neither executive police powers nor direct control over budgetary resources with which to compel compliance from others (Horowitz 1977; Rosenberg 1992). Indeed, judicial decisions typically are restricted to specific parties—for the Supreme Court, involving mostly governmental actors—in particular cases. For unspecified others, each ruling is akin to a weather vane showing which way the judicial wind is blowing. For these reasons, it thus is not surprising that studies assessing whether courts unilaterally cause great change come to mostly negative conclusions.

The problem, however, is that linear impact approaches also tend to overlook the many complex, subtle ways that the courts do greatly matter in our society. For scholars interested in strategic interaction, this means evaluating forms of influence beyond capacity to obtain behavioral compliance (see Brigham 1987a, 205). After all, judicial decisions do not simply dictate particular types of behavior; rather, they identify potential opportunities and costs, resources and constraints, which become meaningful only in the diverse strategic responses from differently situated public and private actors in society, many of which are unintended and unanticipated by judicial authorities. "The messages disseminated by courts do not . . . produce effects except as they are received, interpreted, and used by (potential) actors," notes Galanter (1983, 136). As such, judicial power is understood in relational and intersubjective terms, and it includes symbolic and communicative as well as material dimensions.[8] The positivist emphasis on relative "determination" of behavior by discrete social forces is replaced with the attention to dynamic processes of ongoing, contingent dialectical interaction among reasoning human subjects and institutional actors.[9]

One classic way of conceptualizing this strategic influence of courts is in terms of the "shadow" they cast on "bargaining" relationships among officials, citizen subjects, or both. (Mnookin and Kornhauser 1979; Galanter 1983). In this view, court actions provide various strategic "endowments" to parties engaged in different relationships throughout society. Such judicially authorized endowments thus typically become "bargaining chips" or resources in negotiations that flow from predictions about what the parties would get if they ended up in court or before other legal authorities. These chips include considerations about both the expected outcomes of adjudication and the expected financial, organizational, emotional, and symbolic costs imposed by participation in formal legal processes. Judicially constructed legal endowments influence not just the terms of specific negotiated relationships, moreover, but the very formulation of particular claims and the willingness to act on them, to escalate disputes, and even to negotiate at all. The assumption is that courts not only resolve discrete disputes over law's meaning through clear commands; they also routinely deter, invite, structure, displace, and transform disputing activity throughout society. Courts, "as institutions, are not therefore unimportant," for various political actors' "strategic options and resources and even goals are to some extent supplied by the law and the institutions that 'apply' it" (Galanter 1983, 119). Critical to this understanding is the fact that such judicial influence on strategic action usually is manifest in relationships prior to, and often wholly apart from, the filing of legal charges, consultation with lawyers, or even the expectation that courts or other official third parties actually might intervene in particular relationships (McCann 1994).

The preceding conceptualization was developed to make sense primarily of trial court influence in routine civil disputes, but it is equally applicable to the high profile workings of the Supreme Court in our national public life. In particular, the strategic approach aims to provide important insights into the political dynamics of shared government authority—including the checking and balancing interplay among various institutions at the national level as well as the interaction among different levels of federal jurisdiction—that is at the heart of our nation's constitutional design. Furthermore, while the Supreme Court for the most part considers only cases involving government officials, the strategic approach is sensitive to how Court actions indirectly create important expectations, endowments, incentives, and constraints for public and private actors alike in institutional venues throughout society.

Most contemporary scholars agree that the Supreme Court has exercised significant influence in shaping the strategic terms of political debate and struggle in this way throughout American history, as my examples will support. But it is worth recognizing that this role has increased considerably in scope during the last half century.[10] Although the Court has significantly withdrawn from the major constitutional disputes over the regulation of capitalist development that dominated its agenda for nearly 150 years, it played a huge role in vastly expanding the public agenda of attention to issues of constitutional liberties and civil rights for decades after World War II. Moreover, the federal courts generally, following the lead of the Supreme Court, have expanded the scope of the judicial intervention in many aspects of government regulatory procedures and practices. Indeed, some analysts have characterized this "judicialization of government administration" as one of the most significant changes in American governmental processes over the last century (McCann 1986; Stewart 1975). The increasing recognition and anticipation of such judicial intervention is one factor that renders courts as powerful authoritative bodies in contemporary American public life.[11]

The reach of the Court's influence on strategic interaction has been too extensive and varied for a comprehensive coverage here. Instead, I outline five general ways that are suggestive of how the Court shapes the terms of strategic interaction among political actors in society. For each, I provide very brief examples of influence among different types of actors, including coequal (executive, federal, judicial) branches of national government, local and state government officials, and organized social groups (business, labor, social movements) who interact with government.[12]

THE JUDICIARY AND THE DISPLACEMENT OF POLITICAL CONFLICT. One of the most important conclusions of behavioral social science studies is that the Supreme Court generally has only rarely exercised bold or independent policy initiative. Rather, conventional accounts suggest, the Court typically follows the policy agenda and preferences of legislative majorities at the national level; its most salient actions often involve enforcing this agenda on resistant officials at state and local levels (Dahl 1957). The primary exception is in periodic moments of "critical realignment" in national politics, when the Court might continue to represent for a short time the policy agenda of a previous lawmaking coalition (including a president who appointed key judges) against a new or ascendant policy coalition (Funston 1975; Adamany 1980).[13] There is much truth in this view, but it also is incomplete and overly simplistic about the relationship between the Court and other coequal branches of national government (Casper 1976; Graber 1993).

Frequently the Court has entered as an independent actor into major conflicts where dominant lawmaking coalitions are either unwilling or unable to act in a concerted, decisive manner. Sometimes judicial majorities simply impose their own judgment in matters where other actors lack power or will to deal effectively or successfully with a policy matter (Epstein and Walker 1995). Yet other branches also at many times have welcomed, even "invited," judicial action on significant issues that are too divisive or politically costly for elected officials to address.[14] In this way the Court often becomes an access point for social interests rebuffed elsewhere, a forum for the "displacement of conflict" from other institutional arenas (see Schattschneider 1975). One significant, if seemingly ironic, implication is that "independent" judicial review of this sort serves both the reigning national party coalition and the party system itself as often by removing disruptive issues from the agenda of majoritarian electoral politics as by following explicit majoritarian policy preferences (Graber 1993).

One excellent historical example of this phenomenon was the infamous *Dred Scott* decision (Newmyer 1968; Fehrenbacher 1978; Potter 1976; Graber 1993). Jacksonian era moderates in both parties sought to sidestep the deeply divisive slavery issue as much as possible for decades. Conflicts over new territories thus were settled by a series of legislative compromises dividing jurisdictions between slave and free labor status, and federal appellate courts generally refrained from ruling on the key constitutional issues at stake. The spirit of legislative compromise and electoral insularity from conflict was undone, however, by the Mexican War, which fueled fears that the newly acquired territories would be opened to slavery, and with the resulting Wilmot Proviso of 1847 aiming to prevent that possibility. As prospects for congressional compromise gave way to sectional rancor and the promise of "popular sovereignty" was ravished by the bloody Kansas-Nebraska experience, party leaders openly appealed to the Supreme Court for a legal resolution. Several bills in the 1850s ceded authority to the Court to adjudicate individual conflicts over slave ownership, and the newly elected president James Buchanan declared that the status of slavery in the territories was a "judicial question, which legitimately belongs to the Supreme Court of the United States" (cited in Graber 1993, 48). However lamentable the Court's specific response in *Dred Scott,* the justices arguably acted less to circumvent political compromise than to insulate electoral politics from growing sectional divisiveness through appeals to higher constitutional principles. The Court's ultimate failure should not obscure the strategic relationships at stake among the key actors.

The Court's more widely celebrated action *in Brown v. Board of Educa-*

tion can be interpreted in much the same terms. Presidents Truman and Eisenhower consciously worked to sidestep the issue of racial segregation as a national electoral concern while at the same time appointing justices supportive of civil rights and pushing the Supreme Court through amicus briefs to take the lead in challenging southern apartheid on constitutional grounds (McAdam 1982). Only later, once public opinion outside the South galvanized in support of civil rights advocates and against white violence, did partisan lawmakers take action in passing legislation against racial segregation. Likewise, political scientist Mark Graber convincingly argues that the Court's controversial rulings interpreting antitrust legislation in *U.S. v. E. C. Knight* (1895) and constructing a constitutional privacy right protecting women's choice in abortions (*Roe v. Wade* [1973]) both exemplified similar patterns of displacing conflict from divisive electoral arenas to less politically vulnerable judicial venues. Indeed, to a large degree the Court's overall "double standard" doctrine regarding constitutional rights following the New Deal reflects this same strategic logic of institutional relations. Relative partisan consensus about the legitimacy of economic regulation rendered it a fairly safe issue for legislators to act on in the decades following the 1930s, while more divisive social issues such as civil rights, abortion, local policing techniques, censorship, and the like were displaced into the hands of the High Court.[15]

THE COURT AS CATALYST: LEGAL AGENDAS, OPPORTUNITIES, AND RESOURCES. A second way that the Court often influences strategic politics is by stimulating or inviting positive responses to its directives from government actors or citizen groups usually not directly involved in specific cases. When the Court acts on a particular disputed issue, it can at once elevate the salience of that issue in the public agenda, privilege some parties who have perceived interests in the issue, create new opportunities for such parties to mobilize around causes, and provide symbolic resources for those mobilization efforts in various venues.[16] Responses from various audiences might address the specific issue to which the Court speaks or some other issue that the Court's action is interpreted to concern, at least potentially. Moreover, such mobilizing action often involves primarily further litigation. As Christine Harrington and Daniel Ward's classic study of federal litigation has suggested, court rulings not only rarely "settle" political conflicts; they often serve to encourage or generate further litigation on public issues (1995). At the same time, however, court rulings can just as often stimulate or "invite"—often unintentionally—other types of political action, including unilateral official initiatives, lobbying of officials for such action, media publicity tactics, and grassroots organizing, to name a few. In short, the process of displacing controversial issues from electoral venues into judicial forums often ends up catalyzing as much as discouraging political mobilization around them among various political audiences (Johnson and Canon 1984).

For example, the Court's construction of the "double standard" logic, extending minimal scrutiny to federal economic regulation, opened the floodgates for federal legislative initiatives, often urged by interest-group coalitions, regulating corporate behavior in a host of ways since the 1930s (McCann 1986). Likewise, actual and expected Court actions often shape the specific terms in which congressional initiatives are framed. We know, for example, that legislators both anticipate judicial statutory interpretation when writing new laws and "rewrite" laws in response to judicial rulings "inviting" clarification of previous policy actions (Eskridge 1991; Katzmann 1997; Spiller and Tiller 1996). In similar fashion, local officials often welcome judicial rulings as an opportunity to take action on long-neglected matters. This was the case, for example, with many liberal bureaucrats at the state and local as well as federal levels in responding to opportunities opened up by judicial rulings authorizing race- and gender-based affirmative action in the 1970s (Burstein 1991). The rapid increase in abortion clinic openings after *Roe v. Wade* was another response to opportunities opened up by the Courts (Rosenberg 1991).

Perhaps the best documented responses to judicially created opportunities and catalysts to action involve the mobilization of political interest groups and social movements. Stuart Scheingold demonstrated decades ago that Court actions could be a resource in mobilizing activity in a variety of ways, including *activating* and *organizing* core constituent groups members as well as *realigning* support from third parties (1974). My own research on the politics of gender-based pay equity (or comparable worth) reform provided a detailed account of this process (1994). The very reform strategy itself was conceived by union and civil rights lawyers responding to emerging Court rulings that demonstration of race- or sex-based discriminatory impact could establish a judiciable claim under the 1964 Civil Rights Act. Wage discrimination claims were filed in federal courts during the 1970s in an attempt primarily to develop new case law, but in many local contexts such lawsuits also became key resources for organizing women into unions or activating grassroots involvement among the already organized. This activity increased dramatically in local and state venues around the nation after the 1981 Court finding of sex-based wage discrimination against female prison guards in *Co. of Washington v. Gunther.* In short, the movement was conceived, born, and developed as a formidable political force from opportunities and resources created by federal court, and especially Supreme Court, rulings. Parallel accounts have been provided for a variety of both national and local political movements for environmental causes, civil rights, women's rights, animal rights, and the rights of the physically and mentally disabled (McCann 1986; Melnick 1983; O'Connor 1980; H. Silverstein 1996; Olson 1984; Milner 1986).

STRATEGIC LEVERAGE AND RELATIONAL POWER. Judicial influence extends beyond just encouragement of new disputes and strategic mobilization initiatives, of course. In addition, courts often influence the strategic positions of parties already engaged in ongoing policy bargaining or relational struggles. As such, judicially distributed "endowments" can significantly influence the relative leveraging power available to various parties locked into prolonged patterns of conflict. In this regard, Court actions might either alter *or* reaffirm the preexisting status of relevant parties, thus often providing a critical resource or bargaining chip that determines the outcome of the conflict itself. And, as such, court actions can significantly shape the inclinations of parties to continue, to escalate, to settle, or even to withdraw from the dispute or relationship at stake. In these cases, it is worth noting that Court intervention rarely "legalizes" an extralegal relationship but is more likely simply to refigure the legal terms of a relationship already thoroughly legalized in various ways.

One good example involved the situation of Richard Nixon during the Watergate affair. The president refused to turn over (eventually damaging) tape recordings of White House conversations to two subsequent special prosecutors appointed by his own attorneys general, thus sending the conflict to the Court. Once the justices ruled against Nixon, the position of his adversaries was significantly enhanced, his support in Congress and the public plummeted, and he was left with few alternatives to resignation (Cox 1976). Judicial action can increase institutional leverage of various parties in more routine and subtle ways as well. For example, expansive readings of civil rights law by the Court in the 1970s provided considerable support for aggressive affirmative action policies by many divisions in the Department of Justice during the Carter era (McCann 1994).

Court actions often influence the balance of power between the executive branch and Congress at the national level on specific types of issues. For example, Epstein and Walker show how the Court supported and thus enhanced presidential opposition to radical Republican congressional designs for strong reconstruction efforts after the Civil War in *Ex Parte Milligan* (1866) while reversing its leveraging authority in a similar case involving military tribunals just a few years later in *Ex Parte McCardle* (1869). As formal game theory modeling demonstrates, strategic judicial action at once responds to *and* shapes the institutional power relationships among governmental actors. Another more contemporary example illustrates the point well. The primary thrust of Court rulings in this century—most directly framed by Justice Sutherland's "sole organ" doctrine in *U.S. v. Curtiss-Wright* (1936)—has been to grant the president considerable authority to act unilaterally, without congressional approval, in many types of foreign policymaking activity. The result has not only been to provide fairly routine post hoc constitutional support for disputed presidential actions but actually to enable, even to invite and generate, continued monopolization of foreign policy action by the chief executive. "The courts have steadily fed the springs of presidential power," writes David Gray Adler (1989, 177).

Other Court actions have served to protect existing government practices of many types against various forms of continuous political challenge. In recent decades alone, such practices include abusive police investigative and interrogations practices, racially discriminatory death penalty policies, government inaction on race- and gender-based inequities in employment, and legal protection provided to lucrative private production and sale of pornographic materials. At the same time, Court rulings also have often sustained the bargaining leverage of various social groups organized to *challenge* government actions (or inaction). Leverage provided by the expectation of favorable judicial action was a critical factor in the relative success of gender-based pay equity reform activism in the 1980s as well as by other campaigns for women's rights, environmental causes, animal rights, disability rights, and freedom of speech for political dissenters in previous decades (McCann 1994; McGlen and O'Connor 1980; Melnick 1983; Silverstein 1996; Olson 1984; Shiffrin 1993).

COURT ACTION AS A STRATEGIC CONSTRAINT ON OPTIONS. It is worth noting that virtually every invitation, opportunity, and leveraging resource created for some parties by Court rulings at the same time creates potential constraints or disincentives for other parties. These constraints might be felt directly, or they might indirectly result from the privileging of rivals. For example, the Court's line of reasoning following *Curtiss-Wright* has limited congressional authority as much as it has bolstered presidential boldness in foreign policy matters (Adler 1989). Richard Nixon's options in the imbroglio over Watergate surely were limited as much by the Court's ruling as was the position of his critics enhanced.

The impact of judicial constraints is not always so clear-cut or zero-sum, however. For example, the line of decisions beginning with *Buckley v. Valeo* (1976) has at once significantly constrained, channeled, and justified recent congressional deliberations over federal campaign finance reform, although this limitation has hardly been unwelcome for many legislators (Schockley 1989). And though full compliance has hardly been achieved, Court rulings surely have worked to constrain (or at least to redefine) the options of police officers in investigating crimes and interrogating suspects (Skolnick and Fyfe 1994; Leo 1996) as well as school administrators supportive of integrating religious practices in public schools (Dolbeare and Hammond 1971).

The same constraining influence is also true for social groups and organizations. Since the 1930s, for example, the Court's "double standard" logic has provided few constitutional resources for corporate challenges to legislation as an infringement on property rights or as a violation of commerce clause authority.[17] At the same time, the Court also placed important constraints on the strategic options—both on particular substantive goals and tactics—of the evolving labor movement in early-twentieth-century America (Forbath 1991; Hattam 1993). Indeed, the Court can close opportunities for social-movement strategic action and even undo whole movements that its own actions previously had generated or encouraged.[18] This clearly happened with the gender-based pay equity movement in the 1980s. Although seemingly favorable decisions by the federal courts early in the decade opened the way to "disparate impact" claims of discrimination in the workplace, a series of Court rulings significantly narrowing the reach of the 1964 Civil Rights Act took away an important legal resource and considerably crippled the movement just as decisively by the end of the decade (McCann 1994). The demise of the Civil Rights movement was more complicated, but increasingly conservative Court rulings on affirmative action beginning in the late 1970s dramatically limited the options of advocates for people of color in the nation as well (Scheingold 1989).

STIMULATING COUNTERMOBILIZATION. Court actions can generate various types of countermobilization aiming either to undo directly or to circumvent the effects of judicial rulings.[19] As such, Court rulings may facilitate or catalyze waves of political mobilization quite contrary to what the justices intend or expect. For example, various presidents and legislators have led the way in (so far, unsuccessful) efforts to overturn by either constitutional amendment or statutory authority High Court rulings on constitutional issues regarding prayer in public schools, flag burning, and privacy rights to abortion. Moreover, Congress regularly writes new legislation to overturn, "correct," or bypass judicial interpretations of earlier statutes and increasingly has worked to write legislation in more careful ways that reduce the potential for discretionary judicial readings of law (Eskridge 1991). One good example of this is the Civil Rights Act of 1991, which was passed under pressure from a coalition of liberal groups to "restore" elements of the "disparate impact" test for discrimination that the Court had virtually eliminated from civil rights law through a series of rulings in the 1980s. It is relevant to emphasize here that both coequal branches and local officials often have challenged judicial supremacy and have acted on their own constructions of constitutional law in various policy areas (see Burgess 1992). The widespread evasion and even open defiance of the Court's desegregation mandate in *Brown* by local southern officials provides perhaps the most dramatic example of this in modern times (Rosenberg 1991). Other forms of countermobilization action have been far more subtle, yet still important. For example, most commentators agree that the invalidation of the legislative veto in *Chadha* did not greatly limit congressional oversight of administrative agencies, largely because legislators developed a variety of other resources and strategies for achieving their ends (Korn 1996).

Landmark Court rulings more than a few times have generated mass social movements of considerable significance in their commitment to undoing judicial "wrongs" as well. Examples include the Populist movement's response to various procorporate Court decisions in the late nineteenth century (Westin 1953), the white prosegregation movement defying *Brown* again in the 1950s (McAdam 1982), the right-to-life movement following *Roe v. Wade* since the 1970s (Rosenberg 1991), and the antipornography coalition in the 1980s (Downs 1989). In each case, opposition to the Court became a critical rallying cry around which citizens and official representatives mobilized, often producing significant political clashes for substantial periods of time.

A Composite Case: The Court and the Civil Rights Movement

History is generally far more complex than the five preceding analytical categories and specific anecdotes suggest. Indeed, many analysts have insisted that the Court's influence on strategic politics must be understood in multiple terms of subtle, indirect, unanticipated interactions over long periods of time. No case better illustrates this confluence of different judicial influences than the legacy of the civil rights movement briefly touched on previously (see McAdam 1982; Morris 1984; Scheingold 1989).[20] Those observers who are skeptical about judicial influence rightly point out that the initial impact of the Court's landmark *Brown* decision (1954) was to galvanize defiant reaction from the white southern power structure while the president, Congress, and even the Court itself passively watched, designating it as a largely local problem. Leading lawmakers looked for the Court to exercise leadership on constitutional grounds in part to minimize the development of the issue as a divisive partisan matter. At the same time, however, the *Brown* victory emboldened and encouraged middle-class black leaders in the NAACP, who "spearheaded the resistance of the black community" (Morris 1984, 32). On the one hand, the ruling raised the hopes of southern blacks by "demonstrating that the southern white power structure was vulnerable at some points" and by providing African Americans new practical resources and alliances for reform action. "The winning of the 1954 decisions was the kind of victory the organization needed to rally the black masses behind its program; by appealing to blacks' widespread desires to enroll their children in the better-equipped white schools it reached into black homes and had meaning for people's personal lives" (Morris 1984, 34).

On the other hand, increasing white coercion and violence stimulated more radical forms of grassroots organization and protest action in the black community itself. "The two approaches—legal action and mass protest—entered into a turbulent but workable marriage" (Morris 1984, 39). Again, the judicialization of the racial issue ended up catalyzing as much as discouraging political mobilization. The escalating clashes between the nonviolent civil rights protesters and often violent white segregationists—some directly in response to court rulings mandating desegregation—expanded the scope of the dispute to include federal officials, local courts, the northern media, and national public opinion. In short, the *Brown* victory alone surely did not "cause" social change in any direct or mechanical sense, but it figured significantly into the complex chain of events that we understand as the civil rights movement leading up to congressional passage of the 1964 Civil Rights Act a decade later. "It would be misleading to present the courtroom battles in a narrowly legal light," concludes Morris (1984, 26). And I have already outlined subsequent efforts by shifting judicial majorities to expand and later to restrict interpretations of the 1964 act, thus documenting further the complex role of the Court in the politics of civil rights over the last half century.

Supreme Court Authority and Law's Constitutive Power

The second dimension of Court influence identified by sociolegal scholars is more diffuse and elusive but every bit as pervasive and important as are its manifestations as strategic signals and resources. In short, it concerns the ways in which the Court's practices of legal construction are constitutive of cultural life. Analysis of how the Court figures into strategic political interaction has drawn attention from many social science traditions, but attention to the Court's constitutive power has been the exclusive concern of interpretive sociolegal scholars.[21] As such, it is worth summarizing some of the social constructionist assumptions that underlie interpretive theories of legal practice and that take us to the heart of the constitutive framework.

Interpretive Sociolegal Theory

We begin with how interpretivists understand the *character* of law itself. In the interpretive framework, law is understood to entail more than just the rules and commands that behaviorists emphasize and even more than the discrete but open-textured signals or messages from legal officials (such as judges) that strategic approaches specify. Rather, law is understood capaciously as distinctive "ways of knowing"—as specialized knowledges, symbolic logics, or discursive conventions—that develop from and are expressed through legal practice. In short, legal conventions do not dictate behavior so much as convey recognizable "rationalities of action" through which social life is understood, transacted, and generated by legal actors. The core insight at stake here is that legal conventions contribute to the intersubjective bonds of *ideology* and discursive logic from which human agents develop their very capacity for meaningful interaction. As Sally Engle Merry puts it, "Ideology is constitutive in that ideas about an event or relationship define that activity, much as rules about a game define a move or a victory in a game" (1986, 254; Brigham 1987a). This point underlines the view that legal constructions are more than abstractions. Rather, they are embedded within material practices and relationships; they are a form of *praxis* (Klare 1979). As will be demonstrated, legal norms authorize actions and institutional relations with great material consequences in collective life—for example, discriminating between those whose fates are poverty or wealth, freedom or imprisonment, life or death (Cover 1986).

Moreover, legal conventions are understood to be inherently ambiguous, indeterminate, and contestable in character. Law's meanings are not self-evident, after all, but are subject to multiple constructions and contestation over time by differently situated legal actors. Hence, constitutive approaches shift the terms of analysis away from political conflicts among discrete agents with predefined interests to contests over the very cultural (and, specifically, legal) frameworks, categories, and concepts by which political struggles are defined and become meaningful (Brigham 1996; McCann 1994). This does not mean that the possibilities of legal interpretation and contestation are boundless or arbitrary, as legal realists tend to assume. Growing out of learned conventions and long-developing social relations, even highly innovative legal practices carry with them their own limitations, biases, and weighty baggage. Legal cultures "provide symbols and ideas which can be manipulated by their members for strategic goals," instructs Merry, "but they also establish constraints on that manipulation" (1985, 60). Interpretive sociolegal scholars have debated the extent and implications of law's indeterminacy. But all acknowledge the relatively mutable, adaptive, and contingent character of law as a medium for reproducing social order.

This understanding about law's inherent character is related to different understandings about the very *location of law.* Most traditional behavioral perspectives—often manifest in many strategic action studies as well as in judicial impact studies—tend to assume a fundamental separation between law and society. In this view, law is formulated by legal elites (such as judges) in insular institutional settings of the state (such as the federal courts) and *imposed* as an alien, exogenous force upon a society otherwise structured largely by extralegal interests and conventions. This assumption again sustains the view that identifying law's discrete effects in social practice is a relatively clear-cut matter for empirical investigation.[22]

Interpretive sociolegal scholars once more take a quite different view. As they see it, legal knowledges are not imposed upon society so much as inscribed within the very institutional fabric of social relations. Specific constructions of law thus are not divined from mystical sources and cast down like thunderbolts from on high.[23] Rather, they develop continuously from established legal conventions widely recognized and materially embedded within both specialized and general community practices. As such, sociolegal scholars emphasize that all members of a polity are *at once* subjects and, at least potentially, active "mobilizers" of law in routine social interaction (Zemans 1983). "Efforts to create and give meaning to norms . . . often and importantly occur outside formal legal institutions such as courts . . . [and constitute] an activity engaged in by non-lawyers as well as by lawyers and judges," affirms Martha Minow (1987, 1861–62).

The Supreme Court and the Legal Constitution of Politics

The premises just outlined inform interpretivists' understandings about how courts, and especially the Supreme Court, contribute to the legal constitution of social life. Courts are integral institutional agents of law's constitutive power in that they produce, reproduce, and transform fundamental legal conventions and knowledges. Indeed, legal conventions both produce to a large extent what courts themselves "do" in practice as well as end up as the courts' most significant products in society. These legal practices communicate far more than discrete signals about institutional opportunities, resources, and constraints, which political actors consider in their strategic deliberations about action. More fundamentally, the activity of courts in "policing" official legal meanings and practices contributes to the legal construction of shared cultural understandings about how society is organized, the reasonable expectations that citizens extend to each other, the terms for framing claims about ills and injustices in our society, and the public status accorded to various citizen subjects—in short, to the very foundations of authoritative knowledge that inform our politics and public life. As political scientist John Brigham has argued (1987a, 196), the legal logics and symbols generated by courts are to many terrains of social interaction what language is to the act of speaking:

> In a political sense, the impact of appellate courts is on how they structure political life. . . . As an opinion enters the political environment it joins with a configuration of defined interests and values operating around institutions, doctrines, and perceptions of what is possible. . . . Here, by interpreting the authoritative concepts governing politics, the courts exert their greatest influ-

ence. By refining the language of politics they contribute to the association of what is possible with the authority of the state.

Again, judicial demarcation of "what is possible" refers not just to those discrete options for action that engaged political actors consciously assess, but to the very frameworks of understanding, expectation, and aspiration through which both citizens and officials *interpret reality* or, to quote Geertz, "imagine the real" around them (1973). Specifically, judicial constructions of legal norms act as practical "filters" that simplify the complex welter of social experience and make it accessible, meaningful, manageable. As Carol Greenhouse has argued, legal logics provide specific authoritative terms for cultural "differentiation" among things, relationships, persons, and events— the very stuff of social life (1988). The legal norms articulated by courts provide an array of classificatory schemes, categories, and taxonomies that provide significant criteria by which we sort out experience into comprehensible and "appropriate" groupings (Kessler 1993). Such legal frames enable us to make sense of who we are (who we are like and unlike), that to which we aspire (what we want and do not want), what we can rightly expect of others (what is appropriate and inappropriate action, who is guilty and innocent), and so forth. In short, legal norms and discourses become part of the basic cultural material from which we develop our very perceived interests, identities, and inclinations. These knowledges thus enable and facilitate our very capacity to function as meaning-making subjects within society. But, of course, they also constrain us as social actors in important ways as well. The very process of classifying and organizing into meaningful terms tends to recognize and privilege some features, characteristics, and relationships in social life while ignoring, slighting, or distorting others. Law enables some ways of knowing and imagining while precluding or impeding other potentially valid interpretive perspectives.

Furthermore, Court practices work to impart *legitimacy* to its preferred legal constructions and authorized practices. This legitimation process encompasses many elements. It includes, most obviously, the explicit arguments provided by officials to justify their actions or prevailing institutional arrangements. These arguments are typically advanced through distinctive modes of "legal reasoning" by which adjudicated incidents and relations are decontextualized, treated as prototypical examples of broader categories, and assessed according to abstract principles and highly stylized discursive conventions. Such abstract, distancing practices, along with the characteristically "formal," rationalistic language of appellate legal construction, are important techniques for characterizing judicial action as objective, neutral, and principled (Kairys 1982; Scheingold 1974). At another level, appellate courts, and especially the Supreme Court, carry out their duties through an elaborate array of rituals, ceremonies, and regalia in elaborate architectural settings that invest their actions with an almost religious sense of higher authority. This authority is further supported in turn by an infrastructure of institutions—including lower courts, the legal profession, the mass media—that virtually canonizes the Court's words, logics, and practices, contributing to what Brigham calls the "cult of the Court" (1987a). And behind these institutional trappings looms the often unspoken yet very real coercive, violent capacity of the state to enforce official judicial logics on those subjects insufficiently bound by fidelity to prevailing legal conventions (Cover 1986).

Such constitutive power is not the identifiable product of individual legal decisions by the Court, of course. Rather, this power is manifest in the accumulated cultural legacy of judicial actions and routine practices over time. These legal conventions are in turn learned, internalized, and *normalized* by citizens through many forms of cultural participation—through formal education, mass media, popular culture, and personal experiences directly within legalized institutional settings.[24] And in these ways the foundational legal knowledges, conventions, and justifications transmitted by courts are reproduced and reinforced within the manifold practices, relationships, and arrangements that structure daily life throughout society. Together, argues Mark Kessler, "these processes mystify law's power, transforming the arbitrary and cultural features of social life into that which is considered natural, inevitable, and perhaps most important, universal" among the citizenry (1993, 565). In this regard, the constitutive power of law generated in part by courts is more deeply formative and enduring in its impact on subject identities, consciousness, and constructions of interest than are its manifold signaling effects on particular strategic interactions.[25] Indeed, law's constitutive power is perhaps greatest when we are least aware of its manifestations in the taken-for-granted "common sense" that facilitates our social interaction and informs our routine strategic and moral reasoning processes (see Brigham 1996; McCann 1994). "There is ample evidence that perceptions of desires, wants, and interests are themselves strongly influenced by the nature and content of legal norms," argues Frances Kahn Zemans (1983, 697).

Finally, it is important to point out that, though often de-emphasized or obscured in interpretive studies, law's constitutive power is inextricably intertwined with its influence on strategic action. This recognition is implicit in Tocqueville's famous words routinely cited in scholarship on American legal culture (1966, 270). His most commonly cited phrase recognizes the frequency of legal mobilization and interventions in American public life: "Scarcely any political question arises in the United States that is not resolved sooner or later into a judicial question." But his less often cited words that follow are equally important in recognizing the related constitutive power of legal discourses: "Hence all parties are obliged to borrow, in their daily controversies, the ideas, even the language, peculiar to judicial proceedings. . . . The language of the law thus becomes, in some measure, a vulgar tongue. And the spirit of the law penetrates into the bosom of society, even into the lower classes." Among contemporary scholars, "legal mobilization" theorists in particular have attempted to identify the interrelated aspects of law's constitutive power and influence in strategic action. Scheingold's seminal *Politics of Rights* stressed how the authoritative status of constitutional language, the Supreme Court, and legal rights conventions invest legal reform tactics with great symbolic power (1974). This power of legal conventions simultaneously can render legal action an effective mobilizing resource for reformers *and,* unwittingly, divert them from alternative ways of understanding social relations, framing claims, and formulating political tactics. Whatever the outcome, he argued, law's capacity to facilitate strategic interaction is directly related to its deeper constitutive capacity to construct a shared intersubjective culture of common symbols, myths, and meaning-making conventions.[26]

My own research on the legal mobilization strategies of unionized women to achieve equitable wages during the 1970s and 1980s provides a similar but more detailed picture of this relationship (1994). The very idea of pay equity as a reform cause was consciously shaped in response both to specific rulings by federal courts signaling opportunities for further claims and by the general legal frame of "antidiscrimination" that had come to dominate political debates over race- and gender-based inequality in American society. Federal courts—and especially the Supreme Court in the key *Griggs* and *Gunther* cases—thus not only shaped the conscious formulation of particular goals and tactics of the movement, but they generated the very normative and conceptual framework within which the movement was imagined. As the movement developed, litigation was utilized to publicize reform claims, to mobilize active grassroots constituencies, to leverage bargaining power with employers, and to pressure for effective reform implementation. These legal tactics varied in their effectiveness in different locations of strategic interaction. But even where wage gains were modest, my study shows, the legacy of legal action shaped and reshaped—constituted and reconstituted—the political identities of individual actors and the institutional context in which they acted. "Legal rights became increasingly meaningful both as a general moral discourse and as a strategic resource for ongoing challenges to status quo power relations" (1994, 281). In short, federal appellate courts contributed in important ways to reproducing and transforming the intersubjective legal terrain of interaction in many female-intensive workplaces around the nation.[27]

The Legal Constitution of Ideology, Interest, and Identity: Historical Examples

A host of other examples can be cited from both distant and recent American history to illustrate the High Court's contributions to law's constitutive power. The Marshall Court played a critical role both in establishing the power of judicial review and in using that review to sustain traditional Federalist commitments to protecting the ideological sanctity of property rights in the volatile young republic (Nedelsky 1990; Newmyer 1968). A litany of landmark rulings added salience and content to public norms such as federalism, police power, contractual obligations, commercial enterprise, and "property" itself in ways that significantly structured both the practices of capitalist development and the politics surrounding it. The Marshall Court, writes R. Kent Newmyer, "worked for a powerful, self-sufficient, centralized nation resting on an economic foundation of commerce and free enterprise. . . . Without doubt, American history has favored the principles Marshall worked for" (1968, 148). The Taney Court not only continued as it reformed this tradition, but it played a critical role in authorizing limited constitutional understandings about the rights of propertied slaveholders and the rightslessness of their slaves. Though the Court of that era is rightly maligned for its nefarious ruling in *Dred Scott,* it should not be forgotten that expectations and even invitations of judicial intervention shaped national political debate over slavery in largely constitutional terms framed for decades by earlier judicial rulings (Fehrenbacher 1978; Newmyer 1968).

Equally notable was the Court's role in shaping and constraining political debate about the proper scope of governmental regulation of corporate production in the fifty years prior to 1936. Often remembered as the *Lochner* era for its most famous decision, the Court invoked constitutional principles of (substantive) due process and commerce clause authority to restrict what was considered "class-based legislation" protecting workers and consumers (Gillman 1993). These restrictions on progressive reform legislation were joined by constructions of antitrust statutes and use of common law injunctions directly to constrain the collective action of working-class, agrarian, and other reformers. Following the lead of the Supreme Court, the judiciary took the lead in structuring the terms of newly developing industrial relations rife with open class conflict. On the one hand, the Court's bold actions not only invalidated existing state laws and eventually federal New Deal legislation, but they further discouraged even the formulation of many other regulatory restrictions that were sure to defy judicial constructions of constitutional principles. Likewise, Court opinions provided grand opportunities for rapid expansion and reckless or exploitive behavior by manufacturers and other business interests for many decades. The Court significantly defined the strategic options for action by key players—big and small business, labor, farmers, crafts workers—in the high stakes struggles over the form of capital growth in the United States.

On the other hand, however, the Court's legal constructions also constituted more profoundly the very terms of the ideological debate, expressed interests, and group identities that bound the contestants in those political battles. For example, the agrarian Populists targeted the Supreme Court as the enemy of small farmers and working people in the 1890s and struggled to use various political and legal means to overcome judicial "tyranny" (Westin 1953). But what is interesting is that the Populist platform appealed to the very same legal principles—constitutionalism, property rights, equal citizenship, republican freedom, states' rights—with which the Court thwarted their political designs. In short, the Court, and the legal legacy it authorized, defined to a large extent the very normative terrain on which political struggle was waged. This is equally true for evolving labor politics early in the century. William Forbath and other scholars have demonstrated that constitutional rulings, repeated labor injunctions, and other actions by the federal courts contributed toward shaping the labor activists' identities, material interests, and capacities for collective action (1991; see also Orren 1991; Hattam 1993). Specifically, judicial action encouraged a more liberal, voluntarist, workplace-centered, antistatist, rights-oriented ideology focused on revoking specific court constructions instead of the more radical logic of

European unions sustained by class-based solidarity, national reform legislation, and socialist ideals. "Courts shaped labor's strategic calculus; in more
subtle ways, law also altered labor's ideology. . . . Labor leaders at all levels
began to speak and think more and more in the language of the law" (Forbath 1991, 7).

Other judicial constructions in the same era further constrained dissent
as well, delegitimating certain groups and claims while encouraging or
acknowledging others. Mark Kessler's compelling study of free speech doctrine in the post–World War I era is a fine case study in point (1993). He iden-
tifies two ideological strands in free speech doctrine: a libertarian tradition
valuing free speech as a critical part of our political tradition that must be
protected except in the most unusual cases, and a "pragmatic" approach that
balanced protection for speech with the need for restrictions where expression might prove "dangerous." When combined with other ascendant ideological currents such as nativism, scientific racism, and nationalism, the clear
and present danger doctrine was widely embraced to authorize intolerance
and punishment of those working-class dissenters viewed as "alien," "un-
American," and hence subversive and "dangerous." "Because the institution
from which this discourse emanated, namely, the Supreme Court, was held
in such high regard—perceived as objective, neutral, nonpartisan, and
authoritative—it legitimated the appropriation of social constructions of
'otherness' in other cultural contexts to distinguish between 'acceptable' and
'unacceptable' political expression" (589). In short, the Court played an
important role in demarcating both the boundaries of legitimate ideological discourse and the selective identities of those entitled to speak in one of
the more politically charged moments of our nation's history.

Much the same type of judicial influence—at once enabling and delim-
iting the terms of political challenge—was evident among the civil rights
movement of the 1950s and 1960s. The initial legal strategy of middle-class
black activists was to undo the legacy of the separate but equal jurisprudence
that provided constitutional protection to institutionalized segregation in
the nation, especially in the South. Once again, opposition to inherited law
was framed in essentially legal terms and was waged substantially through
legal institutions. The eventual victory in *Brown* not only created strategic
opportunities and leverage for further collective action, but it also consolidated the liberal, legalistic, civil "rights" logic of antidiscrimination at the
heart of the movement.[28] And this basic legal logic continued to prevail even
as movement tactics gravitated toward grassroots nonviolent protest and

demands for more radical social agendas were voiced. This experience with legally oriented rights claims and appeals to the federal courts has left an enduring legacy—one entailing both transformation and constraint—in the African American community and the nation overall (see Sarat 1997). As Kimberle Williams Crenshaw has argued, "Antidiscrimination law represents an ongoing ideological struggle in which the occasional winners harness the moral, coercive, and consensual power of law" (1988, 1335). Once again, the strategic potential of legal tactics has depended on the constitutive legal authority of general normative logics largely shaped by federal courts. This pervasive power of law in framing much of the debate for egalitarian change among people of color is clearly demonstrated by notable writings such as Derrick Bell's *And We Are Not Saved* (1987). This fascinating collection presents a wide array of fictional narratives about racial injustice that, although taking quite diverse views toward the implications of legal categories and tactics, confirm the powerful pull of legal "equality rights talk" as a framework for making sense of racial relations in our society.

Many other examples could be cited. Indeed, many of the most salient public issues—discrimination against women, ethnic minorities, gays, and lesbians; the incendiary abortion issue; pornography and hate speech; campaign finance regulation; the relationship between religion and public education; gun control; restrictions on police abuse; the death penalty policy, to name a few—have been understood and contested in distinctly legal terms delineated by the federal courts over time. In fact, the rise of rights-oriented politics generally as a characteristic political phenomenon in twentieth-century America is greatly indebted to changes in the Court's basic jurisprudential practices. Likewise, the very faith that formalizing disputes and taking them "all the way to the Supreme Court" can promote justice—captured by Scheingold's "myth of rights" (1974)—is another expression of law's power in constituting our political imagination. Even those citizens who oppose prevailing court constructions and legal frames typically pose their own counterclaims in terms of legal traditions authorized by the courts.[29] In sum, what the Supreme Court does and says clearly has a significant effect on the range of possibilities that even receives attention in our polity.

Hegemony, the Court, and Legal Authority

The recognition of law's constitutive power in our culture raises, for many critical scholars in the new institutionalist tradition, the issue of the Court's role in sustaining systemic hegemony. The term "hegemony" refers to the aggregate of socio-cultural-political forces that generate consent and induce acquiescence in status quo power relations (R. Williams 1977, 110).

I would argue in this regard, however, that the Court's contributions to such acquiescence include both its strategic influence and its deeper constitutive power. Attention to strategic influence emphasizes how courts invite and discourage, and hence shape and channel, conscious disputing activity (or inactivity) in the polity. Such a focus tends to identify types and degrees of changes in relative power relations that are far more complex than just designations of winners and losers. I have noted already how studies attuned to strategic interaction have taught us much about the dialectical relationships between the Court and other state institutional actors, including especially dominant lawmaking coalitions. Many scholars have contended that the Court rarely challenges prevailing national electoral coalitions, often enforcing that consensus against resistant local interests and taking on controversial issues that party moderates would prefer to keep out of electoral politics (Dahl 1957; Graber 1993). Of course, other scholars in this tradition disagree about the conclusions from such studies. In any case, however, such debates surely have contributed to our understanding about the continuities, transformations, and points of contestation in the prevailing constellation of expressed preferences and group positions that rule the nation in particular eras.

Likewise, legal mobilization studies have shown that "have-nots" and subaltern groups sometimes do improve their situation through legal tactics while the "haves" and dominant groups sometimes are forced by law to relinquish some of their power. This is the heart of the claim by legal mobilization scholars that law can "cut both ways—serving at some times and under some circumstances to reinforce privilege and at other times to provide the cutting edge of change" (Scheingold 1989, 76). Nevertheless, most legal mobilization studies confirm that even meaningful changes arising from particular contests rarely alter, and in fact often only reinforce, the overall patterns of social hierarchy and group power relations within society. Overall, both types of studies regarding political interaction have much to teach about what Schattschneider called the "mobilization of bias" in American society—that "set of predominant values, beliefs, rituals, and institutional procedures . . . that operate systematically and consistently to the benefit of certain persons and groups at the expense of others" (cited in Gaventa 1980, 14).[30]

This last point is where constitutive theory begins to add its significant insights about the contributions of law to sustaining hegemony. Constitutive theorists emphasize that, even when law serves as a strategic resource for various parties in or out of government, at the same time it constrains those parties by limiting other options and channeling action into prevailing institutional processes and normative frames. To the extent that judicial constructions of law facilitate disputing activity at all, regardless of immediate outcomes, they thus also *incorporate* social action into familiar, well-established ways of doing and understanding things. "Popular struggles are a reflection of institutionally determined logic and a challenge to that logic. . . . Demands for change that do not reflect the institutional logic . . . will probably be ineffective" (Crenshaw 1988, 1366–67). This incorporative role of courts in preserving the general legal structure of relations—and especially inherited patterns of class, racial, gender, sexual, ethnic, and religious hierarchy—even as they enable specific legal challenges and changes is a critical dimension of how hegemony is sustained as a dynamic interactive process of meaning-making activity (see McCann 1994, 304–10). By recognizing this, constitutive analysis does not discount strategic legal interaction in the shadow of courts but interprets such activity from a more systemic ideological perspective.

At the same time, constitutive analysts tend to probe further the Court's capacity to legitimate and normalize prevailing power relations in ways already discussed. On the one hand, this requires attention to the routine practices by state authorities aiming to justify prevailing institutional arrangements, relationships, and "rationalities of action" that structure social life. This practice of recurrent justification for established ways of doing things as reasonable, right, even natural—regardless of outcomes in specific cases—is one of the most important roles played by our appellate courts, and especially by the Supreme Court. On the other hand, every action encouraging and legitimating one set of arrangements at the same time precludes, obscures, and delegitimates other possible arrangements and understandings. Even when its justifications for status quo arrangements are not convincing, therefore, the accumulated traditions of knowledge production by the courts over time place real constraints on alternatively imagined forms of community. According to Austin Sarat (1985, 31):

Law is . . . most powerful when it stifles demands before they are voiced or destroys them before they acquire access to any important arena. Law works not only when it overcomes resistance, that is, when it wins the contest, but when it effectively prevents the fight. . . . The power of law is found in the dispersion and penetration of legality as an ideological form and in the legitimating effects of that form.

We can see this institutional dynamic at work in historical events. For example, the triumph of an "exceptionally" legalistic, voluntaristic, rights-oriented political strategy within the American labor movement was due to many factors. But most analysts agree that the federal courts' authorization of state coercion to quell labor protests, narrowing of opportunities for effective legal reform, and justification of prevailing market relations and republican values in society were key in shaping labor movement strategy and ideology. The result was not necessarily that most union workers were convinced of the rightness of judicially constructed law but that modest legal alternatives to the courts' vision were rendered as the only ones that were sensible, or even plausibly imaginable, for many leading labor activists in that historical context. Much the same dynamic was at work in the civil rights movement (see Scheingold 1989; McCann 1992). Although Supreme Court decisions giving new meaning to equal rights did facilitate significant struggle and important changes in social relations (especially in the South), that same legal legacy privileged certain claims and modes of action while delegitimating others as dangerous, costly, unrealistic, or senseless. The promise of inclusion and voice offered by the Court's integrationist logic of equal rights to a large degree thus ended up excluding, silencing, or repressing other possible visions of social justice—at least for a time, until the severe limits of the legal promise became palpable amid the increasingly reactionary environment of the 1980s.

Even distrust of the Court's legal constructions typically produces little challenge to the status quo, which is the message of Kristin Bumiller's important research. Her study illustrates how many victims of race and gender discrimination avoid formal legal action because their dependent status—as welfare recipients, tenants, employees, students, and the like—leaves them vulnerable to reprisal or ruin. Indeed, the legal promise of redress for discrimination only "reinforced . . . the bonds of victimhood," offering few remedies through law, little escape from law, and few alternatives to law (1988). In short, those whom Bumiller studied were to a large extent constituted as victims by law, powerless to challenge its hegemonic power.[31]

It is worth adding, however, that all systems of hierarchy and domination are not equal. A distinguished line of critical interpretive scholarship has contended that legally constituted modes of hegemony are preferable to other, more arbitrary forms of rule. As E. P. Thompson has argued, for example, the rule of law and the courts that administer it provide alternatives to, as well as authorizations for, naked coercion and violence (1975). Moreover, law's intrinsic promise of equal treatment both imposes constraints on the powerful and provides opportunities and resources to subaltern groups to challenge their subordination through resort to the courts and other legal tactics (McCann 1994; Silverstein 1996). This has led yet others to characterize liberal legal regimes as tending toward a more "soft" or "open" mode of hegemony where law and its institutional authorities, such as the Supreme Court, are more responsive to the less powerful than in other regimes (Scheingold 1989; McCann 1994).[32] Whatever one's position in this debate, however, attention to law's constitutive power and strategic influence alike seem critical elements in debates over the Court's role in sustaining hegemonic power and status quo relations.

I have outlined two different aspects of Supreme Court influence in American politics addressed by recent social science studies of legal institutions. Attention to both strategic and constitutive dimensions tends to confirm that the Court matters significantly in our public life, although that influence is complex, contingent, and often quite subtle in character. Moreover, each perspective points to, parallels, and often intersects with identifiable trends in what is called new institutionalist analysis (R. Smith 1988). Yet, so far, there have been relatively few efforts at constructive dialogue between adherents of these different modes of sociolegal analysis. The discussion that has occurred has been mostly in the form of an argument—especially between formal game theorists in the positivist tradition who emphasize "strategic" action and interpretive or historical analysts who stress law's constitutive power—about the relative merits of rival epistemologies and methodologies. Few serious efforts to develop complementary approaches integrating or synthesizing both strategic and constitutive dimensions of analysis have been undertaken by public law scholars to date. This is lamentable in light of the inherent connections between these aspects of law's power in actual social practice.

The emergence of the new institutionalist movement thus could be propitious in that it provides both opportunity and motive for intellectual engagement and synthesis. It offers an opportunity in that scholars committed to research in both strategic interaction and constitutive power have identified themselves with the movement (R. Smith 1988; Gillman 1999; Epstein and Knight 1997). The movement might generate a motive, moreover, in that efforts to develop broader frameworks of analysis that integrate or at least balance attention to both dimensions could represent major achievements in intellectual analysis of courts, and of political institutions generally. After all, fruitful dialogue about combining these different frameworks has taken place in other areas of political analysis, such as international relations studies and political theory (Klotz 1995; Finnemore 1996; Johnson 1991). One possible route to this end for new institutionalist legal scholars might simply entail combining rational choice or other behavioral approaches focusing on strategic activity with more historical and interpretive analytical approaches to the subject.[33] This effort is intriguing, but it requires combining several very different conceptions of agency, power, and institutional relations as well as of method and interpretation—indeed, quite contrary epistemologies altogether. A rather different tack for new institutionalists might involve attempts to incorporate attention to strategic interaction within a consistent interpretive framework emphasizing law's constitutive power. Some steps have been taken in the latter direction, but much more remains to be done.[34] In any case, such efforts provide at least some further reason to think that labors to develop integrated, multidimensional analyses would be productive for new institutionalist scholarship regarding appellate courts.

Acknowledgments

The author would like to thank Stuart Scheingold and Beth Harris as well as the book's coeditors, Howard Gillman and Cornell Clayton, for their valuable commentary on various versions of this chapter.

Notes

1. Of course, skepticism about the automatic consequences of court action is hardly new. Some legal realists such as Roscoe Pound emphasized in an earlier era the "limits of effective legal action" (1917).

2. See Becker and Feeley (1973) and Canon (1977); Dolbeare and Hammond (1971); Rodgers and Bullock (1972).

3. Both "strategic" and "constitutive" frameworks have been invoked to explain the intrinsic motivations or rationalities of judges as well, but the focus here will be on the external "effects" of judges' actions.

4. These approaches differ, to be sure, in their most basic understandings of human subjectivity, legal conventions, social power, and causality; indeed, positivist and post-positivist interpretive projects disagree about the very goals of analysis. I shall address such differences to some degree, although extended discussion is limited by space.

5. Most of the analysis by rational choice scholars has focused on how the social context of multiple institutional actors shapes or conditions strategic choices that judges make. But these accounts also at least imply or point toward insights about how judges likewise shape the strategic context of action by other actors in the state (Congress, president, bureaucrats) and out of it (interest groups, social movements, business interests).

6. Different analytical frameworks vary in the degree to which law is viewed as indeterminate and subject to multiple interpretations. Game theorists often identify law with "rules," but their focus on the strategic interaction between judges and other political actors implies a fair amount of indeterminacy in "law." By contrast, intepretivists explicitly ground their analysis in assumptions about the underdetermined but socially constituted character of legal action.

7. Rosenberg, for example, emphasizes changes that occur within only a couple of years of most decisions and deems as significant only those changes that affect bureaucracies on a nationwide basis (1991).

8. One very inviting and useful way to conceptualize these distinctions among types of power is provided in the three-level approach developed and illustrated by John Gaventa (1980). The positivist impact method tends to approach matters of judicial influence at the "first" level of instrumental, unidirectional power. Scholarship that focuses on strategic interaction tends to develop the second level of power, which focuses on interactions within consciously recognized social structures of opportunity and constraint. Interpretive approaches to law's constitutive power work primarily at the third level of power, which has to do with how cultural conventions prefigure and shape the intersubjective norms and understandings that bind officials and citizens alike.

9. It is worth noting at this point some significant disagreements among different traditions of strategic interaction analysis in this regard. Rational choice or game theorists root studies in a microeconomic model of subjects as narrowly self-interested utility maximizers. Actors' preferences or goals themselves tend to be understood as relatively fixed, exogenous, and largely beyond the scope of study. Moreover, rational choice models largely assume that patterns of institutional relations, and law, emerge as the product of individual, short-term strategic actions by discrete actors. Finally, most, but not all, rational choice approaches claim fidelity to goals of assessing and demonstrating relative causal factors in positive fashion, although causality is understood in more dialectical and dynamic terms than is entertained by compliance-oriented impact models. Interpretive scholars, by contrast, focus more on how legal constructions and norms shape the very formulation of specific ends, goals, interests, and aspirations of subjects as well as on the instrumental means for advancing those ends. As such, interpretive scholars focus research more on the very processes of interpretation and deliberation about ends and means by historical subjects, and especially on contests over the social construction of subject claims and under-

standings (see my discussion of constitutive theory for elaboration; see also the debate between Epstein and Knight [1997] and Gillman [1996–1997]).

10. This is not to say the issues on which the Court has intervened are more important today, however. It strikes me that the significance of issues where the Court's influence has been felt in recent decades is no greater—and perhaps is less so—than those disputes over the direction of capitalist economic development into which the Court intervened during the nineteenth and early twentieth centuries.

11. Other factors that have augmented the prestige, role, and authority of the Court in modern times include increased access to varied constituent interests and causes; growth and democratization of the legal profession; the expanded authority of federal government generally; the enlarged discretion assumed by the Court in defining its own agenda; the increasing bureaucratization and interdependence with other branches; and, arguably, changing social patterns of discourse centering on rights.

12. A major contribution to the focus on how appellate court impact is conceptualized in terms of different types of populations was pioneered by Johnson and Canon (1984). Their approach frames influence and analysis in relatively positivist terms, but their work points toward more interactive understandings of power than do traditional impact studies.

13. This phenomenon is distinguished from two other types of majority action in partisan elections. "Maintaining elections" are those in which the majority party retains the loyalty of the electorate expressed in previous elections and wins the presidency. "Deviating elections" involve a short-term defeat of the majority party (due to specific issues or circumstances) that does not reflect changes in longer-term voter allegiance. "Realigning elections" occur when party loyalties are redefined to create a new majority party and give it control of government over an extended number of subsequent elections. The most commonly cited examples of the latter are the elections of Jefferson in 1800, of Jackson in 1828, of Lincoln in 1860, and of Roosevelt in 1932. See Adamany (1980).

14. The best discussion of this phenomenon is Graber (1993); the examples I cite here are drawn largely from his discussion.

15. It is relevant to note that the right-wing Republican reaction to these trends in the last two decades—which was most prominent and explicit during the Reagan presidency—attempted to reclaim various social issues like abortion, affirmative action, police authority, and censorship as partisan matters while stacking the Courts with conservative judges averse to earlier liberal activism.

16. Legal mobilization and other interpretive theorists attuned to law's constitutive power would add here attention to how the Court contributes to the "framing" of particular issues and disputes (see the later sections of this chapter).

17. This is not to say that corporate capacity to fend off government regulation and to shape government policy is not great, by any means (see McCann 1986).

18. In an important sense, every opportunity also constrains action in that it privileges certain ways of doing things over other ways. This is a central insight of the constitutive perspective, which I shall discuss.

19. Judicial impact studies tend to discount countermobilization activity as an indicator of judicial influence because it defies the compliance standard; indeed, political reaction is considered a sign of judicial impotence. Scholars who focus on strategic interaction, by contrast, find countermobilization as an important indicator of how courts matter in social life.

20. For a very different view from an impact perspective, see Rosenberg (1991).

21. This includes again a variety of different traditions, but one can find examples of this type of interpretive analysis by some critical legal studies scholars (Gordon 1984), many legal philosophers (Cover 1986; Minow 1987), and a growing number of post-positivist social scientists (Brigham 1996; Gillman 1993; Merry 1985; Sarat 1990; McCann 1994).

22. Traditional institutionalists in the realist/positivist mode tend to argue that judicial "law," as rules and precedential rulings, is not a particularly significant constraint on either judicial officials (judges, administrators) themselves or on the general public (see Gillman 1995a).

23. The more common legal realist position that judges simply construct law to advance their own policy preferences or attitudes is equally problematic from the interpretivist view. In the latter perspective, a judge's very interests, preferences, understandings, and acts of legal construction are shaped by the learned conventions of institutionalized legal practice (see Gillman 1999; Brigham 1987a).

24. The concepts of "legitimation" and "normalization" have been used somewhat interchangeably by some scholars, but I employ them to refer to slightly different social processes. As I see it, legitimation refers to processes of explicit justification as right or just, but normalization involves processes that render certain understandings as "natural," inevitable, taken for granted. Although analytically distinct, however, these processes surely are often interrelated in practice.

25. It again is useful to invoke the conceptual distinction between the second and third levels of power designated by Gaventa (1980). The second level of power refers more to the "mobilized bias" inherent in the identifiable rules, arrangements, and relational structure of social organization. It refers to more or less conscious deliberations about what is possible, desirable, or feasible in particular situations. The existing rules favor some parties and exclude others, render plausible some arrangements while discouraging others, make some actions rewarding while others are highly costly. The third level of power addresses the more general "social myths, language, and symbols" in a culture through which arrangements are perceived, understood, and accepted as "natural" or given. It refers to that aggregation of learned knowledges that prefigure and facilitate, but only rarely are subjected to, conscious critical interrogation itself.

26. This linkage between law's constitutive power and its facilitation of strategic interaction is nowhere better developed than in studies of civil disputing processes, and especially in recent scholarship on law and everyday forms of resistance. Because such studies focus mostly on local trial courts and other "lower"-level legal institutions, however, they are not discussed in this chapter; but see Mather (1997).

27. Helena Silverstein more recently has concluded much the same thing in her analysis of legal mobilization practices by animal rights activists. She explicitly argues that "the relationship between practice and legal meaning highlights the importance of examining strategic uses of legal forms. If, as suggested here, legal meaning structures and is structured by action, then the exploration of strategic action is crucial to an exploration of legal meaning. Attempts to strategically deploy, for example, legal languages, legal statutes, or litigation are shaped and informed by legal meaning; in turn, these attempts shape and redefine legal meaning" (1996, 13).

28. Actually, the movement drew on a mix of liberal legal rights and traditional Protestant ideological elements in the appeal, as so often has been the case in American politics.

29. Although much of such discourse focuses on rights-oriented claims, this hardly exhausts the types of claims and counterclaims that emanate from the legal conventions articulated by courts. John Brigham develops several alternative constitutive legal forms, including realism, remedy, and rage (1987b).

30. Again, it makes sense to view the contributions of sociolegal scholarship regarding strategic interaction in terms of the "second level of power" outlined by Lukes (1974) and Gaventa (1980).

31. In my view, however, this line of thinking often tends to overstate the ideological grip of law. My own research tends to emphasize the degree to which citizens often are aware of law's power to make sense of things as well as law's role in sustaining hierarchies, indignities, and harm. Moreover, official legal categories and logics are often contested. See McCann (1994); see also the interesting literature on law and everyday forms of resistance (McCann and March [1996]).

32. Sociolegal scholars disagree somewhat over the degree to which legal forms sustain hegemonic order and constrain the development of counterhegemonic possibilities. In general, it strikes me that scholars in the United States who focus primarily on the practices and constructions of federal courts take a more skeptical view while those who focus more on legal action—especially on the "politics of rights"—by groups and individuals in society often find more room for resistance and transformative struggle (see McCann 1994), although not necessarily for legal "success." For a fine discussion in the latter mode, see Hunt (1993).

33. One important contribution in this regard is Lynn Mather's recent effort to integrate different approaches in her interesting analysis of tobacco litigation politics (1997). The study is very much in the spirit of the argument advanced here. However, Mather's study is about legal mobilization in trial court litigation rather than about appellate courts per se; it draws distinctions among key categories (identifying strategic concerns strictly with behavioral anlaysis) in ways somewhat different from those I have developed here; and (perhaps prudently) it eschews the potential epistemological tensions at stake.

34. Legal mobilization scholars (see Mather 1997; H. Silverstein 1996; also McCann 1994) again have been most interested in this integrative effort. Most interpretivists, however, have expressed little interest in theorizing about "micro" level strategic or instru-

mental aspects of legal interaction and instead have focused their attention on broadly constitutive dimensions (but see Gillman 1999). Moreover, interpretive studies of appellate courts have been directed primarily to analysis of judges' actions and practices (internal studies of courts) rather than to how those practices affect political interaction and processes generally ("external" concerns). In this regard, unfortunately, the interpretivist version of the new institutionalism may end up only reinforcing the long-standing obsession of political scientists with more or less traditional doctrinal study of appellate courts in historical context.

Chapter 6

The Supreme Court and Partisan Change: Contravening, Provoking, and Diffusing Partisan Conflict

John B. Gates

An institutional perspective in the study of politics balances a tendency often found in behavioral research to microanalyze the actions of individuals. As one student observes, "A common concern with the behavioral methodologies of individualism was that they lacked a theory of political equilibrium and, equally, a theory of political change"(Rockman 1994, 145). This criticism applies to the study of judicial politics but to a more limited extent than is commonly claimed. An institutional focus is, however, especially revealing in understanding the role of the U.S. Supreme Court in national policy making.

The interaction of political change that is sometimes blurred by the lens of individual behavior is manifested in the ways that institutional policies or decisions affect public opinion, the consensus among political leaders, and the course of the political parties. The concern with the shaping of collective choice cannot ignore the importance of institutions, and this is certainly true with respect to the role of courts, especially the U.S. Supreme Court. The institutional approach is, of course, not without possible analytical blind spots since it could lead many observers to more historical, atheoretical description instead of to explanation (Gates 1991). Fortunately, there are several studies dating from the 1950s that examine the role of the Supreme Court in the course of major change in national policy making and that do so from a social scientific and institutional perspective (e.g., Dahl 1956; Beck 1976; Lasser 1985).

These studies focused attention on rare transformations in the allegiance of Americans to the two major political parties. The dynamics of such significant changes in the party system are the subject of much investigation, including studies examining the role of the U.S. Supreme Court in provoking or contravening partisan change. In several decisions before the onslaught of critical presidential elections and partisan change, the Supreme Court either highlighted volatile electoral issues or forced political leaders to stake out polar positions that demanded a definitive choice by voters.

The Supreme Court may also block the reforms ushered in by realignments of the party system denoted by one or more critical presidential elections. These elections either produce or culminate in a durable change in electoral support for the major parties, and most important, in the long-term direction of national policy making. After a new majority party takes power, it confronts a Supreme Court often reflecting the policy views of the older regime vanquished in the critical election. Extant research on the role of the Court both before and after major partisan changes relies almost exclusively on the Court's decisions overturning federal (Funston 1975; Casper 1976) or state legislation (Gates 1987; 1992).

The role of the Supreme Court in more conventional or less transformational partisan change has not been subject to significant theoretical or systematic empirical analysis. There are also few analyses examining the importance of Court decisions that uphold, rather than strike down, legislation or constitutional precedent. In these instances, the Court may diffuse partisan conflict and contribute to partisan changes that have significant long-term effects on the course of less transformational changes than those associated with critical elections. A more thorough understanding of the Supreme Court's role in national policy making and partisan change must incorporate a concern with the variety of Court decision making as well as a concern with more conventional partisan changes. After examining the role of the Court in provoking critical elections and sometimes in standing as a barrier to the majoritarian reforms through its exercise of judicial review, an analysis of the 1992 election shows how an understanding of Court policy making must also include its more subtle and complex impact in diffusing major partisan controversy. Although less sensational than the Supreme Court declarations of unconstitutionality surrounding critical elections, the Court is often an important component in the course of national politics through both the upholding and striking down of majoritarian preferences.

The Supreme Court and Critical Elections

The Supreme Court's Role Following Critical Elections: Contravening Partisan Changes

There is perhaps no more cited and discussed study of the role of the Supreme Court in national policy making generally than Robert Dahl's (1957) examination of the Court's decisions overturning federal laws. According to Dahl, these decisions were premiere instances of the Court procedurally acting in the interest of some political minority. Though the protection of minority rights was and continues to be a role attributed to the Court, Dahl found little supportive evidence.[1] Of the important pieces of national legislation, almost all were subsequently overturned by either the Court or Congress within a few short years.

Dahl concluded that the Court was generally part of the "enduring alliances" of national politics because presidents have frequent opportunities to appoint justices who share their political preferences on the most pressing issues of the day. Writing over forty years ago, Dahl computed the turnover on the Supreme Court at one vacancy every twenty-two months. The president's power of appointment serves to synchronize the policy views of the executive and the Court, or as Dahl described the partnership, the "enduring alliances." Hence, the relationship between the unelected Supreme Court and the broader field of partisan politics was not digitated but interconnected.

It is difficult to underestimate the importance of Dahl's study of the Supreme Court. He focused attention on the Court's exercise of judicial review and the persistent tension in democratic theory of majority rule and minority rights. Most important, however, Dahl's analysis was soon incorporated into the emerging theory of critical elections (Key 1955; Sundquist 1973). There are few areas in the study of American politics that so intimately link voter preferences, partisan change, and policy change than critical elections and realignment. Partisan realignment is boldly consistent with visions, and perhaps the reality, of democratic governance.[2]

Partisan realignment occurs with one or more critical presidential elections. These elections constitute significant and durable shifts in partisan allegiance among voters in both major parties and represent long-term consequences for the course of national policy making (McMichael and Trilling 1980, 23). As the first to identify such elections, V. O. Key noted over forty years ago that a critical election is one in which "the depth and intensity of electoral involvement are high, in which more or less profound readjustments occur in the relation of power within the community, and in which new and durable electoral groups are formed" (Key 1955, 4). The forces behind such changes may be long-term issues and tensions in society, or they can arise from a sudden and dramatic crisis (Key 1959).

The most important consequence is that these elections coincide with a long-term redistribution of partisan support and begin distinctive periods in American political history. Political historians identify five fairly precise party "systems" in American history. They coincide with the rise and fall of the victorious party in critical elections: the Federalist-Jeffersonian (1789–1828), the Jacksonian (1828–1860), the First Republican (1860–1896), the Second Republican (1896–1932), and the New Deal era (1932–1968).

Although V. O. Key was instrumental in identifying critical elections, the precise theoretical reasons for understanding why such changes occur were not developed until James Sundquist (1973) persuasively argued that certain political issues can divide coalitions within each of the major parties, and thus supporters and defenders of a particular policy position can be found in each party. Hence, these issues are "crosscutting" in partisan terms. These issues may disrupt the existing ideological cleavage within the major parties, but they may also be the source for third-party formation.[3]

Critical or crosscutting issues do not raise partisan passions over the long-term policy differences between the major parties; instead they create new regional, class, or ideological cleavages in each party. Crosscutting issues that provoke partisan changes include governmental policy on slavery in the 1850s, the inequality of wealth and the money supply in the 1880s and 1890s, the regulation of the economy and economic interests in the midst of the Great Depression, and racial equality, rising crime, school prayer, and matters of lifestyle from the 1950s and into the 1960s.

Crosscutting issues may eventually consume political debate and polarize the parties and the electorate. The central and most crucial causal mechanism in realignment occurs when party leaders take distinctive and polar positions either by choice or because of exogenous forces.[4] At such a time, political rhetoric becomes passionate and moralistic. Sundquist (1973, 290) notes: "A realignment crisis is precipitated when the moderate centrists lose control of one or both of the major parties—that is, of party policy and nominations—to one or the other of the polar forces." Sundquist (1973) shows vividly how central certain political issues are to partisan changes.

The theory of realignment does have a number of skeptics (e.g., Shafer 1991). A few challenge the scale of macrolevel policy changes, but most critics question the nature and dynamics of changes among the populace and their voting. Many scholars have suggested that realignment incorrectly magnifies the nature of both issue evolution and change in durable voting patterns. In some sense, this is not surprising; Key wrestled with precisely the same question of long-term versus short-term partisan changes (1955; 1959). The strongest challenges appear at the theoretical level. Carmines and Stimson correctly observe that abandoning the perspective of partisan change goes "equally awry" in considering the theoretical gaps surrounding realignment (1989, 20). Moreover, Poole and Rosenthal (1997) present strong evidence of realigning dynamics among members of Congress in the 1990s despite the lack of extreme polarization among the electorate.

Whether approached from the perspective of realignment or a concern simply with partisan change more generally, the evidence on the role of the Court in national policy making is in rather stark contrast to Dahl's earlier characterization of a Court serving majoritarian interests or the "enduring alliances." With few exceptions, scholars approached the issues surrounding the Court and realignment by examining the Court's controversial exercise of judicial review of federal statutes (Adamany 1973; Funston 1975; Beck 1976; Canon and Ulmer 1976). David Adamany (1973) argued that Dahl's characterization of the Supreme Court may have understated its role in the course of national policy making when viewed within the framework of critical or realigning elections (Adamany 1973; 1980).[5]

Adamany argued that the probability of conflict with a new majority party was greater following a critical election. The logic for conflict is straightforward; a realigning election would precipitate policy conflict between a Court appointed by the "old regime" and the new majority party victorious in a critical election.[6] There is only mixed interpretive (Adamany 1973) and quantitative evidence (Gates 1989; 1992) to support such a straightforward policy conflict thesis.

The Supreme Court's Role Before Critical Elections:
Provoking Partisan Conflict

In contrast to the contravening of partisan change following critical elections, Supreme Court decisions before these elections were often pivotal to provoking the changes. The Court contributed to the process of placing the critical issue on the national agenda or served to redefine the constitutionally permissible positions available to party leaders, leading to polarization (Adamany 1980; Lasser 1985; Gates 1992). The Supreme Court was, for example, a central component in the critical election of 1860, which ushered in a long period of Republican dominance. Many scholars see a similar agenda-setting role in the 1960–1968 critical elections (Adamany 1980; Gates 1992). In each period, Supreme Court decisions were fundamental to the course of national policy making, either by setting the agenda for partisan change or by defining and altering the nature of constitutionally permissible policy stances for each of the major parties' presidential candidates.

The agenda of the critical elections of 1960–1968 was a product of many events, including Supreme Court decisions that focused national attention on issues such as criminal justice, racial equality, and matters of lifestyle. These issues soon led to durable and significant electoral changes, albeit, the changes were novel from a critical election perspective because they represented a dramatic shift away from both major parties and to the growing ranks of independents. This was not a minor change but one persisting into the 1980s and 1990s (e.g., Wattenberg 1990; Shafer 1991). From *Brown v. Board of Education* (1954) to decisions relating to matters of lifestyle and expression as well as a number of cases expanding the rights of criminal defendants, the Supreme Court served an important agenda-setting role. The 1964 Republican presidential candidate, Barry Goldwater, for example, made the Supreme Court's decisions on criminal justice a consistent issue in his campaign as he dedicated time in each campaign speech to criticize the Warren Court for "coddling criminals" (Murphy 1972, 280, 381).

Moreover, the Supreme Court's decisions on racial equality matters were an important consideration despite its rather sporadic foray into the area from *Brown* until a decade later. Though some observers doubt the impact of the end of public school segregation as important to the course of civil rights politics (Rosenberg 1991), there is strong evidence that *Brown* produced significant changes in elite opinion that subsequently influenced national sentiment (Zaller 1992).

Yet another important consideration in understanding the Supreme Court and partisan change is the consequences of its policy decisions on campaigns and elections. The "dealignment" of the 1960s and the movement to more candidate-oriented and independent candidates was aided by Supreme Court decisions such as *Buckley v. Valeo* (1976), upholding the thrust of campaign-finance reform. *Buckley* and the Federal Election Campaign Reform Act of 1974 and its myriad amendments were instrumental in a number of key developments that weakened the role of parties in elections. In sum, the Supreme Court appears as an important actor in setting the agenda of the critical elections of the 1960s and the ensuing long-term and durable change *away* from both major parties.

The dynamics of Supreme Court policy making provoking partisan change before the critical election of 1860 move far beyond simply contributing to a volatile issue agenda. In *Dred Scott v. Sanford* (1857), the Supreme Court forced party leaders to take distinctive and polar stands on an issue that was often on the political agenda of the colonies and the new nation—slavery. The Jacksonian Democratic party system established in 1828 had avoided significant partisan change over the issue of slavery through such measures as the Compromise of 1820. In this vital compromise, one free territory would be admitted into the Union only with the admission of one slave territory.

The potential for regional division was a huge incentive for party leaders to engage in such compromise and bargaining. In *Dred Scott,* however, Chief Justice Taney's opinion declared that Congress lacked the power to control the issue of slavery in the territories and thus invalidated the Compromise of 1820. In the critical election of 1860, the Supreme Court played an even greater role than in the 1960s by not only contributing attention to a long-term crosscutting issue but in defining that which was constitutionally permissible by each candidate. No longer could the candidates take a moderate course. Constitutionally, the Supreme Court made the moderate course impossible for party leaders and the presidential candidates.[7] The typically cautious constitutional historian Charles Warren has concluded: "It may fairly be said that Chief Justice Taney elected Abraham Lincoln to the Presidency" (1932, 357).

To evaluate both the agenda-setting and policy-conflict theses, I examined Supreme Court decisions invalidating both federal and state policies and focused on both the timing of such decisions relating to the critical issues and on the individual behavior or voting of the justices. The analysis produced mixed results on a consistent role in either provoking or contravening partisan change. Nevertheless, the most prevalent role in various critical elections between 1837 and 1964 appears to be to provoke partisan change either by reducing the constitutionally permissible moderate position on a critical issue or by heightening concern over the issue through a series of decisions. Yet a definitive role for the Supreme Court in periods of transformational partisan change remains elusive, due primarily to the uncertainty of membership change on the Court and the indefinite response of party leaders to crosscutting issues (Gates 1992, 180–87).

The Supreme Court's Role in Diffusing Partisan Change: The 1992 Presidential Election and Abortion

The literature's concern with the important power of judicial review and realignments neglects a third important role for the Supreme Court and partisan change: diffusing partisan conflict by upholding legislation or Court precedent in less dramatic elections. This much more subtle type of issue formation or diffusion is nonetheless important to the course of national policy making and can be seen in the months preceding the 1992 presidential election. The Supreme Court upheld state policies making abortion services more difficult, such as a twenty-four-hour waiting period between the signing of the surgery-consent form and the performance of an abortion— a position consistently struck down in the 1980s (Hinkson-Craig and O'Brien 1993). At the same time, the five-justice majority struck down the spousal notification provision of the Pennsylvania law and announced that *Roe v. Wade* (1973) continues to be good law and worthy of Supreme Court respect. This is of no minor consequence as groups and the executive branch called for the overturn of *Roe*.

In upholding some of the most restrictive state laws on the availability of abortion services as well as sustaining the principle of pro-choice advocates, the Court took a moderate course that did *not* reduce the constitutionally permissible policy choices available to party leaders. Hence, the Court avoided the *Dred Scott* of the 1990s. It is thus important to examine how abortion, like slavery, has the potential of provoking partisan change as well as the Court's decision and to explore the issue's significance for the campaigns of the Republican and Democratic candidates.

Abortion: A Crosscutting Political Issue

The Supreme Court's decision in *Roe v. Wade* (1973) is arguably the most volatile decision since *Brown v. Board of Education* (1954) (e.g., Cook, Jelen, and Wilcox 1992; Hinkson-Craig and O'Brien 1993; Adams 1997). The Court announced that a Texas law forbidding abortion services to women except in life-saving situations was an unconstitutional violation of a woman's right to privacy. In *Roe,* the Supreme Court raised a crosscutting issue for the American party system. Similar to slavery in the 1850s, *Roe* has supporters and detractors in both parties.[8]

This division is clear from the many studies on public opinion and abortion (e.g., Cook, Jelen, and Wilcox 1992). Although there are abundant studies focusing on aspects of abortion and public opinion in the aggregate, surprisingly few focus on abortion in partisan terms. Yet the abortion issue cuts across the existing ideological cleavage in the party system (see Fig. 6.1).

Using data from the National Elections Studies (ICPSR 1995), the graph displays the percentage of Democrats and Republicans responding to the most extreme antiabortion position. The American National Election Studies asked, among other alternatives, if abortion should "never be permitted." It is clear that the responses by both Democrats and Republicans are quite similar and stable over this twelve-year period. Roughly 10 percent of both Democrats and Republicans express a desire to ban abortion entirely, and the responses do not change significantly for over a decade before the 1992 election.

The responses to the pro-choice position are even more probative of the crosscutting character of abortion (see Fig. 6.2). This graph displays the percentage of Democrats and Republicans stating that a woman should "always be able to obtain an abortion as a matter of personal choice." These respondents represent the strongest pro-choice position. Over the 1980–1992 period, the percentage of Republicans staking out such a strong stance never fell below a full 30 percent. Although the percentage of Democrats taking the most pro-choice position offered by the survey is almost always greater than the Republican number, the average partisan difference is only 5 percent (5.03 percent) from 1980 to 1992. It is evident that the most extreme pro-choice and antiabortion voices are found expressed within each party, and their levels of support for this position are remarkably comparable and stable over time.[9] This is the making of a crosscutting issue; both parties will suffer electorally by staking out a definitive position.[10]

American public opinion is generally stable over time on most issues (Stimson 1992). Moreover, the portrayal of extreme pro-life and pro-choice responses does not tap the opinion of all Democrats and Republicans. Nevertheless, a significant number of votes within each party could potentially be swayed by a dramatic overturning of *Roe.* Indeed, the moderate course for a large number of both Democrats and Republicans is to be sensitive to the context or the motives underlying the decision to have an abortion,

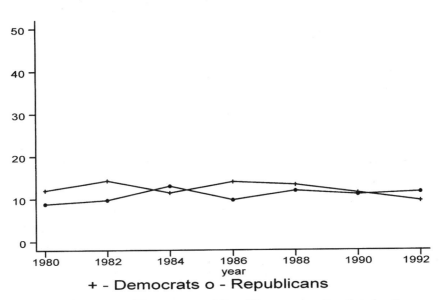

Figure 6.1. Percentage of Democrats and Republicans responding that abortion should never be permitted.

which range from medical reasons to a basic desire not to have a child. Nonetheless, the percentages of both Democrats and Republicans supporting the most pro-choice and pro-life positions (see Fig. 6.2) strongly suggest that a move to an extremist position could turn a presidential election. An overturn of *Roe* or even an implicit denial of its legitimacy would force the presidential candidates either to agree or disagree because the Court would make any moderate course impossible. The potential for the Supreme Court to bring attention to abortion was tremendous by 1991. Studies show precisely how the Court has the ability to focus attention on certain issues through dramatic decisions (Flemming, Bohte, and Wood 1997).

The Supreme Court and Abortion

An opportunity for a dramatic overturn of *Roe* was presented before the Court in *Planned Parenthood of Southeastern Pennsylvania v. Casey* (1992). During the 1980s, the Supreme Court had become increasingly divided on the abortion question and by 1986 was often striking down a number of state laws by a minimum of 5 to 4. In so doing, the Court fashioned doctrine

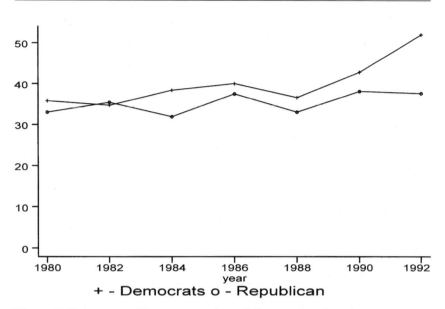

Figure 6.2. Percentage of Democrats and Republicans responding that a woman should always have access to abortion.

supporting the notion that state regulation on the availability of abortion services must be carefully tailored to relate either to maternal or fetal health.

The fragile character of *Roe v. Wade* was perhaps most evident in a 1983 decision, *Akron v. Akron Center for Reproductive Health.* The Court reinforced its increasingly precarious commitment to the principles of *Roe.* Six justices struck down select provisions of the Ohio law at issue. The law required several regulations, including the performance of abortion in hospitals following the first trimester; the written consent of a parent or a judge for minors; the assurance that a woman's consent was truly "informed consent," including a medical assessment of viability before *Roe's* third-trimester demarcation; the increasingly common twenty-four-hour waiting period between the woman's consent and the actual performance of the abortion; and the "humane and sanitary" disposal of fetal remains.

The Supreme Court struck down all nonhealth requirements in *Akron,* including the vague clause relating to fetal disposal. Significantly, Justice O'Connor authored a dissenting opinion, joined by Justices Rehnquist and White, in which she described *Roe's* trimester approach as "unworkable" and "clearly on a collision course with itself." O'Connor argued that *Roe* required courts to assess the state of medical technology and the point of fetal viability. She said a continued commitment to this framework places courts in a demanding position where they "must pretend to act as science review boards." She argued that instead the constitutional question should be whether regulations on abortion services are "unduly burdensome" on a woman's choice.

The issue of abortion was intensified with the retirement of Justice Lewis Powell. His departure left the Court evenly split as pro-*Roe* supporters diminished to four, with an equal number on record opposed to the landmark doctrine. Unprecedented interest-group mobilization accompanied the subsequent nomination of Judge Robert Bork in fall 1986. The nomination hearings and Senate vote illuminate the incredible volatility of abortion as a political and legal issue. The Senate's rejection of Bork only postponed controversy over abortion, the Court, and the course of American politics.

Within two years, the Supreme Court accepted another important case that would test the limits of the *Roe* doctrine and the Court's narrow majority of supportive justices. In *Webster v. Reproductive Health Services* (1989), the Court confronted a restrictive Missouri law that required tests of viability before the third trimester and provisions relating to medical advice regarding abortion as a legal option. Given the appointment of Republican Justice Kennedy to fill the seat of former Justice Powell, it is not surprising that *Webster* generated tremendous interest. Indeed, the case attracted seventy-eight third-party or amici briefs, which represented over 5,000 social interests when one considers the number of brief cosponsors. This was unparalleled in the entire history of the Court but consistent with the volatility one associates with crosscutting issues for the American party system.

A new conservative majority of five justices upheld these restrictions but failed by one vote to overturn *Roe*. Chief Justice Rehnquist's opinion was joined only by Justices Kennedy and White as Justices O'Connor and Scalia wrote separate concurring opinions supporting the judgment. The opinion implicitly invited even more stringent state regulations and revisiting the value of stare decisis (i.e., *Roe*). The four dissenting justices also found it difficult to join a single opinion, as Justice Stevens wrote separately and Justices Brennan and Marshall joined an opinion authored by Justice Blackmun.

In *Webster,* the signs of polarization were becoming clear. Yet it would take the Pennsylvania legislature to enact a statute that directly ignored several Supreme Court decisions by requiring a twenty-four-hour waiting period for women seeking an abortion and a rather novel spousal notification provision. The case would eventually be one of the most important for nontransformational politics and presidential elections: *Planned Parenthood of Southeastern Pennsylvania v. Casey* (1992).

In fall 1991, proabortion forces were adamant on achieving a definitive decision by the Supreme Court on the validity of *Roe* before the upcoming 1992 election. Rarely, if ever, has the Supreme Court's potential action been considered by party activists as so central to a presidential campaign. Pro-choice advocates ironically sought a definitive decision on *Roe* with a realistic expectation that it would be overturned. Since *Webster,* the pro-choice justices Brennan and Marshall had retired and Justices Souter and Thomas had been appointed by a Republican president whose party had, since 1980, an explicit anti-*Roe* plank in the national platform. Although a few observers may have questioned the possibility of overturning *Roe* even with these appointments, it is clear that pro-choice voices understood the nature and power of crosscutting issues that can precipitate durable partisan changes. In a November 7, 1991, press conference, Faye Wattleton, then president of Planned Parenthood Federation of America, noted about the pending case: "Even if [*Casey*] does not come before the election, it will still be a major issue in this election. This is not whether it's better for us politically, but what is better for women. We will not permit the courts to have the last word on this ever again, and we will show our strength in the polls because we simply will not go back" (Hinkson-Craig and O'Brien 1993, 333).

In a 5-to-4 decision, the Supreme Court did not polarize as advocates had anticipated. Instead, the decision pleased few. The variety of complex opinions running some 184 pages suggested that the Court would apply a new, more fully amplified "undue burden" approach to state regulations. At issue in *Casey* were several provisions enacted by Pennsylvania that directly went against established Supreme Court doctrine. The Court addressed five primary provisions of Pennsylvania's law that Democratic governor Robert Casey defended.[11] They included requiring a number of procedures to guarantee that a women's consent was "informed"; a twenty-four-hour waiting period between consent and the performance of an abortion, which had been previously overturned by the Court; parental-consent for minors; public disclosure; and a requirement of spousal notification before an abortion. The spousal notification provision was the only aspect of the law overturned based on the principle of *Roe.* In this case critical for its impact on the presidential election, the Supreme Court pleased no one with its decision that both upheld *Roe* and some of the most restrictive state policies ever enacted.

Justice O'Connor was central to the moderate conservative bloc of Justices Kennedy and Souter that upheld *Roe,* along with Justices Blackmun and Stevens. Significant partisan change was quite probable had this bloc of three moderates polarized and joined their conservative brethren who explicitly voted to overturn *Roe.* The dissenting opinions of Chief Justice Rehnquist and Justices Scalia, Thomas, and White showed that these conservatives clearly wanted to abandon *Roe* entirely. This would have been as dramatic as the overturn of the Missouri Compromise in *Dred Scott* in terms of electoral fortunes and partisan dynamics. The tone of the dissenters in *Casey* was not unlike the harsh criticism O'Connor had launched on *Roe* in her dissent in *Akron* less than a decade earlier. The move of O'Connor and her conservative colleagues provoked Justice Scalia to describe the majority holding as both "contrived" and a decision provoked by "realpolitik." Although the precise etiology of the Supreme Court's response to crosscutting issues is difficult,[12] the dynamics of partisan change provided by Sundquist (1973) are extremely insightful (Gates 1989, 1992; Lasser 1985).

It is useful to recall Sundquist's important insight: "A realignment crisis is precipitated when the moderate centrists lose control of one or both of the major parties—that is, of party policy and nominations—to one or the other of the polar forces" (1973, 290). The moderate centrists gained temporary control over the abortion issue, an issue that has every characteristic necessary to provoke durable change in the American party system. Similar to its relationship with Democrats and Republicans in Congress during the 1850s, the Supreme Court could have easily declared *Roe* unconstitutional and forced the presidential candidates to polar stances. *Casey* cannot be ignored for an understanding of the Supreme Court and partisan change. The Court did not polarize but averted partisan change.

The responses of pro-choice and pro-life advocates are extremely insightful into how the moderate position of the Supreme Court provided little support to either side and avoided polarization. Kate Michelman, then president of the National Abortion Rights Action League, announced *Roe* as an "empty shell," and others declared "*Roe* is dead." In contrast, the founder of Operation Rescue, Randall Terry, announced that the decision "stabbed the pro-life movement in the back" (quoted in Hinkson-Craig and O'Brien 1993, 324). These anecdotal quotes are only suggestive of the major diffusion of partisan change created by the Supreme Court's decision in *Casey.*

The decision highlights how both upholding and striking down legislation are important to the course of national politics. Greg Adams (1997) shows precisely how abortion as a national issue proceeds through a period of evolution consistent with the work of Carmines and Stimson (1989). From 1972 to 1994, Democrats and Republicans did seem gradually to polarize, with information cues flowing from the party leaders or opinion leaders to the general public. *Casey* represented a reprieve for leadership in both parties on abortion. It was also a significant demonstration of how the Court may play an important role in the course of national policy making beyond precipitating or blocking partisan change. Moreover, this is not to suggest that the Supreme Court's diffusion of partisan conflict is necessarily a new role, but it is definitely unexplored and the territory uncharted.

The Supreme Court in National Policy Making

Clearly, the revival of a concern with institutions compared to attitudes and individual behavior offers insights, regardless of whether the institutional approach is interpretive-comparative, bounded rationality, or rational choice. As long as analysts are not moved to mere ethnographic depiction, the concern with institutions can assist in developing non-neutral but generalizable and reliable observations regarding politics. This is certainly true of major partisan change and the U.S. Supreme Court.

Major partisan realignment of the scale known in the past may be a phenomenon that is unlikely, given recent changes in the political party system and the lack of a highly volatile crisis similar to the Civil War and the Great Depression. Yet these differences should not move students of courts, and of the Supreme Court specifically, to ignore how judicial decisions are important in national elections. Whether precipitating tensions in the midst of changes in the political party system or forestalling major shifts in partisan reform, the Supreme Court is an important and much neglected actor in understanding the course of national policy making. By analyzing more carefully Supreme Court policy making that deals with less dramatic exercises of judicial power and by continuing to place these decisions within the context of partisan conflict, we can come to understand that the Court's role is much greater and more complex than Dahl suggested in his classic analysis.

The study of the Supreme Court and partisan change also shows vividly how it is necessary to incorporate an understanding of the Court, its relationship with other political structures, and the historical forces that dynamically interact with political change. As the ultimate arbiter of constitutional conflicts, the Supreme Court confronts the increasingly complex issues arising from socioeconomic change (Unger 1976). Sundquist suggests that the American two-party system is often unable to deal with new issues that did not define the partisan battles of the past. If the late nineteenth century is probative, the Supreme Court's agenda reflected the increasing concerns regarding economics, as the era of massive industrialization following the Civil War ushered in unseen and complicated legal and political issues.

Though lacking both the power of the purse and the sword, the Supreme Court is an important actor in appreciating the complex and subtle changes involved in the transformational, and less dramatic, shifts in the American party system. Understanding the Supreme Court's role in partisan change and national policy making must move beyond both an analysis of the dramatic instances of judicial review and a focus on critical elections. Elmer Schattschneider (1975) argued persuasively how important expanding the scope of political conflict is for a richer understanding of political struggles. It is clear that the Supreme Court's decisions have either expanded the scope of conflict or made such conflict inevitably more intense. A focus on how the Supreme Court can diffuse rather than expand political conflict is also meaningful in attaining a more mature and accurate portrayal of a complex institution in a representative democracy.

Notes

1. One of the most insightful and thoughtful interpretive analyses of this issue is Commager (1943).

2. Some of the problems of divided, as opposed to one-party, rule in the United States are the subject of concern regarding its precise causes and repercussions as seen, for example, in Jacobson (1990) and Fiorina (1992).

3. Crosscutting issues are a necessary condition for a critical issue but are not a sufficient condition. Third parties, for example, can raise crosscutting issues, but party leaders in one or both major parties can endorse as their own the third-party position and thus dilute their appeal. This is seen vividly in the early years of this century as both Democrats and Republicans came to endorse many of the reforms urged by the Progressive movement. This strategy is also evident outside the American context. In the late nineteenth century, the first chancellor of the German Empire, Otto von Bismarck, embarked on a similar strategy in dealing with the growing strength of the labor movement. He proposed national health insurance, which was one of the key reforms underlying the popular appeal of labor.

4. Because crosscutting issues threaten each major parties' coalition, party leaders will initially attempt to straddle or compromise on the issue.

5. See Funston (1975), for a quantitative attempt to assess conflict, and his critics (Beck 1976; Canon and Ulmer 1976).

6. The preeminent example of such policy conflict is the New Deal realignment of the 1930s. As President Roosevelt and the new Democratic Congress sought to deal with the economic crisis of the Great Depression, a conservative and predominantly Republican Court gave tentative support to state-level policies based upon notions of unprecedented governmental regulation of the economy, including price controls (*Nebbia v. New York* [1934]). Yet in spring 1935 and continuing until an abrupt judicial turnaround in 1937, the predominantly Republican Court polarized and handed down a series of decisions that left thirteen provisions of federal legislation declared unconstitutional as well as many more state laws. These policies were directed at unprecedented federal intervention in economic matters (Gates 1992, 118–21). The New Deal era appears as the only period of extreme and prolonged policy conflict between a new majority party and the Supreme Court following a critical election. The remaining periods of realigning partisan change, when a new majority party inherits a Court of the "old regime," show the more probable outcome: the Supreme Court may be just as divided as the party system because it is composed of justices appointed by presidents more concerned with either downplaying critical, crosscutting issues or unlikely to foresee their rise on the political horizon. Given the nearly random nature of turnover on the Court (King 1987) and the crosscutting nature of critical or volatile issues for the Supreme Court and the party system (e.g., Brady and Stewart 1982), it is not surprising that a definitive policy-conflict role has so little systematic empirical support.

7. Alan Westin (1953) detected a similar role in the critical election of 1896, writing before the seminal work of V. O. Key on critical elections.

8. Graber (1996) provides tremendous insight into the democratic role the Court may serve in dealing with an issue so explosive to the political system and the practical implications of the legacy of *Roe.*

9. Adams (1997) is perhaps the best source on the issue of abortion and partisan politics.

10. The debates within the Republican party in 1997 over the issue of partial birth abortion, for example, vividly illustrate a classic tension with crosscutting issues between party moderates and the most extreme sides within a party. Republican leaders sought to downplay the issue as others called for it to be a litmus test for party funding of their candidates.

11. This was a position that moved the Democratic National Convention to ban his speech before the 1992 convention. See especially Hinkson-Craig and O'Brien (1993, 325–26).

12. It is difficult to decipher the underlying motive(s) of the moderate conservative bloc. Their concern with legal policy rather than with Justice Scalia's characterization of "realpolitik" could indeed account for the decision. I would suggest that it is some complex combination of legal, policy, and political elements.

Chapter 7

The Supreme Court Bar and Institutional Relationships

Kevin T. McGuire

Perhaps more so than any branch of the federal government, the U.S. Supreme Court is dependent upon individuals outside of government to provide it with information and analysis to support its policy making. Congress boasts some 24,000 legislative personnel who better enable its members to fulfill their mission of legislation and representation, and roughly 1,700 members of the executive office of the president help to oversee the day-to-day responsibilities of the chief executive. Unlike its counterparts, however, the Court has only a modest staff to which it can turn; with less than 350 full-time employees, the Supreme Court has the smallest contingent of staff in the federal government.[1] All three branches must face the demands of their relative constituencies, as diverse interests compete against one another for the time and attention of decision makers. Organized groups pressure Congress; lobbyists advocate the causes of a myriad clientele before federal administrators; litigants of every stripe seek authoritative resolution of any number of complex legal questions. Yet the Supreme Court is quite distinct from its institutional peers; the nine justices, aided almost exclusively by a talented but small group of law clerks, bear the burden of responding directly to the scores of pleadings that annually land on the steps of the Court.

Such limited resources might be less of a concern if the justices were not burdened with the necessities of processing a substantial caseload. If the Court could ignore the thousands of petitions brought to it each year, its members might be free to pursue their own policy designs on whatever legal issues most concerned them, creating, at their own initiative, abstract constitutional and statutory questions from whole cloth.[2] Despite its considerable autonomy, though, the Supreme Court does not have such luxury. The justices must establish their plenary agenda only from among the cases that litigants have seen fit to bring to them. Sifting through a profusion of requests for review—most of which are of no interest to the justices—the members of the Court labor to locate the limited number of cases presenting the issues of genuine legal import that are worthy of the Court's attention (H. Perry 1991).

In those few cases that are ultimately slated for decision on the merits, the Court naturally values intelligence regarding the likely policy consequences of its decisions (S. Shapiro 1984; R. Stern et al. 1993). With only two competing parties presenting focused arguments, however, the nature of the judicial process works against the Court's becoming more broadly educated about the impact of its policies (Horowitz 1977). Fortunately, the justices remain open to a larger array of input through the advocacy of an ever-growing cast of "friends of the Court" (Caldeira and Wright 1990). With only rare exception, however, the Court does not solicit such legal analysis from the segments of society most likely to feel the impact of its rulings; rather, as with the process of selecting cases, the justices must await affected interests to make their views known.

With a limited staff, large volumes of information, and little control over the manner of facts and analysis that flow to it, the Supreme Court puts a premium on reliable information that genuinely aids its decision making. Thus, individuals who are dependable sources of such information—those to whom the Court has learned it can turn for helpful knowledge that consistently better informs its decisions—are bound to enjoy a favorable relationship with the justices. Who plays such a supporting role?

Virtually all the facts, issues, and arguments that are brought to the Court are filtered through its legal community. Petitions for review, briefs on the merits, the filings of amici curiae—all are prepared and submitted by lawyers. Moreover, the Court's only immediate interaction with outside actors, oral argument, is a structured dialogue taking place exclusively between the justices and members of the Supreme Court's bar. In this sense, the Court again stands in marked contrast to its fellow branches. Congress, for instance, is remarkably open to the voices of a kaleidoscope of characters. Certain segments of the legislative process (such as committee hearings) and less formal settings (such as face-to-face discussions in the home district, office, or the halls of Congress) serve to ensure that members have every opportunity to hear from constituents, lobbyists, laborers, business and industry representatives, regulators, and the like. At the same time, institutional actors like the General Accounting Office and the Congressional

Research Service provide thorough policy analysis for the House and Senate. At the other end of Pennsylvania Avenue, modern presidents are likewise close students of the ever-shifting concerns of economic, social, and foreign interests; and they work vigorously to maintain similar contacts with those interests through a variety of forums—public meetings, cabinet discussions, negotiations with legislative leaders and bureaucratic decision makers, and diplomatic summits, to name but a few. Of course, a vast network of executive branch institutions, providing the president with a wealth of expertise to guide the development of public policy, exists as well.

Congress and the president, then, are much more pluralistic than the Supreme Court with respect to their openness to the voices of outside interests. Certainly, this is not to suggest that the Court is hostile to the involvement of those not directly involved in litigation; indeed, the justices are quite receptive to the advocacy of a large and varied band of organized interests, which routinely participates in the business of the Court (Caldeira and Wright 1990). Furthermore, the legislature and the executive are far better equipped to generate and organize vast amounts of policy information. Accordingly, while actors of many different guises may seek to influence the choices made by the legislative and executive branches, the Supreme Court's institutional arrangements effectively guarantee that virtually all the relevant data that contribute to its decisions is filtered through a single source, a relatively small group of individuals whose common denominator is the practice of law. It is not that the nature of the judicial process keeps relevant information out but that the structure of its decision-making process tightly constrains how it is presented.

Does this control that lawyers exercise over the flow of information to the Supreme Court have any consequences for its policy making? In this chapter, I argue that the Court's decisions are affected in important ways by its relationship to the legal community. In particular, the norms and practices of its principal players—their ability to shape alternatives, their legal craftsmanship, their capacity both to advocate and provide genuine assistance to the Court—are significant determinants of how the justices understand and process their caseload. Notwithstanding the importance of the justices' ideologies (Segal and Spaeth 1993), much of what the Court does may be governed by legal concerns, norms internal to the Court, or institutional imperatives (see Clayton and Gillman 1999; Smith 1988). Exploiting a decision-making process that is unique to the judiciary, these sophisticated actors help to determine which alternatives will be brought to the Court and how they will be presented. In turn, the Court's policies are conditioned, to some extent, by the way in which issues and information are channeled to it.

The idea that the structure of governmental decision making might affect public policy is not new (March and Olsen 1984), and scholars of the judiciary have variously sought to link those structures to its decisions (see, e.g., Hall and Brace 1993). Here I argue that the attitudes of the justices have been and continue to be affected by their legal community (see R. Smith 1988). In brief, a largely reactive Supreme Court, with a dependence upon the legal system for its formal input, facilitates a potentially influential role for a set of leading institutional actors, Washington's contingent of experienced Supreme Court lawyers. I begin by tracing the early link between the Supreme Court and the lawyers of the capital city. I then turn my focus to the Court's more recent reliance upon Washington's leading legal lights.

Historical Context

Washington, D.C., was a mere swamp when it was selected as the location for the capital of the republic in 1791 (Reps 1991). Unlike the existing and thriving cities of the day, such as Baltimore, New York, or Philadelphia, Washington was largely undeveloped land with little infrastructure, a fact frustrating ready transportation to and from the young capital. Cases began to wend their way to the Supreme Court, but the absence of rapid transportation, combined with Washington's relative inaccessibility, made traveling to the federal city to appear before the Court a tremendously arduous trek (Frank 1958; Warren 1939). As a consequence, many lawyers were virtually precluded from arguing their cases before the justices.

To their aid came a small number of lawyers who lived in and around Washington. Unable to make the journey, lawyers from distant parts of the country often referred their cases to lawyers practicing within the capital city. Given their proximity to the Court, active advocates of the era were chosen to represent a variety of interests before the justices; luminaries such as William Pinkney, Daniel Webster, and William Wirt, engaged as counsel in case after case, became prolific and respected Supreme Court practitioners (White 1988). As a consequence, these Washington lawyers came to command substantial proportions of the Court's time, and an identifiable Supreme Court bar developed. What is more, quite apart from their professional interactions, these lawyers often lived alongside the justices in local boardinghouses, facilitating personal as well as professional ties to the judiciary (Krislov 1965).

Working closely with the Court and handling a substantial proportion of its docket, these experienced Washington advocates exercised a good deal of control over how legal issues were framed and presented to the justices. As much as the modern Court relies upon its legal community, the justices of the early nineteenth century were almost completely dependent upon the lawyers who appeared before them to provide them with information relevant to informed decision making. "Advocacy before the Marshall Court was an essentially oral medium. Written briefs were rare and . . . not required; collected volumes of precedents were sparse; written treatises were neither numerous nor widely available" (White 1988, 203). Not surprisingly, these lawyers had a considerable influence on the development of federal law; the views of the justices seem to have been shaped, to a considerable extent, by the lawyers who appeared before them.

One way to illustrate that influence is to compare the arguments made by these lawyers against the text of the Court's opinion (see Ivers and O'Connor 1987; Spriggs and Wahlbeck 1997). How do the propositions that these experienced lawyers advanced compare with the rationales that were ultimately adopted by the majority? Did the legal analysis of the Supreme Court's bar inform the development of the law, or did the justices derive their opinions independently of the arguments of counsel? It is one thing to suggest that the justices may have been persuaded to vote in a fashion favorable to a lawyer's interests; it is quite another to say that the actual supporting doctrine was drawn from counsel. If, in the absence of other competing information, the justices incorporated the arguments, reasoning, and legal interpretation of those men who appeared before them, then that would serve as fairly persuasive evidence of the legal community's impact on early constitutional law.

An excellent candidate for such a test is William Pinkney. A Baltimore-based practitioner, Pinkney was a noted Supreme Court expert in the early 1800s, whose value to clients was reflected in his dozens of appearances before the Court (Ireland 1986). In the 1814 Term of the Court alone, for instance, roughly half the cases on the docket bear his name as counsel (White 1988, 245). Clearly, he earned the admiration of the Court, as evidenced by Chief Justice John Marshall's averment that "Mr. Pinkney was the greatest man I have ever seen in a court of justice" (Warren 1939, 260). Two of Pinkney's most notable victories in the Court were the decisions in

McCulloch v. Maryland (1819) and *Cohens v. Virginia* (1821). In *McCulloch,* Pinkney successfully defended the supremacy of federal law as well as the implied power of the national government to establish the Bank of the United States. His argument in favor of federal judicial review of the decisions of state courts enjoyed similar support in the *Cohens* decision. To what degree, though, did Chief Justice Marshall's opinions in these cases actually derive from Pinkney? The evidence seems to provide a clear answer (see boxed text, pp. 122–23).

In both cases, the final text of the Supreme Court's opinion bears a stunning resemblance to the substantive positions advocated by Pinkney. In *McCulloch,* for example, his arguments on the sources of sovereignty are incorporated almost verbatim into the decision: Pinkney disavows both federal and state sovereignty, asserting that ultimate authority resides with the people; Marshall adopts this logic wholesale. Similarly, Marshall's construction of the necessary and proper clause—one supporting Pinkney's argument for the congressional discretion to charter a bank—seems to be fairly lifted from Pinkney's oratory; the word "necessary" in this context, argues Pinkney, cannot be understood to mean "absolutely necessary," a proposition that Marshall clearly endorses. Likewise, the *Cohens* decision reveals an apparently strong influence of Pinkney on the Chief Justice, as Pinkney's analysis on the jurisdiction of the federal courts tracks Marshall's all too closely: paralleling Pinkney's peroration, Marshall concludes that a case's subject matter—not its parties—determines the scope of federal judicial power.

Obviously, not all decisions of the early Supreme Court provide such dramatic evidence of the apparent impact of the bar on the minds of the justices. Other comparisons would surely reveal only limited connections between the legal interpretations advocated by the Washington contingent and Supreme Court doctrine (see White 1988, 291). Still, these limited illustrations mark the potential reach of the legal community's influence on the thinking of the justices. No less than the members of the modern Court, the justices in any given case had to rely heavily upon lawyers for an understanding of what issues were at stake, how they might reasonably be resolved, and what the probable consequences of a decision might be. They were, in effect, the primary filters through which the Court's information had to pass. As such, the lawyers of this era could not but affect a justice's legal orientations. "When the breadth of oral advocacy before the Marshall Court is compared with the relative paucity of other authorities, and when one recalls that the arguments of counsel were regarded as themselves sources of law, one must conclude that Marshall Court advocacy had a significant effect on Marshall Court decisions" (White 1988, 291). Even if in varying degrees, then, the Supreme Court relied upon the Washington legal community to provide it with information and legal analysis. These actors, therefore, aided the justices in weighing the competing legal interests of the day, and through their advocacy, they became a primary mechanism for helping to shape the Court's policies. With such collective expertise, the Washington bar was a principal institutional force within the Court.

Washington Expertise in the Modern Supreme Court

What kind of impact does the Washington legal community have upon the Supreme Court today? Does the bar enjoy a similar relationship with the justices, and if so why? Obviously, modern transportation has eliminated the geographical causes of the Washington bar's early dominance before the Court. Long gone, too, are the shared living quarters of the lawyers and justices. Nonetheless, Washington practitioners are once again central figures in the politics of the High Court.

The resurgence of the Supreme Court bar is best understood in the context of larger changes in political representation and the legal profession. Over the last thirty years, Washington has become home to an increasingly large number of individuals who represent assorted organized interests. These lobbyists have advocated their positions, largely before decision makers in the halls of Congress and before administrative agencies (Berry 1989; Schlozman and Tierney 1986; Walker 1983). Many of these representatives are lawyers; and given that they frequently come to their positions after having left service within the federal government, they quite often enjoy firsthand knowledge of both the policy process and its principal actors (Heinz et al. 1993). At the same time, the legal profession more generally has become quite specialized, with lawyers offering highly focused practices of one brand or another (Heinz and Laumann 1982). With the rise in interest representation in Washington and the fragmentation of the bar, it is not surprising that talented lawyers with expertise in appellate advocacy have begun to appear there, specializing in Supreme Court litigation. Thus, for example, former members of the solicitor general's office—H. Bartow Farr III, Andrew L. Frey, Kenneth S. Geller, Kathryn A. Oberly, Carter G. Phillips, and Richard Taranto, as well as the late Erwin N. Griswold and Rex E. Lee, to

Comparison of the Arguments of William Pinkney and the Opinions of Chief Justice John Marshall

Pinkney in *McCulloch v. Maryland* (1819)

Marshall in *McCulloch v. Maryland* (1819)

It is said, too, that the powers of the State governments are original, and therefore more emphatically sovereign than those of the national government. But the State powers are no more original than those belonging to the Union. There is no original power but in the people, who are the fountain and source of all political power. . . .

The constitution by which those authorities and the means of executing them are given, and the laws made in pursuance of it, are declared to be the supreme law of the land. The legislatures and judges of the States are to be bound by oath to support that constitution.

We are told that the [necessary and proper clause] . . . excludes all such [means] as are not strictly and absolutely necessary. But it is certain that this clause is not restrictive. . . . Compare [its language] . . . with the qualified manner [of the language of] the 10th section of the [first] article. In the latter, it is provided that "no State shall, without the consent of the Congress, lay any imposts, or duties on imports or exports, except what may be *absolutely necessary* for carrying into execution for foregoing power," etc. There is here, then, no qualification of the necessity. It need not be absolute. It may be taken in its ordinary grammatical sense. The word *necessary,* standing by itself, has no inflexible meaning; it is used in a sense more or less strict, according to the subject. . . . It may be qualified by the addition of adverbs of diminution or enlargement. . . . But that it is not always used in this strict and rigorous sense may be proved by tracing its definition and etymology in very human language.

The powers of the general government, it has been said, are delegated by the States, who alone are truly sovereign. But when . . . it was deemed necessary to change [the confederation] into an effective government . . . the necessity of referring it to the people . . . was felt and acknowledged by all. The government of the Union, then . . . is emphatically and truly a government of the people. In form and substance it emanates from them. . . .

The nation, on those subjects on which it can, must necessarily bind its component parts. . . . This question is not left to mere reason; the people have, in express terms, decided it, by saying "this constitution, and the laws of the United States, which shall be made in pursuance thereof, shall be the supreme law of the land, and by requiring that the members of the State legislatures, and the officers of the executive and judicial departments of the States, shall take the oath of fidelity to it.

The argument on which most reliance is placed is drawn from the peculiar language of the clause. . . . The word "necessary" is considered as controlling the whole sentence. Does [the word] always import an absolute physical necessity? We think it does not . . . A thing may be necessary, . . . absolutely or indispensably necessary. . . . This comment on the word is well illustrated . . . by . . . the 10th section of the 1st article of the constitution. It is . . . impossible to compare the sentence which prohibits a State from laying "imposts, or duties on imports or export, except which may be *absolutely necessary* for executing its inspection laws," with that which authorizes Congress "to make

*Comparison of the Arguments of William Pinkney and
the Opinions of Chief Justice John Marshall, continued*

all laws which shall be necessary and proper for carrying into execution" the powers of the central government, without feeling a conviction that the convention understood itself to change materially the meaning of the word "necessary" by prefixing the word "absolutely." This word, then, like others, is used in various senses.

Pinkney in *Cohens v. Virginia* (1821)

It is an axiom of political science, that the judicial power of every govern-ment must be commensurate with its legislative authority: it must be ade-quate to the protection, enforcement, and assertion of all the other powers of the government. . . . [In] suits between citizen and citizen on con-tract . . . the State courts must neces-sarily have original jurisdiction; but if the party defendant gets up a defence . . . and the decision of the State Court is in favour of the law thus set up, the judicial authority of the Union must be exerted over the cause. There is nothing in the consti-tution which prohibits the exercise of such a controlling authority. On the contrary, it is expressly declared, that where the *case* arises under the con-stitution and laws of the Union, the judicial power of the Union shall extend to it. It is the *case*, then, and not the *forum* in which it arises, that is to determine whether the judicial power of the Union shall extend to it.

Marshall in *Cohens v. Virginia* (1821)

The powers of the Union, on the great subjects of war, peace, and com-merce, and on many others, are in themselves limitations of the sover-eignty of the States. . . . The main-tenance of these principles within purity is certainly among the great duties of government. One of the instruments by which this duty may be peaceably performed, is the judi-cial department. It is authorized to decide all cases of every description, arising under the constitution or law of the United States. From this gen-eral grant of jurisdiction, no excep-tion is made of those cases in which a State may be a party. When we con-sider the situation of the Union and of a State, in relation to each other; the nature of our Constitution; the subordination of the State govern-ments to that constitution . . . are we at liberty to insert, in this general grant, an exception of those cases in which a State may be a party? . . . We think . . . not. We think a case arising under the constitution or laws of the United States, is cognizable in the Courts of the Union, whoever may be the parties to that case.

Source: G. Edward White. 1988. *The Marshall Court and Cultural Change, 1815–1835.* Pp. 248–50. Abr. ed. New York: Oxford University Press. Emphasis in original.

name but a few—have often elected to remain close to the Court as Washington lawyers specializing in Supreme Court advocacy (Caplan 1987). Former law clerks to the justices have followed much the same pattern (Grogan 1991; McGuire 1998). As a result, there exists once again a relatively small number of lawyers within the capital community to whom litigants routinely turn for representation in the High Court (McGuire 1993).

That the reappearance of a Washington bar would coincide with larger changes in how competing interests are represented is neither coincidental nor inconsequential. The literature on interest groups has long documented a strong link between the Washington pressure community and the process of political decision making; government officials need reliable information about the likely consequences of diverse policy alternatives; and lobbyists, with considerable intelligence from their interests, are willing providers of this information (Milbrath 1963; Truman 1951). This relationship holds with particular force in modern political life, as government officials seek trustworthy analysis from within a cacophony of competing voices (Hall and Wayman 1990; Hansen 1991; Schlozman and Tierney 1986). By this means, an important informational link is established between reputable constituent groups and members of government.

This link is no less significant for the judiciary. The Supreme Court's informational needs are enormous; with thousands of petitions for review and multiple briefs on the merits, the justices face the burden of locating the kind of legal analysis that will best enable them to reach informed decisions (see, for example, Caldeira and Wright 1988; H. Perry 1991). Once again, the Supreme Court's lawyers in Washington—no less than their peers in the executive and legislative branches—have served this function. Thus, the return of the Washington Supreme Court bar is really a reflection of a more general phenomenon of American national politics: decision makers, in their need to make sense of complex problems, rely upon representatives in the capital community for guidance. How has the Washington bar affected the Supreme Court's perceptions and decisions?

Controlling the Flow of Information

To an extensive degree, the Washington bar controls what information reaches the Supreme Court. During the 1996–1997 term of the Court, for example, roughly 60 percent of the decisions on the merits featured Washington lawyers on one side or another.[3] Naturally, since many of the cases the justices elect to hear involve the participation of the solicitor general, the Court's most frequent litigator, this figure is explained, at least to some extent, by the participation of the U.S. government (Salokar 1992). This is by no means the whole story, however; leaving aside lawyers for the federal government, advocates from within the federal city still represented interests in some 44 percent of the cases on the plenary docket.[4] Simply in descriptive terms, these data illustrate the renewed dominance of the Washington bar in the politics of the Supreme Court. Like so many others who endeavor to shape the choices of the federal government, when parties seek resolution of pressing policy issues of national concern, they rely upon representation from lawyers within the Washington community, a city that ironically lays claim to little more than 5 percent of all the attorneys in the country (Curran et al. 1986).

Of greater significance, though, is what these data reveal about the flow of policy-making information to the Supreme Court: in a majority of cases, virtually all the analysis relevant to effective and informed decision making—the factual circumstances; what is at issue; how the lower court's judgment comports with the existing decisions of other tribunals; which Supreme Court precedents govern the decision and to what extent; the legal and prudential arguments for resolving the case in a particular way; what social, political, and economic interests are affected and how—is channeled to the Supreme Court through a rather narrow funnel, the Washington contingent of the bar. In short, the justices' perceptions of a case are governed, to a significant degree, by the Supreme Court bar in the capital.

To be sure, the lawyers in the federal city exercise no monopoly over this flow of information. Affected groups, through their numerous briefs amicus curiae, present their own distinct perspectives (Caldeira and Wright 1990). These briefs are designed—at least in theory—to afford outside interests the opportunity to provide the justices with knowledge not contained in the parties' briefs; in practice, though, amicus briefs often merely recapitulate those of the parties as well as of one another (Spriggs and Wahlbeck 1997).

Furthermore, the Washington lawyers must compete with their colleagues beyond the beltway for the attention of the justices. A critical factor, however, distinguishes the Washingtonians from the balance of the bar: expertise. Of the lawyers who appear in the Supreme Court, the Washington lawyers—including those outside the solicitor general's office—are significantly more likely than are lawyers from other cities to come to the Court with the benefit of having handled previous cases before the justices

(McGuire 1995). By implication, obviously enough, they are more prone to return as counsel in future cases, as well. Why might this be important?

In the context of governmental advocacy, anticipated future interactions give structure to the relationship between organized interests and members of government. "The importance of recurrent dealings with advocate groups is apparent enough. If [legislators] expect their relationships with a group to recur, they know they may have the chance to retaliate if their ally deserts them. They know, furthermore, that lobbyists know this. Thus, legislators know that expectations of a recurrent relationship will constrain pressure groups from exploiting their immediate advantage" (Hansen 1991, 17). What is true for Congress applies more generally; those who hope to enjoy the continued goodwill of members of government in the future have incentives to provide genuine aid in the present. Scholars of the judiciary, for some time now, have been cognizant of the benefits of institutionalized representation (see, for example, Galanter 1974). Thus the justices, like all governmental actors who submit themselves to outside pressures, need to identify the suppliers of credible information; and it is the prospect of repeated interactions in the future that promote reliability from those who litigate again and again. In this case, it is the Washington bar (McGuire 1993).

At the same time, because they, like their nineteenth-century predecessors, exercise a fair amount of control over which issues are brought to the Court as well as how those questions are framed, the lawyers in the capital are in a position to shape the Supreme Court's conceptualization of an issue. As a more general matter, "The legal system functions as an entrepreneurial market in which development of law is affected by . . . decisions to mobilize the law, and decisions to mobilize the law depend on [the] capacity to do so, which depends partly on . . . access to resources" (Epp 1996, 766; see also McCann 1994). Stated differently, the expertise of the bar has a good deal to do with the nature of the issues that courts confront. Therefore the collective view of Washington's lawyers—in particular, their judgments about which cases are important enough to bring to the Supreme Court—should have measurable consequences. To the extent that they are successful, for example, their access to the agenda should signal the Court's interest to other litigants, shaping the way litigation resources are mobilized in future cases (Epp 1996; H. Perry 1991). Similarly, the competing formulations of issues by the bar and the manner in which they are cast should also be institutionalized in judicial opinions (see Lamb 1976); consequently, just as William Pinkney's hand can be seen in the opinions of Chief Justice Marshall, so too should the wording and language of the modern Supreme Court's decisions be shaped by the views of the Washington bar.

Given the sheer presence of the Washington legal community as well as its expertise, the justices' understanding of the legal problems brought before them—and thus their more general sensitivity to the issues confronting the judiciary as a whole—is apt to be conditioned to some degree by the experienced Supreme Court advocates in the capital. After all, it is their analysis that the members of the Court are likely to regard as most relevant to their deliberations, all things being equal. Of course, this does not inhibit the ability of the justices to act on the basis of their policy predilections (Segal and Spaeth 1993). Nevertheless, those lawyers who consistently enable the justices to identify clearly their preferred alternatives—Washington's experienced Supreme Court practitioners who seek to maintain their reputations—may be extended more serious consideration. How that consideration might manifest itself is a subject to which I now turn.

Shaping the Supreme Court's Agenda

In deciding which cases to decide, the Supreme Court confronts the perennial problem of separating the handful of truly meritorious cases from a cast of thousands whose social and political ramifications are marginal, at best. There is little doubt that the process of case selection is driven by the ideological preferences of the justices (Songer 1979). Nevertheless, there are still nonideological factors—whether there are conflicts among the federal courts; whether the issue requires further percolation among the lower courts; or whether a case represents an attractive legal vehicle for addressing an issue, to name a few—that affect the decision to grant certiorari (H. Perry 1991). Obviously, each of the justices has his or her own ideas about whether these criteria are met in any given case, but to what extent might the Washington legal community help to affect those judgments?

Access is a primary goal of Washington representatives (Berry 1989; Hansen 1991; Heinz et al. 1993; Schlozman and Tierney 1986), and like so many other actors who endeavor to influence political outcomes, Washington lawyers seek space on the Supreme Court's plenary agenda, the chance to make their case on the merits directly to the members of the Court. With so many candidates and so few spaces to allocate, the Supreme Court can ill afford to make uninformed choices. The justices want to locate cases that matter to larger cross-sections of society. For that reason, the trustworthiness of the information that litigants present to the Court is especially crucial; reliable resources who can offer legitimate assistance in clarifying the issues presented in their cases are likely to be looked upon with favor in the process of setting an agenda (see, for example, Caldeira and Wright 1988; H. Perry 1991). For their part, the lawyers in Washington who petition the justices—at least those who want to be taken seriously in the future—will naturally cultivate favorable relations with the Supreme Court by consistently supplying dependable information regarding the certworthiness of their pleadings (see McGuire and Caldeira 1993). "Most of the bar are probably not aware of what the Court or individual justices might be interested in. . . . Undoubtedly, some people, such as the solicitor general, a few New York and D.C. attorneys who argue with some frequency in the Court, and some court watchers, have a sense of the Court's, or an individual justice's interest. But most of the nation's best attorneys are not likely to be aware of the type of cases that might interest many of the justices" (H. Perry 1991, 213). Accordingly, the actions of the Court's leading legal actors—those who work in close proximity to the Court and who provide accurate assessments of the possible implications of a case—have the potential to affect the justices' understanding of which cases merit the Court's time and which do not.

Does the Supreme Court's relationship with the Washington bar affect the process of case selection? A variety of evidence certainly suggests that it does. One primary illustration in this regard is the solicitor general, probably the leading figure among the Washington heavyweights. Representing the interests of the United States before the Court, the federal government enjoys unrivaled success in gaining access to the justices' plenary agenda; this success, like that of repeat players more generally, is widely interpreted to be a function of the government's credibility (Caldeira and Wright 1988; Galanter 1974; H. Perry 1991; Salokar 1992; Tanenhaus et al. 1963). That is, because the United States needs to foster a long-term relationship with the Supreme Court, its natural tendency is to restrict itself to cases of genuine consequence.

Aside from the pleadings of the solicitor general, the odds against most petitions for review are tremendous; indeed, fewer than 5 of every 100 paid cases are granted review (H. Perry 1991). In marked contrast, though, the Supreme Court veterans in Washington fare much better; even after the solicitor general's cases are excluded, these representatives still boast success rates as high as 25 percent (McGuire 1993). That one in four petitions drafted by the capital bar succeeds in capturing the attention of the High

Court speaks well both of the careful work of the Washington lawyers and the implicit trust that the justices extend them.

Such expertise is not merely a product of laboring in the shadow of the Supreme Court; many lawyers derive expertise from prior experience in the federal government. Practitioners working within the federal bureaucracy derive considerable knowledge and proficiency in the machinations and policies of the federal courts (Clayton 1995). Some lawyers in particular, such as members of the solicitor general's staff, have turned their governmental service to private advantage by joining firms within Washington and marketing their skills in Supreme Court advocacy (Caplan 1987). Likewise, former law clerks to the justices enlist in disproportionate numbers within the ranks of the capital legal community, and their knowledge gleaned from direct exposure to the Court appears to influence the justices as well (McGuire 1998). Thus, decisions made by expert counsel within the federal city about which cases matter have a lot to do with the small number of issues to which the justices elect to address themselves.

Affecting Decisions on the Merits

The value of the Washington bar's reputation need not end with the process of case selection. These Supreme Court practitioners may continue to be a guiding force in determining judicial choices at the merits stage. In evaluating their influence on the justices, one must begin by conceding that, at least as a statistical matter, there is not a great deal of influence for a lawyer to wield; the evidence is fairly clear that the voting behavior of the justices is determined primarily by their policy preferences (Segal and Spaeth 1993). This does not mean that Washington's veterans of Supreme Court advocacy have no impact. It does mean, though, that their influence must be evaluated against the justices' strong disposition to follow their ideological dispositions.

Since the experienced Washington lawyers value their ongoing relationship with the justices, it would be in their interest to continue to provide the Court with reliable and useful information for the Court's consideration of the merits. Still, if the justices are motivated by their personal preferences, then it should not matter who the lawyers are in any given case: no matter what manner of insightful analysis and evenhanded argument is offered, the members of the Court should remain unaffected. If, however, an experienced member of the bar can mold the Court's conception of a given legal problem, that may at least serve to make acceptance of an argument more palatable.

Judging by some of the more prominent practitioners of the Washington bar, the experienced advocates would seem to wield considerable influence. In the 1996–1997 term, for example, Bruce J. Ennis Jr., a leading private lawyer in the capital, appeared as counsel in three of the most noteworthy cases on the plenary docket, successfully arguing each one (Coyle 1997). Obviously, such an illustration presents an amplified sense of the success of the Washington contingent. A more systematic look at the impact of the lawyers in the federal city suggests that, on a modest but regular basis, the justices actually pay particular heed to their advocacy. Although the justices still reverse approximately 65 percent of the decisions they review, the rate of reversal increases or decreases by at least as much as 10 percent, depending upon which party has the benefit of veteran Washington counsel (McGuire 1995). Again, if the Supreme Court's perceptions about the wisdom of legal policy were not shaped to some extent by the Washington bar, then they would enjoy no greater success than anyone else. Yet the lawyers in the capital do much better than other lawyers, even the non-Washington lawyers with similar levels of experience in litigating before the High Court.

These patterns of influence for the legal community emerge in sensible ways. The evidence suggests that Washington lawyers have only a marginal measure of impact; other factors—such as attitudes about policy, views of the law, the facts of the cases, and the like—clearly drive the justices' decisions. Still, given the importance of such factors, the efficacy of these veteran counsels is rather impressive. That they are able to affect the judgment of the justices from time to time indicates that, despite strongly held views on the bench, the Supreme Court's practitioners are still capable of captivating the thinking of the justices and helping to chart the course of constitutional policy.

Putting the Washington Bar in Perspective

Despite its discretion, the Supreme Court remains remarkably dependent upon its legal community. Lawyers are ultimately responsible for what facts and ideas reach the Court; the issues of public policy confronting the judiciary, as well as their proposed solutions, are conveyed to the justices through the Court's bar. Like other members of government who face substantial demands on their time and attention, the justices must rely upon certain of the representatives who advocate causes before them to provide reliable intelligence that can be used to make meaningful decisions. It seems only natural, then, that the Court would develop a strong relationship with its institutional players, those members of the Supreme Court bar who, working in close proximity to the Court itself, return to appear before the Court in case after case. It is these individuals in whom the justices invest particular trust; they stand, therefore, to affect the Court's view of what constitutes both a worthwhile case and its sensible resolution. The unique features of the judicial process, then, facilitate the opportunity for Washington's legal elites to shape and animate the views of the justices. Stated more generally, "The world view of judges is constituted by institutional norms, jurisprudential traditions, and related social structures of power" (Gillman 1996–1997, 9).

This marriage fashioned between the Washington bar and the Court is by no means new to judicial politics. Lawyers in the capital city, as I have argued, have long had an impact on the thinking of the justices. At least as early as the days of Chief Justice John Marshall, the elite lawyers in the federal city became the Supreme Court's constituency; they, together with lower court judges, were diligently hammering out early doctrines that the justices quickly came to support (McCloskey 1994, 47–48). Thus, for example, in the Court's adoption of an expansive view of the contract clause (49),

> The startling thing about the *Dartmouth College* case is . . . the fact that [it was] announced so confidently and seem[ed] to have provoked so little dissent. . . . How did it happen that Marshall could forge such an instrument so off-handedly? How did the tentative suggestion of *Fletcher [v. Peck]* in 1810 become the confident assertion of *Dartmouth* in 1819? The explanation is that the Court's "constituency" had been at work on its behalf in the meantime. The idea that the contract clause might serve to protect private property from the states and the corollary idea that corporate charters could be included in such protection—these embryonic ideas had caught hold in the minds of lawyers and judges, had been fostered and developed by them, and had thereby been raised to the status of mature constitutional doctrines. By 1819, they were so well entrenched that the Supreme Court needed to do little more than stamp them with its formal sanctions.

Marshall, hardly a weak personage lacking in notions about the scope of federal authority and the role of the judiciary, took his cues from the lawyers who labored to provide the Supreme Court with the kind of tested rationale upon which stable doctrine could be built.

Today the Supreme Court continues to draw from the expertise within the legal profession. The members of the Washington bar, like all lawyers, work to vindicate the interests of those whom they represent; still, valuing their long-term relationship with the Court, they protect their access by ensuring that dependable, informed advocacy and sound rationales undergird the legal causes that they champion. As a result, some of the justices' most important judgments—decisions regarding which questions merit their time and how those questions should be resolved—are enlightened by the experienced efforts of the lawyers within the federal city.

Thus, an identifiably strong link has emerged—indeed, reemerged—between the Supreme Court and the larger legal community within which it functions. Whether one examines the Washington bar's early exploration of new constitutional waters during the Marshall era or its pervasive presence in more recent years, it seems clear that the justices have remained open to some amount of persuasion. Lawyers in the Washington community, in various ways, contribute to what the justices think about a case. That, after all, is what lawyers are supposed to do. However much the members of the Court may wish to etch their personal policy preferences into law, the legal context in which those preferences operate is affected by the active participation of the Washington bar.

Notes

1. Figures for the staff within the federal government are taken from Ornstein, Mann, and Malbin (1996), Ragsdale (1996), and Epstein et al. (1994).

2. Although they cannot decide nonexistent cases, the justices are, of course, still free to modify the issues presented by a case. The justices have been willing to do so in a small but noteworthy number of instances over the past forty years (McGuire and Palmer 1996).

3. Data on the 1996–1997 term of the Court was collected by the author.

4. This does not mean that the federal government was involved in only 12 percent of the Court's decisions. Washington lawyers often serve as counsel in opposition to the solicitor general (i.e., the participation of the federal government on one side of a case does not preclude the involvement of a Washington lawyer on the other side). Thus, although the solicitor general appeared in 37 percent of the cases during this term, the percentage of cases involving Washington lawyers from outside the federal government can still range from 0 to 100 percent.

Chapter 8

Bill Clinton's Excellent Adventure: Political Development and the Modern Confirmation Process

Mark Silverstein

The Invisible Man

In retrospect, it was a most telling moment in the annals of both the American presidency and the federal judiciary. On Friday, May 13, 1994, Pres. Bill Clinton met with reporters to announce his nominee to succeed retiring Supreme Court Justice Harry Blackmun. Unfortunately the nominee—Stephen Breyer, chief judge of the First Circuit Court of Appeals—was not present. Although Justice Blackmun had announced his retirement from the Court in early April (and by all accounts had notified the president privately months earlier of his intention to retire), Clinton had spent the weeks following Blackmun's announcement seemingly careening from one potential nominee to another in a very public and rather undignified process of choosing the retiring justice's successor. Unwilling to assume even the risk of a confirmation fight, the administration floated names and carefully gauged public and senatorial reaction. The effort to find a suitable nominee intensified (and became more public and even more disorderly) when Sen. Joe Biden, then chair of the Senate Judiciary Committee, reminded the White House that his committee would need six to eight weeks to prepare for confirmation hearings. Clinton's goal of having the new nominee confirmed by the full Senate prior to the August recess (and hence fully prepared to join the Court for the opening of the new term in October) ultimately forced the president's hand. The denouement was a hastily announced, late-Friday-afternoon press conference that left Judge Breyer, the man of the hour, home in Boston unable to arrive in Washington in time to attend the announcement of his nomination to a seat on the Supreme Court of the United States.

The fact that the president stood on the South Lawn sans nominee was, however, merely a curious preface to what followed. After paying tribute to Judge Breyer's unquestioned qualifications, the president segued into what could only be termed a lament for what might have been, drawing attention to the two men who, according to many reports, had been his preferred choices for the High Court. He turned first to the secretary of the interior Bruce Babbitt, as of that moment a man with the dubious distinction of being very publicly considered and passed over for both the vacancies on the Supreme Court during Clinton's first term in office:

> Secretary Babbitt was Attorney General and Governor of his state, during that time a colleague of mine. He was a candidate for the Presidency in a race which, everyone acknowledged, raised the serious and substantive issues of the day. He has been a very effective Secretary of the Interior for me, one of the most sensitive, complex and difficult posts in this Administration. He would bring to the Court the responsibility and discipline of service in public life. He would bring forth a feel for law at the state level and, most important, perhaps, for life at the grass roots.
>
> Although I know he would be a good addition—indeed, a superb addition—to the Court, frankly I came to the same conclusion I have every time I've thought about him: I couldn't bear to lose him from the Cabinet, from his service at Interior, from his service as an adviser to me and a vital and leading member of our domestic policy team.

Then to Judge Richard Arnold of the Eighth Circuit Court of Appeals, an old friend of the Clintons and a judicial moderate who enjoyed considerable bipartisan support:

> Judge Richard Arnold, the chief judge of the Eighth Circuit, has been a friend of mine for a long time. I have the greatest respect for his intellect, for his role as a jurist and for his extraordinary character. I think a measure of the devotion and the admiration in which he is held is evidenced by the fact that somewhere around 100 judges, one-eighth of the entire Federal bench, wrote me endorsing his candidacy for the Supreme Court.
>
> But, as has been widely reported in the press, Judge Arnold has cancer and is now undergoing a course of treatment. I have every confidence that that treatment will be successful. And if I am fortunate enough to have other opportunities to make appointments to the Court, I know I will be able to consider Judge Arnold at the top of the list.[1]

Understandably, the president made no mention of the fact that key Republicans had reacted to Secretary Babbitt's possible nomination with a vow to resist the confirmation of a "liberal" who would undoubtedly "legislate" from the bench. And, perhaps even more telling than Judge Arnold's battle with cancer (it was in remission) was the fact that several important women's groups had expressed misgivings about him as a successor to Justice Blackmun because of his votes while on the Court of Appeals in cases dealing with abortion rights and all-male clubs. Both Babbitt and Arnold appeared to have the votes for confirmation but, in the end, the president chose to switch rather than fight. His eloquence on behalf of those not chosen perhaps inadvertently accentuated the actual nominee's most consequential attribute: unlike the others, the nomination of Stephen Breyer was certain to produce little if any organized opposition.

On the other hand, it was a nomination that was equally certain not to excite the imagination of the general public or to invigorate the Democratic party faithful. A quarter of a century separated Lyndon Johnson's inspired choice of Thurgood Marshall in 1967 and Bill Clinton's nomination of Ruth Bader Ginsburg in 1993. During those years successive Republican appointments decidedly shifted the Court's center of gravity to the right, and safeguarding the Supreme Court from further Republican domination was one of the very few campaign themes that appeared to unite the disparate factions of the Democratic party. Candidate Clinton had stirred the hearts of the party faithful when, during an MTV town hall meeting, he had mentioned Mario Cuomo as an ideal nominee to the Court because Cuomo "understands the impact of the law on real peoples' lives" (Fulwood 1992). Walter Dellinger, then consultant to the Clinton campaign on judicial matters, let it be known that Clinton also believed the Court suffered from the lack of any members who had achieved political prominence before coming to the bench (Phelps 1992). The message, if implicit, was unmistakable: Clinton's understanding of Court and Constitution was in stark contrast to that of recent Republican presidents and, if elected, he could be counted on to bring to the Court men and women of political stature and prominence who would, in turn, restore the Court to a prominent place in the nation's political life.

Clinton's preference for a nominee with "a big heart" only added to the peculiar nature of the scene on the South Lawn. Much could be said on behalf of Judge Breyer, but he certainly was not the political luminary that Clinton claimed to be seeking.[2] Indeed that he was invisible during the proceedings only highlighted his relative anonymity; he was, quite obviously, no Mario Cuomo, and the appointment of Stephen Breyer (or, for that matter, Ruth

Bader Ginsburg) was not an appointment to capture the public's fancy and rekindle the activism of the Warren era. As Bill Clinton listlessly introduced his absent nominee, one had the distinct impression that the high hopes associated with being the first Democratic president in twenty-five years given the opportunity to shape the Supreme Court had quickly faded.

From Presidential Asset to Political Liability

Presidents traditionally treasure the opportunity to appoint Supreme Court justices, and Bill Clinton was doubly blessed not only with vacancies on the Court but also with a solid (albeit not filibuster-proof) Democratic majority in the Senate. Nevertheless, the entire selection process (as opposed to the Senate confirmation proceedings, which, in the case of both Ginsburg and Breyer, went off without a hitch) emerged as an unexpected burden rather than a cause for celebration. For the Clinton White House the naming of a new justice became a nerve-racking enterprise in which the president often appeared weak and indecisive, torn between the desire to seek a "home-run" nominee and the fear of a costly battle over confirmation. Part of the difficulty rested with Clinton's presidential style; early in his term he had evidenced a disturbing tendency to abandon nominees who engendered anything approaching controversy. Notwithstanding the president's personal foibles, however, it was apparent that even the selection (quite apart from the confirmation) of a new justice had become a daunting challenge. Politics had produced a peculiar, but quite fascinating, transformation, converting a vacancy on the Supreme Court from a presidential asset into a new political liability.

Throughout a good deal of the twentieth century (from the late 1890s through the late 1960s) the process of selecting and confirming Supreme Court justices might be characterized as marked by the politics of acquiescence.[3] During this period, the president was, of course, expected to consult with key legislators and party supporters in selecting the nominee, and behind-the-scenes deals might need to be struck. For the most part, however, presidential choice was respected. There were occasional battles— Louis Brandeis in 1916 or Charles Evans Hughes in 1930—but from the turn of the century through 1967 the executive branch enjoyed an astounding success rate of 98 percent. During this time frame only one nominee (of a total of forty-three), John J. Parker, was rejected, and a vacancy on the Court typically provided the president with a welcome opportunity to exercise the prerogative of office and perhaps shape the development of American law for decades.

The failure of the Senate to confirm Abe Fortas in 1968 signaled a pronounced change in this state of affairs, the arrival of the politics of confrontation. Since 1968, seven nominations have produced more than twenty-five negative votes in the Senate, and four nominations have been defeated. Two sitting justices—Thomas and Rehnquist—have the uncertain honor of eliciting more negative votes than any other successful nominees in the history of the Court.[4] Televised hearings now escalate the potential for conflict. And despite the lopsidedly favorable votes for Ginsburg and Breyer in the Senate confirmation proceedings, the fierce political infighting during the drawn-out selection stage for both nominees suggests that the politics of confrontation still abounds, albeit perhaps at earlier stages in the selection/nomination sequence (Silverstein and Haltom 1996).

Torn between the desire to "hit a home run" with his nominee and the fear of antagonizing interested parties and senators on either side of the aisle, Clinton's delay and indecision opened the selection process within the White House to intense lobbying and outside pressure. To grasp the degree to which vacancies on the Court may now pose unique political problems for presidents requires that we forsake a preoccupation with the personalities and events of the moment and try to appreciate how institutional development and political change have altered the process of selecting and confirming Supreme Court justices. Modern presidents (both Democrat and Republican) confront a complex and daunting task in placing new personnel on the Court; to appreciate Bill Clinton's particular predicament during his first term demands that we focus our attention on several events that preceded the Clinton presidency.

The Legacy of the Warren Court

Bill Clinton came of age during the chief justiceship of Earl Warren and, like many of his generation, chose to pursue a legal career inspired in no small measure by a Court deeply committed to the application of judicial power in the service of America's disadvantaged. Politics, however, has little room for sentiment, and it was, indeed, the legacy of the Warren Court that rendered President Clinton's task in nominating new justices so very difficult. To be sure, the bequest of the Warren Court that was to haunt the president was not a product of its famous (or, perhaps, now infamous) efforts to anchor the principle of equality more securely in constitutional law. Instead, the modern politics of nomination and confirmation is currently shaped by a remarkable series of Warren Court procedural decisions that dramatically expanded access to the federal courts in the 1960s.

The generation of progressive reformers that preceded the Warren era took as an article of faith that active judicial intervention in the political arena was incompatible with progressive politics. To guard against such judicial overreaching, jurists of the New Deal era developed a complex set of rules designed to limit access to the federal courts and to define narrowly the nature of cases deemed appropriate for federal court review.[5] By the mid-1960s, however, the majority of the justices on the Warren Court found these rules to be outdated obstacles to the Court's quest to equalize and nationalize American politics. Ignoring the caution that marked an earlier generation of judicial liberals, the Court redefined judicial liberalism by disregarding the prudential rules painstakingly developed by earlier reformers to limit the reach of judicial power, expanding the range of litigants permitted access to the federal courts, and subjecting a wide sweep of public and private disputes to judicial intervention.[6]

In opening the doors of the federal courts to further the progressive reform of American politics, the Warren Court, however, made the politics of selecting and confirming federal judges in the ensuing years vastly more complicated. Increased access to the courts begets a willingness to expand the type of cases considered appropriate for judicial resolution, which in turn begets the development of a wider array of judicial remedies to deal with these new issues. In short order the very nature of judicial power in the United States was transformed as the Court emerged as an important player in the policy process, able to provide successful litigants with remedies and relief previously available only through the executive or legislative branches. An unintended side effect, however, was to make the question of who sits on the federal bench a life-and-death issue to an expanding array of powerful interests.

Consider the example of class actions. The class action permits a court to settle issues common to a large number of litigants in a single action.[7] In 1966 the Supreme Court amended Rule 23 of the Federal Rules of Civil Procedure to facilitate class actions, and to virtually no one's surprise (including the justices of the Warren Court) the prime beneficiaries in the years immediately following the revisions were civil rights litigants. Within a decade, however, public interest groups pressing the concerns of often more affluent litigants found the class action a powerful device in asserting consumer, environmental, and antinuclear claims against both private and public defendants. Mass tort class actions, ranging from flight attendants asserting damages from tobacco companies for medical problems linked with secondhand smoke to women seeking relief for injuries resulting from defective silicone breast implants, soon threatened corporate America with enormous potential liability.[8]

The Warren Court's efforts to relax the rules regarding class actions, standing, political questions, abstention, and other judicial rules designed to limit the impact of federal judicial power combined to change the relationship of the federal courts to other governing institutions. Opening up the federal courts to diverse litigants and claims thrust those courts deeply into the policy-making arena. A judicial determination that an action may proceed as a class action, for example, itself escalates the policy implications and the potential liability at issue in the litigation. With judicial attitudes regarding this increased access to the system extending from those who believe that class actions are vital in providing justice to the socially and economically disadvantaged to others who argue that it is a "Frankenstein monster," it can hardly come as a surprise that powerful interests, previously exhibiting only sporadic and often minimal concern in the staffing of the federal judiciary, are now quick to perceive a substantial stake in who sits on the federal bench.[9]

The Rise of the New Right

The principal beneficiaries of the expanded access to the federal courts are groups and interests generally aligned with the Democratic party. Since the days of the New Deal, civil rights organizations have found a home with the Democrats; and during the late 1960s and 1970s upper-middle-class Democratic interests, including environmentalists, consumers, and feminists, also considered the open-door policy of the federal judiciary to be of extraordinary benefit. Important forces within the party continue to believe an activist judiciary to be a significant ally in securing policy goals, and the theme of protecting the Court from further Republican domination has been a surefire, unifying campaign theme in every modern Democratic presidential campaign.

Expanded access to the federal courts, however, has had an indirect impact on the politics of the Republican party, a development that complicated immeasurably Bill Clinton's appointment options. During the 1970s, a new group of conservative activists sought to redirect the Republican party from its traditional concern with preserving the free enterprise system and with battling domestic and international communism to the problems, in the words of Paul Weyrich, one of the movement's early spokesmen, "that people cared about," that is, issues like busing, abortion, and pornography. Of course this New Right did not forsake traditional Republican values, but the emphasis on new hot-button issues and the skillful use of the media linked Protestant evangelicals, Catholic ethnics, and secular blue-collar voters into a new, and potentially powerful, political force in the Republican party.

Ronald Reagan was one of the first to recognize the potential of this new coalition; and during his drive to secure the Republican nomination in 1980 and the subsequent national campaign, Reagan courted the votes of the New Right and made an extended effort to fuse it permanently to the Republican party. Many of the New Right's primary concerns—abortion, school prayer, the return to "family values"—emerged as important Reagan campaign themes, and the coalition quickly became an important component in the national Republican organization. Reagan's effective appeal to patriotism and the "issues people care about" had the remarkable effect of uniting Catholics and Protestant evangelicals, a momentous event in American, if not world, political history (B. Ginsberg 1986).

Once in office, however, Reagan faced a troublesome dilemma. To push effectively for the social changes sought by the New Right risked alienating traditional, upper-income Republicans. Failure, however, to appease the concerns of the religious and secular right posed the hazard of discord from a now-important element of the Republican revolution. Appointments to the federal judiciary provided Reagan an escape valve. Virtually the entire agenda of the New Right was precluded by Supreme Court rulings; however passionate, for example, Reagan's desire to return God to America's public classrooms, little could be done without a willingness by the Supreme Court to reexamine established court rulings. Early on, Reagan made the transformation of the federal judiciary his gift to the New Right and, in so doing, instilled in this politically powerful element of the Republican coalition an obsession with judicial appointments.

Reagan's promise to transform the federal judiciary was an important strategy during his presidency. By focusing the New Right's attention on the judiciary, his administration was freed to pursue more secular goals like tax cuts and deregulation. The New Right's divisive social agenda could be placed on the back burner; the failure to secure its enactment could hardly be blamed on the Reagan administration until, at the very least, a new Supreme Court was in place. Paradoxically, wealthy Republican interests that supported Reagan's economic policy but were alarmed by a radical social agenda could rest easy in the knowledge that a series of Supreme Court decisions precluded enactment of the Radical Right's agenda, regardless of the rhetoric that might come from the White House.

Throughout the Reagan years, a good deal of the energy of the Radical Right was directed toward the staffing of the federal courts. Its focus on the federal judiciary benefited Reagan, but it later haunted Clinton as powerful groups within his own party as well as the Republican party became absorbed over appointments to the judiciary. On the heels of Clinton's victory in 1992, conservatives united under the Free Congress Foundation to establish the Judicial Selection Monitoring Project dedicated to the scrutiny of potential Clinton court nominees and to mobilize grassroots support in preparation for upcoming confirmation battles. When Justice White resigned from the Court in spring 1993, the Monitoring Project quickly moved into action by floating the names of individuals termed potential Clinton nominees (for example, Laurence Tribe and Marian Wright Edelman). Each was associated with an activist judiciary and each name floated by the Monitoring Project was certain to raise the ire of conservatives. The fact that the names of these "potential" nominees came not from the Clinton administration but from the Monitoring Project did not lessen the impact; from the very moment of White's resignation, the right was mobilizing to shape the selection of the new justice. The Monitoring Project continues to flourish, now encompassing some 260 conservative organizations and thirty-five talk show hosts, all seeking greater scrutiny of Clinton's judicial nominees (Carney 1997).

Clinton can now expect to be battered from both the left and right on judicial appointments. Many conservative groups contend that attacking Democratic judicial nominations and limiting the president's options are currently the most effective ways to promote a conservative social agenda. They are poised, even before the president makes a selection, to mobilize supporters to combat the nomination of "activist" judges who "legislate from the bench." Groups within the Democratic fold nonetheless chide the president for the failure to fight for more progressive nominees (Klaidman 1993). With presidential options circumscribed, Clinton's response seems to be a dogged determination to avoid being caught in the crossfire.

A Fragmented Senate and a Separated Presidency

The "advice and consent" of the Senate is the final step in the confirmation of a new Supreme Court justice, but the contemporary Senate is not an institution that can be expected to defer to presidential judgment. Since the mid-1960s, the norms of the U.S. Senate and the behavior of individual senators have undergone a profound readjustment. Barbara Sinclair has written of the transformation of the U.S. Senate from the tightly controlled, hierarchical, less partisan institution of the post–World War II era to the anarchic, individualistic, media-oriented modern Senate; and this evolution has dramatically altered the politics of the selection and confirmation of Supreme Court justices. When the institutional changes that have taken place in the Senate are combined with the reality of what Charles Jones has characterized as the modern "separated presidency," the contention that vacancies on the Court now constitute presidential liabilities rather than opportunities gains added credence (Jones 1990; Sinclair 1989).

The Senate has always been a chamber with a tradition of unlimited debate, few formal rules limiting the autonomy of each senator, and minimal formal leadership. To function as an effective legislative body, the Senate developed a highly refined pattern of unwritten rules and norms governing the institution and constraining the serious power of each individual member to disrupt its work. In fact, for a good part of the twentieth century the Senate resembled the close-knit society of a small town, where conformity to established folkways facilitated day-to-day relations (Matthews 1960). The norm of "apprenticeship," for example, placed newcomers at the base of the Senate hierarchy, demanding deference to Senate elders and postponing effective participation in the legislative process while they learned the ways of the institution. The norm of "specialization" required senators to focus their efforts on particular committee work and to avoid asserting themselves on policy matters beyond their field of specialization. The "reciprocity" norm went beyond expected mutual cooperation and compelled senators to refrain from exercising their individual prerogative to disrupt the orderly flow of Senate business. A senator who frequently engaged in filibusters, for example, was courting the disfavor of his colleagues and was certain to face retaliation.

The acceptance of the norms of Senate behavior made the Senate of the 1950s a highly predictable, stable institution in which a few key elder senators allocated resources to reward those colleagues who played by the rules. It was also a Senate that accommodated presidents in the confirmation of Supreme Court justices (from the 1930s through 1967 not one nominee triggered the opposition of even one-fifth of the Senate). Behind-the-scenes presidential consultation with the appropriate Senate leaders (laced with, at times, the judicious use of the resources of the executive branch) would secure the necessary votes to ensure confirmation. A Senate bound by generally accepted norms that made behavior predictable and that encouraged senators to seek the approval of their peers, to follow the direction of Senate elders, and to avoid public grandstanding substantially increased the likelihood of the confirmation of even visible, controversial nominees.

The norms governing the behavior of the Senate began to lose their hold during the 1960s and early 1970s. Today the Senate is an unruly place where even newcomers arrive with a broad policy agenda and the wherewithal to push that agenda within the institution. Committee assignments no longer define the range of senatorial interest; the extraordinary growth in media coverage coupled with a continuing quest for campaign funds oblige most senators to seek national exposure on a broad range of issues. If the old Senate rewarded the specialist who gained the admiration of colleagues through effort and dedication to the work of the institution, the new Senate rewards the quotable, visible generalist whose face and name are well known to the general public. Media attention leads to national prominence, and opposition to the president (particularly a president of one's own party) virtually guarantees extensive national coverage.

Most important, the norm of reciprocity seems now simply a quaint reminder of times gone by. In the 1950s, the exercise of the filibuster was an extraordinary event, an average of one a year. From 1987 through 1992 the average grew to 26.7 (Sinclair 1995). During those years, the latter figure actually understates the impact of this development, as the mere *threat* of a filibuster from the Republican minority often doomed legislation. By the 1990s the key number for any Senate majority became sixty, the number of votes needed to invoke cloture and to cut off debate. Moreover, the power of individual members to disrupt the orderly operation of the Senate has become a frequently used tactic producing little in the way of retribution. Republican senator Jesse Helms, for example, repeatedly employed such tactics and, as a result, was unlikely to win a popularity contest among his peers. But his defiance of many of his colleagues and Senate norms in a highly contentious and successful effort to block Republican William Weld's nomination to become ambassador to Mexico in all probability had little serious consequence on his Senate career.

As the Senate becomes a more open and unruly arena for the expression of diverse interests, a president's work in securing consent to a Supreme Court nomination becomes a complex and, indeed, often harrowing undertaking. This is particularly the case for a "separated" presidency (Jones 1990). Although the president is separated from the other branches by virtue of the dictates of the Madisonian system, the Clinton presidency, despite unified Democratic rule in 1992 and 1993, was unable to connect with a permanent governing majority in either the Congress or the electorate. Separated from a reliable base of support and confronting an assertive and often polarized Congress, Clinton assumed the awesome task of governing from the center by forging ad hoc coalitions to further his policy goals. Writing of Clinton's initial years in office, Walter Dean Burnham described the man's "inexhaustible energy." "At times," Burnham (1995, 6) noted,

> he almost seems a one-man band. Yet these frenetic bursts of activity are ultimately driven by the inadequacy of his political resources on Capitol Hill: not merely the presence of "too many Republicans," but the glaring extent to which leading archons of his own party in the Senate have repeatedly gone into business for themselves and against his interests and policies. A remarkable ad hoc quality has also emerged: pure reliance on Democrats to get his budget enacted, alliance with Republican leaders (and rank and file) against Democrats in the NAFTA struggle. . . . The presidential coopting of traditional Republican themes . . . [has] been duly noted by Republicans worried about losing control of "their" issues and by Democratic liberals in Congress who are plainly unhappy with these initiatives.

Governing from the center is a most difficult undertaking because, contrary to most conventional political wisdom, there is little long-term, solid political support to be found there. For Clinton, the selection of any nominee to the Court had to be considered against the need to forge yet another new coalition for whatever tomorrow's political battle might be. Prior to the formal nominations of Ruth Bader Ginsburg and Stephen Breyer, friends and foes of the Clinton administration (often a difficult distinction to make when governing from the center) were, in effect, given a veto power over potential nominees. The strategy exacerbated conflict at the selection stage, eliminated it at the confirmation stage, and produced centrist jurists of substantial legal but little political distinction.

Separated from a consistent and cohesive nucleus of support and forced to do business with 100 independent contractors in the Senate, Clinton ceded his professed desire to seek a nominee of broad political and public stature to the "let's make a deal" requirements of governing from the center. A remark once attributed to Groucho Marx long before even Bill Clinton set his sights on the White House captures the new governing philosophy: "These are my principles. If you don't like them, I have others."

Toward a Nonpolitical Supreme Court?

Considered from an institutional and historical perspective, the modern confirmation process provides a president with precious little room for maneuver. Expanding access to the federal courts during the Warren years may have been calculated to aid America's poor and disenfranchised, but that same access also benefited powerful organized interests, making the staffing of the federal judiciary a matter of extraordinary significance to an array of potent political forces. The emergence of the New Right in the Republican party ratcheted the stakes still higher as Republican presidents linked the enactment of a Christian social agenda with the need to alter the makeup of the federal courts. A fragmented, individualistic Senate makes the insider deals and low-visibility transactions that once smoothed the way in Supreme Court judicial confirmations a thing of the past. Separated from a consistent power base, the president must balance Supreme Court nominations against the need to stitch whatever coalitions are available in a never-ending battle simply to govern.

It is not a scenario likely to bring to the Court nominees with the stature of a Frankfurter, the political experience of a Warren, or the inspiring private career of a Marshall. Given the current constellation of forces surrounding the modern confirmation process, the nomination of individuals of public stature appears increasingly unlikely. Ronald Reagan's 1986 gambit of naming Justice Rehnquist to succeed the retiring Chief Justice Warren Burger and elevating the controversial, if not academically distinguished, law professor and court of appeals judge Antonin Scalia to Rehnquist's old seat may be the last successful ideologically charged appointment to the Court for some time. Liberal groups mobilized to challenge their old enemy Rehnquist, generating thirty-three negative votes on the Senate floor. But the energy expended on the Rehnquist battle permitted Scalia a free ride; he was confirmed the same day with a startling 98 to 0 vote. A more accurate indicator of the current state of confirmation politics took place the following year when Justice Powell announced his retirement, and the president nominated Robert Bork as his successor.

Justices Ginsburg and Breyer are superb lawyers and jurists. In fact, aside from gender, they appear almost interchangeable and are perhaps the best the modern process of selection and confirmation can offer. Cautious, centrist jurists who accept a rather limited role for the federal judiciary in the political process may be the only types who can survive the rigors of the process in the 1990s. Such individuals often make excellent lower-court judges. Success on the Supreme Court, however, may demand something more. But over the long haul, eliminating nominees with intensely held political principles and ideological attachments will inevitably produce a less activist and less political Supreme Court. Whether a politically diminished Supreme Court would better serve the nation, however, remains a proposition open to question.

Notes

1. Excerpts from the president's press conference can be found in the *New York Times,* May 14, 1994, p. 10.

2. Neither for that matter was Justice Ginsburg, Clinton's first appointment. Both Ginsburg and Breyer had developed reputations as judicial moderates while serving on the court of appeals although Justice Ginsburg's earlier days as general counsel to the ACLU and as a crusader for women's rights made her the more interesting nominee.

3. In the nineteenth century, however, one out of three nominees was rejected. Before the enactment of the Seventeenth Amendment in 1913, senators were appointed by state legislatures, and powerful state party leaders were often named with the mission to funnel patronage back to the state party organization. In an age of patronage and partisan politics, little deference was paid to presidential prerogative over appointments.

4. Justice Thomas garnered forty-eight negative votes while Rehnquist's elevation to the chief justiceship in 1986 produced thirty-three negative votes. When Rehnquist was originally confirmed as associate justice in 1971, twenty-six negative votes were cast, giving the chief justice the all-time negative vote record for a sitting justice.

5. The classic short description of these rules remains Justice Brandeis's litany of "will nots" appearing in his concurring opinion in *Ashwander v. TVA* (1936): "The Court will not pass upon the constitutionality of legislation in friendly, nonadversary, proceedings . . . will not anticipate a question of constitutional law in advance of the necessity of deciding it . . . will not formulate a rule of constitutional law broader than the precise facts to which it is to be applied . . . will not pass upon a constitutional question . . . if there is also present some other ground upon which the case may be disposed of . . . will not pass upon the validity of a statute upon complaint of one who fails to show he is

injured by its operation . . . will not pass upon the constitutionality of a statute at the instance of one who has availed himself of its benefits."

6. E.g., *Flast v. Cohen* (1968) distinguished almost forty years of precedent to permit a taxpayer suit challenging federal expenditures said to violate the establishment clause. *Baker v. Carr* (1962) in effect removed the political question doctrine as an impediment to judicial review in order to reach the explosive issue of legislative reapportionment. The abstention doctrine, designed to require a federal court to decline jurisdiction when faced with an unsettled issue of state law, was dismissed in the haste to ensure federal protection of constitutional rights (*Dombroski v. Pfister* [1965]).

7. The literature on class actions is extensive. Of particular relevance to the points made here are Garth et al. 1988; Miller 1979; and "Developments in the Law" 1976.

8. Dow Chemical, for example, has offered to set aside $2.4 billion to settle the silicone breast-implant litigation.

9. The Frankenstein view is that of Lombard, C.J., dissenting, in *Eisen v. Carlisle & Jacquelin,* 391 F. 2d. 555, 572 (2d cir. 1968).

Part III

Supreme Court Agenda Setting and
Decision Making in Context

Chapter 9

Law, Politics, and the Rehnquist Court: Structural Influences on Supreme Court Decision Making

Cornell Clayton

The Court's legitimacy depends on making legally principled decisions under circumstances in which their principled character is sufficiently plausible to be accepted by the Nation.
— J. O'Connor, *Planned Parenthood v. Casey,* 1992

During the past few decades the Supreme Court has confronted the destabilizing forces of modernism.[1] These forces simultaneously unsettled established theories of law and destabilized electoral politics in the United States. These broad structural forces, more than the personal predilections of individual justices, have shaped the contemporary nature of Supreme Court decision making. Indeed, to the disappointment of both the left and the right, the 1990s has become a decade of judicial moderation. The constitutional activism that marked the Warren Court and Burger Courts (Blasi 1983) gave way to a Rehnquist Court that is unwilling to expand boldly or to abandon established constitutional rights and doctrines. This retrenchment has been accompanied by a reluctance to discuss substantive values or to articulate defining principles governing constitutional law. Whether speaking in near unanimity while striking down state antigay initiatives (*Romer v. Evans,* [1996]) or in severely divided opinions reaffirming abortion rights (*Planned Parenthood v. Casey,* [1992]), the Court as an institution has become centrist and pragmatic in its constitutional decision making.

The Court's drift toward pragmatism, although widely noted in law journals, has gone relatively unnoticed in political science literature because much of this research neglects to account for the Court as an institution that is historically situated within the larger political system. Although a new and growing body of scholarship seeks to return to an institutionally grounded understanding of Supreme Court decision making (Clayton and Gillman 1999), most contemporary political science research continues in a positivist, social science tradition, following either a behavioral approach pioneered in the work of Pritchett (1948) and developed into the attitudinal model by Schubert (1965) and Rhode and Spaeth (1976), culminating in the work of Segal and Spaeth (1993); or in a strategic approach, first pioneered by W. Murphy (1964) and recently reinvigorated by scholars such as Epstein and Knight (1997) and Maltzman and Wahlbeck (1996). On the whole, this work tends to be ahistorical, reductionist, and positivist, focusing on the votes or actions of individual justices rather than on the Court's doctrinal developments. It also adopts an instrumentalist conception of law, in which the law is seen as an empty shell within which judges pursue a priori policy preferences. In the words of Segal and Spaeth, "Rehnquist votes the way he does because he is extremely conservative; Marshall votes the way he does because he is extremely liberal"; but neither votes the way he does because of the law or judicial norms (1993, 65).

I do not intend a systematic critique of positivist approaches to Supreme Court decision making in this chapter nor a precise defense of historical institutionalism (but see Clayton 1999; Gillman 1999; R. Smith 1988). Rather, I attempt to explain Supreme Court decision making by situating the Court within the broader political and legal systems. The approach thus follows the new institutional framework spelled out by R. Smith (1988), in that it argues justices are influenced by the Court's distinctive institutional perspectives and values. But it also has much in common with work of an earlier generation of scholars who sought to link the Court's institutional norms and values to those of the dominant governing coalition (Dahl 1957; M. Shapiro 1983; Funston 1975; Adamany 1980).

Even at the height of the behavioralist period, there were political scientists who saw the Court as part of the broader political system and examined its role by focusing on doctrinal developments rather than on judicial vote counting (Adamany 1980; Dahl 1957; Funston 1975; M. Shapiro 1964; Scheingold 1974). Still, these scholars tended to adopt the same instrumentalist conceptions of law as other behavioralists. Thus, the Court was generally described as "following the election returns," and its decisions over time were usually explained by the fact that the Court is in important ways dependent on the political branches and that justices are appointed because they share the policy views of the dominant political coalition. Although there is much to be said for this perspective, it ignores the possibility that law and the judiciary's distinctive institutional features may exert an independent influence over judicial attitudes and decision making. Thus, in adopting a new institutional approach, I shall focus on how law and politics are interrelated but nevertheless relatively autonomous forces, each structuring Supreme Court decision making in different ways.

The Collapse of Consensual Jurisprudence and Politics

Two historical developments, one legal and the other political, have profoundly affected the way the Court functions in the late twentieth century. The first is the collapse of a consensual constitutional jurisprudence. During the early part of this century, legal realists such as Oliver Wendell Holmes and Karl Llewellyn effectively undermined legal formalism by emphasizing law's dependence on political and social forces (Llewellyn 1931). The way progressives used realist analysis to attack the Court's *Lochner*-era jurisprudence and to reconcile the political transformations accompanying the New Deal to nineteenth-century constitutional values is well known (Gillman 1993). Between 1932 and 1944, Roosevelt appointed eight new justices to the Court, each infused with New Deal values. Roosevelt's judicial strategy was not only successful at winning judicial acceptance of his legislative program, but the Court's shift in jurisprudence was also so thoroughgoing that it effectively ushered in a new constitutional regime (Ackerman 1991; Leuchtenburg 1995).

Still, realism's impact on the relationship between the Court, the Constitution, and the political system was not fully apparent until much later. In the wake of the New Deal, American politics was marked by broad ideological consensus. Both political parties occupied the center of the ideological spectrum and accepted the values forged during the 1930s. Within the judiciary, that political consensus translated into agreement over constitutional fundamentals, an emphasis on the technical aspects of legal process, and judicial restraint (Hart 1959; Levi 1949; Wechsler 1961). Indeed, during a period when all respectable opinion fell within a relatively narrow political band, it was easy to forget that judging required political choices and to think of it instead as a neutral process concerned primarily with issues of technical competence (Posner 1990).

As the consensual politics of the 1940s and 1950s gave way to ideological polarization in the 1960s and 1970s, realism's impact on the Supreme Court became more clear. Triggered by Warren Court activism, political dissensus in the nation began to manifest itself in normative debates over constitutional values both on and off the Court (Fried 1988; Posner 1990; Seidman and Tushnet 1996). During the past three decades, constitutional theory has become a booming industry in the United States with approaches ranging from critical neomarxism to a conservative brand of law and economics (see generally Seidman and Tushnet 1996). At least four major approaches to constitutional adjudication have been held by members of the modern Supreme Court: (1) *textualism-originalism,* or the view that the Court should adhere to the literal text or the actual historical judgments of those who ratified the Constitution; (2) *deference-restraint,* or the view that the Court should defer to judgments of the elected branches unless those judgments are clearly mistaken; (3) *independent-interpretivism,* which suggests that the Court must make independent, substantive interpretations on the basis of what best makes sense to the justices; and (4) *democracy-reinforcement,* or the view that the Court should act to improve and protect the democratic character of the political process (Sunstein 1996).

Since the 1950s the Supreme Court, as an institution, has been unable to make an official choice among these, or other, approaches to constitutional adjudication. Even individual justices may be inconsistent, adopting one approach in some cases and a different one in others (Sunstein 1996). Without a consensual constitutional jurisprudence the Court's decision making has become increasingly fragmented and fractious. This affects both the nature of cases that the Court can decide and the clarity with which it can express its decisions. Further, many students of the Court have interpreted this dissensus as evidence that the justices simply act on the basis of their own policy preferences or "attitudes" rather than on the basis of "legal" considerations. Justices, in other words, are thought to decide cases in a result-oriented fashion, using law and jurisprudence merely to cloak their own political preferences (Bork 1990; Schubert 1981; Segal and Spaeth 1993; Rohde and Spaeth 1976). Within political science especially, analysis of Supreme Court decision making has become preoccupied with trends in the voting records of justices or the presence of "liberal" or "conservative" voting blocs rather than with traditional doctrinal analysis and normative jurisprudence.[2]

The justices themselves have grown sensitive to the public perception that they decide cases on the basis of political preferences, not the law, and recognize the threat this perception poses to judicial legitimacy and authority. In *Mitchell v. W. T. Grant* (1974), for instance, Justice Stewart warned, "A basic change in the law upon a ground no firmer than a change in our membership invites the *popular misconception that this institution is little different from the two political branches* of the Government. No misconception could do more lasting injury to this Court, and to the system of law which it is our abiding mission to serve" (emphasis added).

The consequences for the Court of the collapse in consensual jurisprudence has been exacerbated by a second development in American politics. Historically, the U.S. electoral system tended to produce relatively stable governing coalitions that unified control over the legislative and executive branches of government and coordinated the work of governments at the state and national levels. Major *realigning elections,* around which governing coalitions emerged, occurred in 1800 (Jeffersonian Republicans), 1828 (Jacksonian Democrats), 1860 (Republicans), and 1932 (New Deal Democrats). In the past, the Court's constitutional role coincided with these periods of electoral realignment, as political-cleavage issues became constitutionalized and were thrust into the courts for resolution. Most of the Court's important constitutional decisions corresponded closely to the timing and the political issues involved in these major electoral realignments.[3] Between these periods of realignment, however, when governing coalitions were stable, the Court returned to a secondary-branch role, acting to legitimize the policies of the dominant national political coalition (Adamany 1980; Dahl 1957; Lasser 1985; Shapiro 1964).

Since the 1950s, however, American electoral politics has been characterized by dealignment. Increasingly, voters disassociated themselves from the major parties and become independents. Split-ticket voting increased, and national politics has been characterized not by a dominant governing coalition but by divided government and gridlock. For all but six years since 1968 (1976–1980 and 1992–1994), the party that controlled the presidency did not have control of Congress.

Much attention has focused on how electoral dealignment impacts Congress and the presidency (Cox and Kernell 1991; Thurber 1991). Less well understood, but equally important, is its impact on the judiciary. Initially, dealignment led to a new judicial politics that made the Court both a more regular and a more independent source of policy innovation. Without a stable coalition controlling the elected branches, the Court has less fear of institutional retaliation if it makes unpopular decisions. Unlike in earlier periods, recent presidents and Congresses have not just been unwilling to coordinate an assault on the Court, but parties controlling each have acted to protect the Court's independence from threats mounted by the other. During periods of divided government it also becomes difficult for the Court to defer to the elected branches even when it is so inclined. Since the 1960s the Court has been deluged with separation of powers cases and a new kind of administrative-law conflict where Congress and the executive branch are regularly at odds over the interpretation of federal statutes (Clayton 1994). As a result, the Court has become increasingly detached from the political agenda of the elected branches in a way that would have been impossible during previous periods of electoral alignment (Ginsberg and Shefter 1990; Silverstein and Ginsberg 1987).

The Court's independence has been further bolstered by an emerging alliance with interest-group constituencies. As the elected branches became less able to address controversial issues, interest groups increasingly turned to courts in order to effect changes they could not secure through legislation. The Warren Court's relaxation of the rules of standing and access to judicial power greatly enhanced and facilitated this trend (Silverstein and Ginsberg 1987). Thus, during the 1960s and 1970s, older, established public-interest litigating organizations such as the NAACP and the ACLU, were joined by a host of new groups such as the Natural Resources Defense Council, the Washington Legal Foundation and the Lambda Legal Defense Fund, all of whom saw the courts as the most effective venue for effecting policy change (Kobylka 1991; O'Connor and Epstein 1989, 1983b). These groups are able to mobilize significant financial and political resources to mount litigation campaigns and to oppose the appointment of judges who threaten the judiciary's new independence, making the courts at once more active policy makers and less susceptible to traditional methods of control by the elected branches (Silverstein and Ginsberg 1987).

The Role of the Supreme Court and Judicial Decision Making in the 1990s

The twin developments of electoral dealignment and a collapse in consensual jurisprudence explain much about the role and decision making of the Rehnquist Court. To begin with, rather than defining moments in the relationship between the Court and the elected branches, appointments of justices during the late-1980s and 1990s have increasingly become defining moments for the relationship between Congress and the president. As such they have become exercises in pragmatism and conflict avoidance. After several contentious confirmation battles during the 1970s and 1980s, presidents and Congress in the 1990s have tended toward an equilibrium process that produces politically centrist and jurisprudentially pragmatic judges (see chapter 8).

The turning point in this process was Ronald Reagan's failed nomination of Robert Bork in 1987. The Reagan administration came to office with a well-articulated strategy aimed at remolding the federal judiciary (Clayton 1992; O'Brien 1988). In many ways, the strategy was inherited from Richard Nixon, who also made opposition to the Court a cornerstone of his electoral platform (Simon 1972). Yet, despite the four appointments to the Court made by Nixon and his successor Gerald Ford, the judicial "counterrevolution" that conservatives hoped for never materialized (Blasi 1983).

Reagan made his first two appointments to the Supreme Court—Sandra Day O'Connor in 1982 and Antonin Scalia in 1986—while the Senate was controlled by his own party and the Judiciary Committee, chaired by Strom Thurmond (R-SC), worked closely with the administration. By 1987, however, Democrats had gained control of the Senate, and the Judiciary Committee came under the chairmanship of Joseph Biden (D-DE). Although Bork had impeccable credentials, he was seen as a conservative ideologue, a leading advocate of original intent jurisprudence, and a sharp critic of the Court's alliance with interest groups and the politically infused style of law it represented. Bork's hearings were televised nationally, and more than 300 groups publicly took stands on the nomination. The American Bar Association (ABA) split on whether to recommend him as "qualified" to sit on the High Court (Silverstein 1994). The political mobilization turned public opinion against Bork, and a Democratic-controlled Senate defeated his nomination by the widest margin ever, 58 to 42 (Gitenstein 1992; for Bork's account, see Bork 1990).

Following the Bork defeat, Reagan selected a political moderate, Anthony Kennedy, for the vacancy on the Court. As an appeals court judge, Kennedy had established a reputation as a careful and pragmatic jurist (Uelman 1987). During the hearings he distanced himself from the administration's and from Bork's controversial legal views, accepting the constitutional status of the right to privacy and explicitly rejecting original intent jurisprudence (O'Brien 1988). His confirmation sparked little controversy, the hearings were not televised, few groups testified, and the Senate confirmed him by a unanimous 97 to 0 vote.

When William Brennan retired from the Court in 1990, George Bush selected an unknown, moderate state court judge, David Souter, in a calculated effort to avoid a Bork-style confirmation conflict. Indeed, Souter's political values were so opaque that the *New York Times* labeled him the "Stealth Justice," and in the Senate, in contrast to Bork's hearings, concerns were raised about confirming someone about whom so little was known. What record Souter had indicated a pragmatic judge who wrote carefully crafted and narrowly tailored opinions. He too won easy confirmation on a 90 to 9 vote. Bush sparked controversy, however, when he named Clarence Thomas, a conservative African American and former head of the EEOC, to fill the seat of the retiring Thurgood Marshall in 1991. Nevertheless, Thomas's race split the opposition of Senate Democrats, and he narrowly won confirmation by a 52 to 48 margin, but only after televised hearings in which Democrats savaged his legal views and aired explosive charges of sexual harassment brought by Anita Hill.

Anxious to avoid a confirmation conflict, President Clinton also steered clear of controversial nominees. The Clinton administration worked closely with Sen. Orrin Hatch (R-UT), ranking Republican on the Judiciary Committee and its chair since 1994, to assure smooth confirmation hearings. Indeed, Clinton twice disappointed liberal supporters by passing over prominent liberals such as Interior Secretary Bruce Babbit, after warnings from Hatch that such a nomination would lead to protracted conflict. Other prominent liberals, such as former New York governor Mario Cuomo, former Senate Majority Leader Paul Mitchell (D-ME), and former secretary of education Richard Riley, headed off controversy by withdrawing their names from consideration. Meanwhile, Clinton was content to appoint two politically moderate technocrats to the Court, Ruth Bader Ginsburg in 1993 and Stephen Breyer in 1994.

Jewish groups and women's groups both supported Ginsburg's appointment. During the 1970s, Ginsburg headed the ACLU's Women's Rights Project and argued some of the most important gender discrimination cases that came before the High Court. Still, Ginsburg had developed a reputation, both as lawyer and judge, for careful and incremental development of legal doctrine. She even infuriated some women's groups by criticizing the Court's decision in *Roe v. Wade* (1973) as "extravagant" and "divisive" (Ginsburg 1992). Her moderate and pragmatic views won her early support on the Judiciary Committee, and she easily won confirmation by the full Senate on a 96 to 3 vote.

Stephen Breyer also had strong backing from Jewish groups and support from Senator Hatch. Prior to his appointment to the federal appeals bench in 1980, Breyer had served as chief counsel to the Judiciary Committee under Sen. Edward Kennedy (D-MA). Hatch knew and liked Breyer for his careful work as chief counsel. During his thirteen years on the appellate bench, Breyer was known as a legal technician. He authored narrow opinions, and his writings had focused on administrative process and regulatory law rather than on constitutional issues. He too won the unanimous support of the Judiciary Committee and an easy confirmation by an 87 to 9 vote in the full Senate.

With Clinton's appointment of Ginsburg and Breyer, the current Court is relatively young, moderate in political outlook, and pragmatic in its approach to the law. With the exception of Justice Stevens (appointed in 1975) and Rehnquist (appointed in 1972 and elevated to chief justice in 1986), the remainder of the Court has been appointed since 1982.

The changing political dynamics of judicial selection during the 1980s and 1990s have led to three ideological blocs on the Rehnquist Court: a conservative bloc consisting of Scalia, Rehnquist, and Thomas; a center-right bloc consisting of O'Connor, Kennedy, and Souter; and a center-left bloc consisting of Stevens, Ginsburg, and Breyer. During the Court's 1995–1996 term, for example, Justice Scalia voted most often with Rehnquist (82.3 percent) and Thomas (87.2 percent), and least often with Stevens (45.5 percent) and Breyer (54.4 percent). Conversely, Justice Stevens voted most often with Breyer (74 percent) and Ginsburg (72.7 percent), and least often with Thomas (44.7 percent) and Scalia (45.5 percent). Meanwhile, Justice O'Connor and Justice Kennedy often found themselves as swing voters; one or the other voted with the majority in each of the eleven cases where the Court's decision split 5 to 4, and both voted with the majority in eight of those cases, more than any other single justice.

Decision making on the Rehnquist Court thus became the product of shifting coalitions around these three blocs, with O'Connor and Kennedy casting deciding votes in most controversial cases and Stevens and Scalia the most vociferous and frequent dissenters. Indeed, Stevens and Scalia wrote thirty-one dissents during the 1995–1996 term, nearly as many as the thirty-six authored by the remaining seven justices combined.

These ideological blocs, however, are further crosscut by jurisprudential cleavages. Justice Scalia, for instance, has been an enthusiastic supporter of a textual/originalist jurisprudence, whereas Chief Justice Rehnquist has been a strong advocate of judicial restraint. Thus, in cases such as *Texas v. Johnson* (1989) and *United States v. Eichman* (1990), where the Court struck down statutes prohibiting desecration of the American flag, Scalia joined with the majority, but Rehnquist wrote withering dissents. Simply pointing to the political-attitudinal alignments on the Court, as political scientists have been inclined to do (Segal and Spaeth 1993), thus obscures and over-simplifies how the breakdown in consensual jurisprudence has affected the Court as an institution.

Even the ability to engage in this type of behavioral analysis of the Court depends on institutional norms governing the Court's opinion writing that are the result of a collapse in a consensual approach to constitutional jurisprudence. Prior to the 1920s, dissenting and concurring opinions were relatively infrequent. Except in extraordinary cases, the Court produced institutional opinions that the justices tended to sign even when they disagreed with their specifics. O'Brien (1998) notes that judicial realism and the conflict between the Court and the elected branches during the 1920s and 1930s led to an initial relaxation of these norms. Justices Holmes and Brandeis earned the title of the "great dissenters" as a result of their willingness to author dissenting opinions critical of the Court's anachronistic jurisprudence (Zoebel 1959). But Holmes's average of 2.4 dissents per term and Brandeis's 2.9 per term pale in comparison to the contemporary level of dissensus. Thus, O'Brien (1999) reports that during the Burger and Rehnquist Courts, the most frequent dissenters include Justice Douglas (38.5 dissents per term), Stevens (21 per term), Brennan (19 per term), Marshall (15.4 per term), and Rehnquist (12.2 per term) (see also O'Brien 1996). Moreover, as an overall percentage of the total number of opinions written by the Court as a whole, the number of individual opinions—dissents and concurrences—went from under 22 percent of the total during the Hughes Court to more than 55 percent of the total during the Rehnquist Court. During the 1994–1995 term alone, in the eighty-six cases the Court decided by full opinion on the merits, fifty concurrences and sixty-four dissents were authored by the justices.

The diminution of consensual norms on the Court had become clear by the early 1970s. For example, in *New York Times v. United States* (1971), the Pentagon Papers case, and in *Furman v. Georgia* (1972), the Court's first major decision on capital punishment, the Court's nine members authored ten opinions in each case—a per curiam opinion, announcing the Court's decision, six concurrences, and three dissents.

But what explains these changing norms? The high rate of concurring opinions is particularly noteworthy because concurrences do not affect the policy outcome of a case. Consequently, concurring opinions can only be explained as an expression of a justice's sincere concern that the Court adhere to proper legal criteria or jurisprudence in the case. As ideological polarization during the 1960s led to competing constitutional visions, justices felt compelled to articulate these visions in individual opinions. Dissensus over constitutional jurisprudence thus led to an increasingly fragmented form of decision making on the Court (O'Brien 1999).

The most obvious consequence of this fragmentation is greater uncertainty and less predictability in law. In the Court's first major decision involving affirmative action, *Regents of the University of California v. Bakke* (1978), for instance, the only part of Justice Powell's opinion for the Court joined by the other justices was a one-paragraph statement of the facts. Even when the Court avoids dissents and reaches a unanimous decision, its holding can be unclear. For example in *Church of Lukumi Babula Aye v. City of Hialeah* (1992), the Court's decision striking down a city ban on animal sacrifices as violating the free exercise clause, the opinion alignment for a *unanimous* Court read:

> Justice KENNEDY delivers the opinion for the Court with respect to Parts I, III, and IV, which Chief Justice REHNQUIST and Justices WHITE, STEVENS, SCALIA, SOUTER, and THOMAS join; Part II-B, which Chief Justice REHNQUIST and Justices WHITE, STEVENS, SCALIA, and THOMAS join; Parts II-A-1 and II-A-3, which Chief Justice REHNQUIST and Justices STEVENS, SCALIA, and THOMAS join; and Part II-A-2, which Justice STEVENS joins.

Opinion alignments such as these have become commonplace in the 1990s. Indeed, the Court has even handed down cases in which two opinions announce different and contradictory parts of the Court's ruling for two different majorities in each case (see *Arizona v. Fulminante* [1991] and *Gentile v. State Bar of Nevada* [1991]). Such decisions would have been unthinkable in earlier periods of Court history, and attorneys and lower courts have understandable difficulty making any sense of them today.

Even when the Court avoids making fragmented decisions, it often does so only by strictly limiting the principled holding of the decision in order to accommodate competing jurisprudential views of the justices. Thus, political and jurisprudential fragmentation has led to a type of decision making that is pragmatic and minimalist (Sunstein 1996; Fried 1995). Increasingly, the Court decides cases on the most narrow grounds available and avoids broad principles that would control other cases, future courts, or the efforts of the elected branches to correct imperfections in their policies. Decisions are narrowly tailored to the specific facts of each case and are usually tied to careful, incremental developments of doctrine.

Although a thorough review of decision making by the Rehnquist Court's is well beyond the scope of this chapter, even a cursory review of its major decisions in important areas of constitutional law reveal the structural tendencies toward political moderation and legal pragmatism already identified. There are only a few exceptions to these trends, and these are in areas of law such as free speech, where a substantial overlap between competing jurisprudential perspectives exists.

The Right to Privacy and Abortion

Few areas of constitutional law led the Court deeper into the political thicket and more clearly demonstrate the Rehnquist Court's retreat to moderate, pragmatic decision making than privacy and abortion. In *Roe v. Wade* (1973), the Court boldly expanded the right to privacy, not just nullifying but effectively rewriting the abortion laws in more than forty-five states. Since 1973, *Roe* has been a focal point of fierce partisan conflict. As with Reagan and Bush, the electoral platform of Bob Dole in 1996 made explicit the Republican party's opposition to abortion and its aim to reverse *Roe* through a constitutional amendment. President Clinton and the Democratic party meanwhile committed themselves to protecting the abortion right, using it as a wedge issue to open up a gender gap over Republicans in the 1992 and 1996 presidential elections (Graber 1996).

Five times between 1980 and 1992, Republican administrations unsuccessfully asked the Court to overturn *Roe*.[4] By 1992, however, with the addition of five Republican appointees since 1980, the Court seemed poised to reverse *Roe*. The opportunity came in *Planned Parenthood v. Casey* (1992), a case challenging five provisions of a Pennsylvania law restricting access to abortion services. Yet the Court upheld the right to an abortion and merely altered *Roe*'s trimester framework. The decision was fragmented, with the Court's opinion authored by Justice O'Connor and joined by Souter and Kennedy. While continuing to acknowledge a woman's right to an abortion prior to viability, O'Connor held that the state may nevertheless regulate the abortion procedure so long as it does not impose an "undue burden" on women.

By protecting the abortion right while allowing greater state regulation, the Court struck a moderate political stance that corresponds closely with the views of a majority of Americans (Graber 1996). At the heart of O'Connor's opinion, however, was a telling discussion of the problems associated with the contemporary Court's jurisprudential fragmentation. The perception that the Court makes decisions on the basis of political preferences, O'Connor warned, undermined its authority and capacity to carry out the judicial function. Regardless of how individual justices viewed *Roe,* she said, the Court should adhere to the doctrine of stare decisis unless it had compelling, principled reasons to deviate. The Court's power lies in "its legitimacy, a product of substance and perception that shows itself in the people's acceptance. . . . The Court must take care to speak and act in ways that allow people to accept its decision on the terms the Court claims for them. . . . The Court's legitimacy depends on making legally principled decisions under circumstances in which their principled character is sufficiently plausible to be accepted by the Nation" (at 2814).

By contrast, Chief Justice Rehnquist and Justice Scalia wrote blistering dissents, chiding the Court's moderates for contriving a "novel" theory of stare decisis. Scalia wrote that "*Roe* fanned into life an issue that has inflamed our national politics in general, and has obscured with its smoke the selection of Justices to this Court in particular ever since."

O'Connor's opinion in *Casey,* and the bitterness of the dissents, illustrates how broad structural forces have pushed the Court as an institution toward a pragmatic, centrist approach to constitutional decision making, even while some of its individual members have become more extreme and divided in their views. This trend is apparent in other areas of privacy jurisprudence as well. In *Bowers v. Hardwick* (1986), for example, the Court, in a 5 to 4 decision with five separate opinions, upheld a Georgia statute that criminalized sodomy and refused to expand the right to privacy to cover homosexual conduct. Likewise, in *Cruzan v. Missouri* (1990), the Court declined to use privacy to establish a broad, open-ended "right to die." Instead, the Court in a 5 to 4 decision relied on common-law principles to conclude that individuals merely possess a "right to refuse lifesaving" medical intervention and said that even this limited right was subject to extensive state regulation. The Court's limited construction of the privacy right in *Cruzan,* and its refusal to recognize a constitutional "right to die," set up the Court's decision in 1997 in *Washington v. Glucksberg* (1997). There the Court upheld a state law prohibiting physicians from assisting terminally ill patients to commit suicide against a challenge that such laws violated rights to privacy.

The Court's pragmatism and its minimalist approach in one area of law, however, often carry costs to other institutions in American government or to other areas of the law. Following *Bowers,* for example, activists on both sides of the gay rights issue redirected efforts away from federal courts and toward the elected branches and state courts. President Clinton, for example, found himself locked in a costly political battle early during his first term when he attempted to reverse the military's ban on gays. The resulting "don't ask, don't tell" policy pleased neither side of the dispute, and it has produced a stream of litigation in the lower courts (see *Steffan v. Aspin* [1993] and *Meinhold v. Department of Defense* [1993]).

Meanwhile, at the state and local level, gay rights groups began lobbying local governments to adopt antidiscrimination policies. Antigay rights groups have fought these efforts by sponsoring statewide referenda or citizens initiatives, such as the one approved in 1992 by voters in Colorado, known as Amendment 2 ("No Protected Status Based on Homosexual, Lesbian, or Bisexual Orientation Amendment"). The Colorado amendment was challenged in the Supreme Court in 1996, and it was struck down in a bitterly divided 6 to 3 decision, not on privacy grounds but under the equal protection clause. Likewise, in 1996, gay rights groups succeeded in persuading the Hawaii State Supreme Court to strike down a state law forbidding single-sex marriages under provisions of the state constitution (*Baehr v. Lewin* [1993]). In response, the Republican-controlled Congress passed the Defense of Marriage Act of 1996 (DOMA), defining marriage within federal law as meaning a "legal union between a man and a woman" and permitting state officials to refuse legal recognition of single-sex marriages performed in other states. DOMA was immediately challenged under the "full faith and credit" clause of Article 4 and under the premise that Congress lacks power to regulate in this area, challenges with which the Court will eventually have to deal.

Equal Protection and Affirmative Action

The Rehnquist Court's pragmatism is also evident in its recent decisions involving equal protection. Like abortion, affirmative action became an important wedge issue in electoral politics during the 1980s. The Court, for its part, had created two separate inconsistencies in its affirmative action decisions. First, under the rationale that the Fourteenth Amendment was intended to restrict states but not the federal government, the Court treated state affirmative action programs more strictly than federal programs (compare *Fullilove v. Klutznick* [1980] and *Richmond v. Croson* [1987]). Second, the Court had been inconsistent with respect to what purposes race-based classifications could be employed, in some cases holding that they could be used only in narrowly tailored efforts to effect a compelling state interest such as remedying the effects of past discrimination (see *Wygant v. Jackson Board of Ed* [1986] and *Richmond v. Croson* [1987]), while other times holding they could be used in a more flexible manner to serve goals such as educational or broadcasting diversity (see *University of California v. Bakke* [1978] and *Metro Broadcasting v. FCC* [1990]). These inconsistencies led the Court to subject affirmative action programs to strict scrutiny in some cases but to a more relaxed means-ends analysis, or "intermediate level" of scrutiny, in others.

The Court attempted to resolve these inconsistencies in *Adarand Constructors, Inc. v. Pena* (1995). In a 5 to 4 decision with six separate opinions, the Court held that all race-based programs would be held to the same strict standard of scrutiny, requiring programs at both the federal and state level to be "narrowly tailored to promote compelling governmental interests." The opinion for the Court, authored by Justice O'Connor and joined only by Kennedy, however, made an important concession; it is not true, she said, that "strict scrutiny is strict in theory, but fatal in fact." The government is not disqualified from using affirmative action to address "the unhappy persistence of both the practice and the lingering effects of racial discrimination against minority groups."[5]

The Rehnquist Court has brought the same equal protection standards to bear in redistricting cases as well. In *Shaw v. Reno* (1993), Justice O'Connor, writing for a 5 to 4 Court, held that districts so bizarre on their face as to be "unexplainable on grounds other than race" were subject to the same strict standards of scrutiny as are other state laws that classify citizens solely on the basis of race. Such districts, O'Connor said, drew upon stereotypical notions about members of the same racial group that were "odious to a free people." In *Miller v. Johnson* (1995), the Court went a step further. In another 5 to 4 decision, Justice Kennedy said that the equal protection clause was violated when Georgia created three majority-minority districts.

The touchstone for strict scrutiny in redistricting cases, Kennedy argued, was not just the bizarre shape of districts but whenever race was used as the "predominant" factor in creating districts.

The decisions in *Adarand, Shaw,* and *Miller* brought coherence to the Court's equal protection jurisprudence, although it did so at the cost of restricting governmental use of race-based programs to effect substantive equality. Still, the Rehnquist Court's decisions were relatively moderate, rejecting more conservative positions that had earlier been advanced by the Reagan/Bush Justice Department and conservative interest groups. The Court did not prohibit considerations of race altogether either in redistricting decisions or government actions tailored for remedial purposes (the position favored by conservatives and advanced by Justices Scalia and Thomas in concurring opinions).

Moreover, at the same time the Rehnquist Court restricted the use of group-based characteristics for "benign purposes," it made it more difficult for private employers and governments to use them for "invidious purposes." In *Harris v. Forklift Systems, Inc.* (1993), for example, the Court expanded actionable sexual harassment under the 1964 Civil Rights Act. Writing for the Court, Justice O'Connor held that sexually offensive behavior that is pervasive and unwanted, even if it is not "psychologically damaging, is actionable as an abusive work environment." And in *Burlington Industries v. Ellerth* (1997), a 7 to 2 Court, led by Justice Kennedy, went even further, holding that victims of workplace harassment can recover against an employer even if they suffer no "adverse, tangible job consequences."

In *United States v. Virginia* (1996), the Court also struck down the male-only admission policy at the publicly supported Virginia Military Institute (VMI). Writing for the Court, Justice Ginsburg said that gender-based government action must demonstrate an exceedingly persuasive justification, which VMI failed to do. Likewise, in *Romer v. Evans* (1996), the Court struck down Colorado's Amendment 2. Writing for the majority, Justice Kennedy said that the amendment targeted a class of individuals for unequal treatment in a way that had no rational relation to a legitimate legislative end. Kennedy explained that the amendment (unlike Georgia's antisodomy statute upheld in *Bowers*) "classifies homosexuals not to further a proper legislative end but to make them unequal to everyone else" and thus could only be explained as an expression of animus toward that group. As such, the amendment failed to meet even the lowest standard of rational basis scrutiny. This prompted a scathing dissent from Scalia, accusing "this most illiberal Court" of embarking on a "course of inscribing one after another of the current preferences of the society . . . into our basic law."

Even when the Rehnquist Court has struck down laws on constitutional grounds, it has tended to limit its holding. In *Shaw* and *Miller,* for example, the Court was careful to instruct lower courts to exercise extraordinary caution in adjudicating claims that a state has drawn race-based district lines and to emphasize that the burden of proof is on plaintiffs to show that traditional race-neutral districting principles had been subordinated to racial considerations. In *Romer,* the Court refused to elevate sexual preference to the level of "suspect" or "quasi-suspect" scrutiny and instead relied on simple rational basis analysis to strike down the Colorado law. Consequently, it is unlikely that *Romer* will have any life beyond the specific facts of that case. Likewise, in the *VMI* case, the Court refused the invitation of the Clinton administration to treat sex-based classifications as "suspect" and continued to treat them as it had since 1972 under an intermediate level of scrutiny (*Frontiero v. Richardson* [1973]). Ironically, given the fact that strict scrutiny was used by the Court to strike down race-based affirmative action, the Court, by refusing to elevate sex-based classifications to a strict scrutiny standard, may have saved affirmative action for women from a similar fate. At the very least, the Court has created a temporary double standard with respect to race-based and sex-based affirmative action that it will be forced to reconcile in the near future.

Church and State

The splintered and fragmented nature of the Rehnquist Court's jurisprudence is probably most apparent in its decisions on religious freedom, where it has been unable to develop a coherent approach either to the establishment clause or the free exercise clause. During the 1980s, conservatives advocated returning prayer to public schools and greater accommodation of religious belief in public institutions. A focal point of controversy has been the establishment test that the Court enunciated in *Lemon v. Kurtzman* (1971), requiring state legislation to have a secular purpose, neither to advance nor inhibit religion, and to avoid unnecessary entanglements with religion. At one time or another, most of the justices currently on the Court have advocated abandoning the *Lemon* test. Still, with its members unable to agree on an alternative interpretive approach, the Court has continued to invoke *Lemon.*

Precisely what kind of religious influences the *Lemon* test precludes, however, is subject to constantly shifting coalitions on the Court. For instance, in *Zobrest v. Catalina School District* (1993), a 5 to 4 majority led by Chief Justice Rehnquist upheld public funding for a sign-language interpreter for a deaf student attending a private religious school. And in *Lamb's Chapel v. Center Moriches Free School District* (1993), a unanimous Court held that public schools that provide after-hours access to facilities to civic groups must also allow religious groups access. But in *Lee v. Weisman* (1992), a 5 to 4 Court, led by Justice Kennedy, rejected the practice of prayer in high school graduation ceremonies. In 1994, a 6 to 3 Court, led by Justice Souter, struck down New York's creation of a special school district accommodating a community of Hasidic Jews (*Kiryas Joel Village v. Grumet* [1994]). Justice Scalia's concurrence in *Lamb's Chapel* and his dissents in *Weisman* and *Grumet* chastised the Court's majority for its pragmatic, case-by-case jurisprudence and its continued reliance on *Lemon,* which he likened to a "ghoul in a late-night horror movie that repeatedly sits up in its grave and shuffles abroad, after being repeatedly killed and buried."

The Rehnquist Court's approach to the free exercise clause has been equally fragmented and fractious. In *Oregon v. Smith* (1990), a 6 to 3 Court, led by Justice Scalia, upheld a state's denial of unemployment benefits to members of the Native American Church fired from their state jobs for using peyote in religious ceremonies. The central part of the Scalia opinion, however, was assailed by Justice O'Connor (concurring) and three dissenters. In that part, Scalia abandoned the test established in *Sherbert v. Verner* (1963), which required state laws not only to have a secular purpose but also to be in pursuance of a "compelling state interest" and to employ the least drastic means when they restrict religiously motivated action. By contrast, Scalia argued that the free exercise clause only required laws to be "neutral" and "generally applicable." This part of the Court's decision, more than the actual holding, alarmed the religious community, who saw the Court abandoning its commitment to protect unpopular religions from majority animus. Three years later, the Court seemed to go out of its way to reassure the religious community that government could not regulate religious activity if it was simply unpopular. In *Church of Lukumi Babalu Aye v. Hialeah* (1993), Justice Kennedy invalidated a city ordinance banning the sacrificial use of animals. The Court held that the law was not passed for a "neutral" purpose but was enacted out of animus to a Caribbean-based religion that practiced Santeria. The Court's decision was unanimous, but no other Justice joined

Kennedy's opinion in its entirety. In three separate concurring opinions, Justices Souter, Blackmun, and O'Connor vigorously disagreed with the Court's continued reliance on *Smith* and urged a return to *Sherbert* as more consistent with the historical purposes of the free exercise clause.

Not persuaded by the Court's reassurance in *Hialeah,* religious groups successfully lobbied Congress for the Religious Freedoms Restoration Act, passed in November 1993. The law essentially reversed the effect of *Smith* by writing the *Sherbert* standards into federal statute. But the law provoked a flood of litigation, and in *Boerne v. Flores* (1997), a 6 to 3 Court led by Justice Kennedy struck it down on separation of powers grounds. Though members of the Court continued to debate the propriety of *Smith,* there was a majority consensus that Congress could use its powers under Section 5 of the Fourteenth Amendment for remedial purposes only and could not impose a substantive determination about what constitutes a violation of the First Amendment on states. Such a power would alter the "traditional separation of powers between Congress and the Judiciary," which gives the Court "primary authority to interpret" the Bill of Rights, wrote Kennedy.

Free Expression

In contrast to religious freedom, free expression is the area perhaps least affected by judicial fragmentation and the collapse in consensual constitutional norms. The Rehnquist Court's decision making in this area has been neither pragmatic nor minimalist. Although Chief Justice Rehnquist has often found himself in dissent, a clear majority of the Court has shown little hesitancy toward striking down state or federal statutes or toward construing the right to free expression in expansive, libertarian terms. In *Texas v. Johnson* (1989), for instance, the Court, led by Justice Brennan, struck down Texas's flag desecration statute on the grounds that it was a viewpoint-based restriction on free speech. Chief Justice Rehnquist wrote a bitter dissent, accusing the majority of abandoning a 200-year-old tradition of protecting the flag as a national symbol. The decision ignited a public firestorm, and Congress responded by passing a federal flag-protection statute, which the Court unceremoniously struck down a year later (*United States v. Eichman* [1990]).

In 1993, in *RAV v. St. Paul* (1992), the Court also invalidated a so-called "hate speech" law, prohibiting speech that "arouses anger, alarm, or resentment in others on the basis of race, color, creed, religion or gender." Such codes had increasingly been used by municipal governments and public universities in an effort to protect minorities from harassing speech. In this case, a group of white teenagers had burned a cross on the lawn of a black family and were charged with violating the St. Paul ordinance. Adhering to its broad, principled protection of free expression against viewpoint restrictions, however, a unanimous Court led by Justice Scalia struck down the city ordinance.

Likewise, in *Colorado Republican Campaign Committee v. FEC* (1996), the Court invalidated an FEC regulation that restricted independent campaign expenditures. And in *DAETC v. FCC* (1996), the Court struck down portions of the Cable Regulation Act of 1992, restricting "indecent programming" on public access channels. Justice Breyer's opinion in this latter case was particularly striking, both because it rejected a categorical rule to be applied to this area of emerging technology and because it was a harbinger for the Court's decision in 1997 invalidating portions of the Communications Decency Act of 1996. In that act, Congress sought to impose indecency standards on internet users and access providers. The act was immediately challenged by the ACLU, and the Court, in *Reno v. ACLU* (1997), struck it down. The Court held that the act's "indecent transmission" and "patently offensive display" provisions abridge "the freedom of speech" protected by the First Amendment.

The Rehnquist Court's willingness to interpret free speech rights expansively continued even when they conflicted with other First Amendment values. In *Rosenberger v. University of Virginia* (1995), for instance, the editor of a student Christian magazine challenged a university policy that denied religious groups access to student-activity funds. Writing for the Court, Justice Kennedy said that the university's funding policy violated the right to free expression and was not required under the establishment clause (see also *Capitol Square Review Board v. Pinette* [1995], where the Court upheld the KKK's right to display a ten-foot cross in a public park).

The Rehnquist Court also expanded protection of so-called "commercial speech." In *Ladue v. Gilleo* (1994), Justice Stevens, in a sweeping opinion, barred government from banning the posting of signs on private property. In *44 Liquormart v. Rhode Island* (1996), the Court limited government's ability to regulate advertisements for harmful products such as alcohol and tobacco. Striking down a Rhode Island statute that prohibited advertising the retail price of alcoholic drinks, Justice Stevens's opinion for a unanimous Court contrasted restrictions on misleading advertising with regulations that ban truthful advertising for paternalistic reasons. In the latter, Stevens wrote, "There is far less reason to depart from the rigorous review that the First Amendment generally demands" (but see *Florida Bar v. Went For It* [1995]).

The Court also expanded the free speech rights of government employees against regulations aimed at keeping them out of partisan politics. In *United States v. National Treasury Employees Union* (1995), for example, the Court struck down the federal Ethics Reform Act of 1989, prohibiting government employees from accepting honoraria for speeches or articles. Writing for the Court, Justice Stevens claimed the law burdened the free marketplace of ideas established by the First Amendment. Again, in dissent, Chief Justice Rehnquist argued that the majority had "understate(d) the weight which should be accorded to the governmental justifications for the . . . ban and overstate(d) the amount of speech which actually will be deterred." And in two other cases the Court, for the first time, extended to independent government contractors the right to criticize their public employers on public matters without fear of losing their contracts (*County Commission v. Umbehr* [1996] and *O'Hare Trucking v. Northlake* [1996]).

In contrast to other areas of constitutional adjudication, the Court's broad, principled, and nonminimalist decision making in free expression cases underscores the fact that more is at play in shaping the Court's role than the justices' policy views alone. Few scholars, for instance, would argue that Justice Scalia was in favor of flag burning or hate speech, yet he voted to strike down statutes prohibiting both. Rather, the Court's free expression decisions have been robust precisely because it is one area where there is significant agreement and overlap between competing jurisprudential approaches. A broad libertarian conception of free speech rights under the Constitution can be supported from any of a textual-originalist, democracy-reinforcement, or an independent-interpretivist view. The only approach that would consistently lead to a more narrow conception of the right is a deference-restraint approach, which also explains why Chief Justice Rehnquist, its most enthusiastic supporter, often found himself dissenting in these cases.

Separation of Powers and Federalism

Divided government and the collapse in political consensus in electoral politics have generated a steady flow of separation of powers disputes during the last three decades. The Rehnquist Court's turn toward a pragmatic and

minimalist jurisprudence is evident in this area as well. The Burger Court
adopted a highly formalist approach to the separation of powers, leading it
to invalidate several major federal statutes during the 1970s and early 1980s.[6]
By contrast, the Rehnquist Court adopted a flexible, pragmatic approach,
leading it to be more deferential to Congress and less interested in using rigid
principles to create air-tight governmental departments. In *Morrison v. Olson*
(1988), for instance, the Court upheld the independent counsel provisions
of the Ethics in Government Act against claims that it gave the judiciary an
improper role in the executive's prosecutorial function. The following year,
in *Mistretta v. United States* (1989), the Court upheld the federal sentencing
reform act and the creation of the U.S. Sentencing Commission against
claims that it violated the appointments clause and improperly gave the
other branches control over the judicial function.

The Rehnquist Court continued this more flexible and minimalist
approach in *Clinton v. Jones* (1997), where it decided that the presidency was
not sealed off from judicial power. Paula Jones had brought a suit asserting
that President Clinton had sexually harassed her while he was governor of
Arkansas. Rejecting President Clinton's claim that sitting presidents are tem-
porarily immune from civil actions, Justice Stevens, writing for a unanimous
Court, held that the president has no such immunity. In an opinion particularly revealing of the Court's pragmatism, Stevens refused even to consider
Clinton's principled claim that without such immunity future presidents
might be harassed by frivolous and harassing suits. Such a problem is only
hypothetical and ought not to form the premise of a new constitutional rule,
Stevens said. Further, if such suits became a problem in the future, Congress
could legislatively immunize the president, and thus no constitutional rule
was necessary. Nor, Stevens held, was a broad constitutional principle of
immunity necessary to protect against the time burdens that such suits
might impose on the president, which, he said, could be adequately managed on a case-by-case basis by lower court judges. The Court's pragmatism
in *Clinton v. Jones* once again proved to have severe costs to other institutions. One year later President Clinton found himself subject to an impeachment referral from Independent Counsel Kenneth Starr on the grounds that
he perjured himself during a deposition in the *Jones* civil suit.

The one clear exception to the Rehnquist Court's more flexible approach
to the separation of powers came in *Clinton v. New York* (1998), where a 6
to 3 Court struck down the Line Item Veto Act (*2 U.S.C. Sec. 691*). Writing
for the Court, Justice Stevens said that the act, which empowered the presi-

dent to cancel individual "items of new direct spending" contained within larger bills, violated the presentment clause of Article 1, Section 7, of the Constitution. Once again, however, even when the Court exercised its power to invalidate a federal statute, it carefully limited its holding. The lower court had invalidated the law both on presentment clause grounds and on the ground that it impermissibly disrupted the balance of powers among the three branches. Stevens went out of his way to emphasize that the Court's decision rested on the narrow presentment clause ground only and that the Court was declining the invitation to endorse a general theory regarding the balance of powers among the branches.

The Rehnquist Court's decisions in federalism cases are more enigmatic, but here too there is evidence that a highly fragmented Court is unable to strike out in a bold direction even though individual justices hold strong preferences to alter the existing constitutional relationship between the federal government and the states. Since the 1970s conservatives have championed the idea of "new federalism" and the devolution of government regulatory authority. The Rehnquist Court's decisions in *New York v. United States* (1992) and *United States v. Lopez* (1995) sparked debate about whether the Court had embraced an extreme form of new federalism. In *New York,* the Court appeared to breathe life back into the Tenth Amendment by striking down a provision in a federal statute that required states to enter into interstate compacts for the disposal of hazardous waste or take title to the waste. Writing for a splintered Court, Justice O'Connor resurrected the idea of "dual sovereignty" and held that Congress may not "commandeer" state legislative processes in order to enact and enforce federal programs. In *Lopez,* the Court again raised the prospect of a revolution in federalism, when, for the first time since 1937, it struck down a federal statute, the Gun-Free School Zones Act of 1990, on the grounds that Congress lacked interstate commerce clause authority to regulate in that area. In a fractious 5 to 4 decision, Chief Justice Rehnquist wrote that the act, which barred individuals from carrying a firearm within 1,000 feet of a school, regulated an area of "traditional" state control and that Congress had failed to justify it as regulating an activity that had a "substantial impact" on interstate commerce.

Some observers saw these decisions as embracing a new federalism jurisprudence that would severely limit Congress' power to regulate in areas ranging from criminal law to health, safety and the environment. Even at the time, however, other commentators pointed out that the Court's decisions were narrowly drawn and fact specific, leaving Congress several ways to correct the deficiencies in their laws (Stewart 1995). Indeed, while Justice Thomas's concurrence in *Lopez* suggested that the Court should reconsider its entire post-1937 federalism jurisprudence, Chief Justice Rehnquist, writing for the majority, went out of his way to emphasize the limited nature of the Court's holding. The Court was not disturbing modern precedents giving Congress broad powers, he said, but was only requiring Congress to explicitly implicate commerce when drafting its statutes, something it conspicuously had failed to do in the School Zones Act of 1990.

Subsequent decisions tend to support the view that *Lopez* was limited to its facts and that the decision was consistent with the pragmatic approach that the Court has taken in other areas of constitutional law. Indeed, one week after deciding *Lopez,* the Court handed down a second commerce clause case, *United States v. Robertson* (1995). In a per curiam opinion the Court reinstated a federal Racketeer Influenced and Corrupt Organizations Act (RICO) conviction thrown out by the appeals court on commerce clause grounds. Then in 1997 the Court, in *Terry v. United States,* without comment, also rejected a commerce clause challenge to the Freedom of Access to Abortion Clinics Act of 1994 that regulated protests around abortion clinics, a controversial statute supported by the Clinton administration but opposed by conservative antiabortion groups.

The Court's treatment of "dual sovereignty" since *New York* is less clear, though here too the Court seems to have moved incrementally. In *U.S. Term Limits, Inc. v. Thornton* (1995), for example, the Court struck down an Arkansas statute that sought to impose term limits on members of Congress. Writing for the Court, Justice Stevens said that laws restricting who could run for Congress violated Article I, Section 2, of the Constitution, which sets out the exclusive qualifications for membership in Congress. Significantly, Stevens rejected out of hand the argument that the power to add qualifications was "part of the original sovereignty that the Tenth Amendment reserved to the States."

Two years later in *Printz v. United States* (1997), however, a divided 5 to 4 Court struck down the Brady Handgun Violence Protection Act of 1993 on the grounds that it "commandeered" state governmental institutions in violation of the Tenth Amendment and the separation of powers. The act required a five-day waiting period on the sale of handguns and imposed on local law enforcement officials a temporary duty to conduct background checks to determine if purchasers had felony records. However, that duty ended in 1998 when the U.S. Department of Justice was required to have in place its own national background check system. In writing for the majority Justice Scalia argued that requiring local sheriffs to conduct background checks "commandeered" state officials in violation of the Tenth Amendment and also violated the separation of powers by vesting federal law enforcement duties in officials removed from direct presidential control and supervision. Although Scalia's opinion included expansive dicta regarding "dual sovereignty," the holding itself was quite limited and had little impact on the operation of the Brady Act. Not only was the provision invalidated by the Court, but it specifically left Congress free to ask states for voluntary participation in the program or to amend the act and provide financial incentives for state participation. Most important, the Court refrained from deciding whether other purely ministerial requirements imposed by Congress on state and local authorities were similarly invalid. Thus, whether *New York* and *Prinz*, and the concept of "dual sovereignty" they embody, will have leverage in future cases remains to be seen.

Between 1932 and 1944, President Franklin Roosevelt appointed eight justices to the Supreme Court, fundamentally transforming its role and ushering in a new constitutional regime (Ackerman 1991). Republican presidents Nixon, Ford, Reagan, and Bush, with an equally clear judicial strategy, made nine appointments to the Supreme Court over a period lasting twice as long (1968–1992) but enjoyed no such success. And Clinton's two appointments to the Court only strengthened its moderate, pragmatic direction. The "counterrevolution" (Blasi 1983) that conservatives hoped for and liberals feared has became nothing more than incremental tinkering with established constitutional rights and doctrines.

Constitutional structures link the role of the Supreme Court to the elected branches of government. But the relationship of the elected branches to each other is equally important in shaping the role of the Court. Mr. Dooley's maxim, that the Court follows the election returns, assumes that the election returns are coherent and intelligible, an assumption that has been inoperative for much of the past quarter century. During that time, the federal judiciary has become increasingly moderate in its political outlook as presidents have appointed centrists as a way of avoiding costly confirmation battles with the Senate.

Moreover, the legacy of legal realism is not nearly as simple as many modern social scientists assumed. The core legal realist insight, that law is dependent on politics, has become even more clear since the 1960s when the collapse of ideological consensus has led to a proliferation of constitutional theory and jurisprudential dissensus on and off the Court. However, though it is true that law and politics are inescapably linked, it is fanciful to assume that judges vote their policy preferences in the same way as would a member of Congress or a state legislator. Politics enters the judicial process in deeper, more constitutive ways, shaping the way judges think about law. As the changing norms of opinion writing on the Court illustrate, judges care deeply about the law, and that solicitude is at the root of the fragmentation that has characterized decision making by the Rehnquist Court.

The pattern of electoral dealignment and divided government that has characterized American politics for at least the past two decades shows little sign of ending. Nor is it likely that constitutional jurisprudence will become less conflictual as we enter the next century. These structural forces, far more than the preferences and proclivities of individual justices, have led to the politics of moderation, pragmatism, and fragmentation that has characterized the Rehnquist Court's decision making. Absent a more systemic transformation in American law and the American political system, it is unlikely that the Court's role in constitutional policy making or its fragmented style of decision making will change, and those hoping for either a judicial revolution or counterrevolution are likely to continue to be disappointed.

Notes

1. Some portions of this chapter are based on Cornell Clayton and James Giordano, "The Supreme Court and the Constitution," in *Developments in American Politics,* vol. 3, ed. Gillian Peele et al. (London: Macmillan Press, 1998), 71–96, and reprinted by permission of Macmillan Press.

2. This form of "behaviorist" analysis is most prominent in political science and other social science literature, but even the *Harvard Law Review,* the bastion of normative jurisprudence, has since the 1960s published voting records of each justice and analyzed block alignments on the Court in its annual review of the Court's term.

3. E.g., *Marbury v. Madison* (1803), *McCulloch v. Maryland* (1819) and *Gibbons v. Ogden* (1823), *Dred Scott v. Sanford* (1857), and *Lochner v. New York* (1905) and its abandonment in cases like *West Coast Hotel v. Parrish* (1937) and *NLRB v. Jones and Laughlin Steel* (1937).

4. On two occasions, *Akron v. Akron Center for Reproductive Health* (1983) and *Thornburgh v. American College of Gynecologists and Obstetricians* (1987), the Court rebuffed restrictions on the *Roe* right. But by the *Thornburgh* case, the original *Roe* majority of 7 to 2 had dwindled to a 5 to 4, following the appointments of O'Connor and Scalia. Then,

with the addition of Kennedy in 1988, the Court, without reversing *Roe,* upheld by a 5 to 4 vote a Missouri law that placed substantive restrictions on abortions in *Webster v. Reproductive Health Services* (1989). And two years later, the Court, by another 5 to 4 vote, upheld the Reagan administration's ban on abortion counseling by organizations that receive federal funding (*Rust v. Sullivan* [1991]).

5. The Court's decision in *Adarand* nevertheless makes it much more difficult to justify affirmative action programs. In the first significant test of affirmative action since the decision, for example, the Fifth Circuit Court of Appeals in 1996 ruled that a University of Texas Law School admissions policy that gave an advantage to minority applicants failed to meet the strict standard of scrutiny required under *Adarand*. When it was appealed in 1996, the Supreme Court declined to hear the case (*Texas v. Hopwood*).

6. See *Buckley v. Valeo* (1976), invalidating portions of the Federal Elections Campaign Act; *INS v. Chadha* (1983), striking down the legislative veto; and *Bowsher v. Synar* (1986), invalidating the Gramm-Rudman-Hollings deficit reduction act.

Chapter 10

Supreme Court Agenda Setting in Gender Equity Cases, 1970–1994

Leslie Friedman Goldstein

Women's rights in America over the past three decades, by a combination of judicial and legislative innovation, have been revolutionized on two topics: gender equity (i.e., a right to be free of discriminatory treatment based on gender) and reproductive freedom (i.e., a right to be free of laws forbidding one either to have or to avoid having children). Supreme Court policy innovation in terms of these rights has patterned itself into three slightly overlapping phases of roughly equal duration. The first, the constitutionalization of reproductive freedom phase, extended from 1965 through 1977; the second, that of the constitutionalization of gender equity, extended from 1971 through 1982; the third phase was that of enhancing gender equity by feminist extensions of federal statutes through what one scholar has called "dynamic statutory interpretation"—that is, interpretation that produces policies probably not within the original intent of the Congress that enacted the statute (Eskridge 1994). This dynamic statutory extension phase seems to have run from 1978 to at least fall 1993.[1] My purpose in this chapter is, first and by way of background, to provide a brief overview of these dramatic policy innovations by the justices, and then, second, to attempt an explanation of the Court's shifts of activity.

As to the first of these phases, the eventual cessation by the late 1970s of dramatic policy innovations on the matter of reproductive freedom is not particularly puzzling, since it naturally takes a certain number of cases presented over a course of years for the details, various applications, and limits of a new judicial policy, or doctrine, to be spelled out by the Court, a period that would normally be followed by a period of stabilization. Other scholars (Caldeira 1981; Likens; Pacelle 1990) have identified a kind of natural life cycle for judicial policy innovation, which seems to fit this picture.[2]

On the other hand, the shift from phase two to phase three cries out for explanation. If the Court still favored changes in public policy in the direction of enhanced gender equity, why would the justices switch from Constitution-based decisions in that direction to statute-based decisions in the same direction? The Court issued numerous important expansions of gender equity by statutory interpretation in the years 1978 through 1993, including such significant policy innovations as the rule that pension plans must treat women as men are treated even though as a group women live much longer than men *(Los Angeles Department of Water and Power v. Manhart, Arizona Governing Committee v. Norris);* the conclusion that the 1964 ban on sex discrimination on employment conditions implies an employer obligation to keep the workplace free of sexual harassment *(Meritor Savings v. Vinson, Harris v. Forklift Systems, Inc.);* and the outlawing (as sex discrimination) of fetal protection policies that restrict women's job opportunities *(UAW v. Johnson Controls).* Yet from August 1982 through March 1994 the Supreme Court did not declare a single gender discrimination unconstitutional.

In other words, beginning in 1971, the mix of Warren Court holdovers and early Burger Court justices contained a group willing to alter constitutional interpretation dramatically on behalf of women's rights. That was not visibly true from the 1982–1983 term until April 1994. But since 1978 the Burger and Rehnquist Courts have continued to be willing to innovate in a feminist policy direction by means of expansive statutory interpretation instead. Why did the Court in its efforts to further gender equity not continue to issue both sorts of opinions—Constitution-based and statute-based?

To address this question, I shall first provide a historic overview of national-level alterations-in-rights policies during the decades at issue; then a survey of potential answers from the judicial agenda-setting literature; and finally an exploration of a couple of plausible hypotheses by a careful examination of relevant data, with an explanation of the thinking that guided the data collection and interpretation.

National-level Innovations on Women's Rights, 1965–1995

Reproductive Freedom

In the first phase of gender policy innovation, the Supreme Court secured as a constitutional right, in their words, "the right of the individual to be free of unwarranted governmental intrusion into those decisions so fundamentally affecting a person as the decision whether to bear or beget a child" *(Eisenstadt v. Baird)*. This phase began in earnest prior to the women's movement, in 1965, when the Supreme Court declared unconstitutional a ninety-year-old Connecticut law forbidding the use of contraceptive devices *(Griswold v. Connecticut)*. It reached its peak in January 1973, with the famous *Roe v. Wade* and *Doe v. Bolton* decisions, which in a single day declared unconstitutional the criminal abortion statutes of forty-six states. It generally concluded by 1977, by which time the Supreme Court had delineated the basic contours of how much abortion restriction it would and would not permit. By that time, the Court had extended the right to obtain contraceptives even to children under the age of sixteen *(Carey v. Pop. Services)*; had indicated that husbands could not be given a veto power over their wives' abortions; had indicated that it would uphold parental consent laws for abortions performed on minors as long as such laws provided the option of obtaining permission from a judge when the minor chose not to face her parents *(Planned Parenthood v. Danforth)*; and had allowed the government to refuse to fund abortions even when funding childbirth costs *(Beal v. Doe, Maher v. Roe, Poelker v. Doe)*.

These contours were slightly altered in 1992 in the *Casey* decision, in that the Supreme Court allowed states to insist that women seeking abortions be exposed to information about fetal development and adoption resources and also to impose a twenty-four-hour waiting period prior to abortion consent *(Planned Parenthood of S.E. Pennsylvania v. Casey)*. Still, the magnitude of the 1992 shift does not come close to approaching that of the 1973 innovation and does not in major ways alter the basic contours of policy crafted in the 1965–1977 period. *Roe v. Wade* survives fairly intact twenty years—and a great many abortion cases—later (with a majority of the Court still committed to what they call its "essential holding"), despite three completed terms of presidents publicly pledged to appoint justices who would undo that decision, presidents who managed to appoint a total of six new justices to the Court. Thus, if one were to examine only judicial policy innovations on abortion (as distinguished from either litigation flow or space on the judicial agenda), one would find clear confirmation of the Caldeira-Pacelle judicial policy life-cycle model (see note 2).[3] The gender equity side of the story, however, is different.

Gender Equity

The story of the constitutionalization of gender equity began somewhat later. As recently as 1968 the Warren Court refused to reconsider its own

1961 rejection of that constitutionalization, in the context of systematic exemption of women from jury duty, an exemption that resulted in trials of women criminals by almost exclusively all-male juries *(Hoyt v. Florida, State v. Hall)*. In 1971, however, Chief Justice Burger led the Court in a new direction by means of a cryptic opinion.

This cryptic opinion, in the case *Reed v. Reed,* purported to explain why the Court was declaring unconstitutional an Idaho law that preferred men to women in selecting among equally connected relatives to appoint an estate administrator for someone who died intestate. Justice Burger called this discrimination "arbitrary" and said it therefore violated the equal protection clause. And in constitutional discourse "arbitrary" was a code word for "lacking any rational connection to any legitimate governmental purpose." But the Idaho Supreme Court had pointedly argued that this law was rationally designed to produce estate administrators more rather than less likely to be familiar with the affairs of the business world and to do so in a quick and approximate way without a lot of bureaucratic paperwork. Recall, this was only ten years after *Hoyt v. Florida,* where the Court had found it "reasonable" to give a blanket jury-duty exemption to women (on the grounds that woman is "regarded as the center of home and family life"), even when it resulted in an all-male jury for the trial of a woman who murdered her husband pursuant to a marital dispute. By the traditional standard that had governed decisions like *Hoyt,* this Idaho law letting males administer estates should have passed muster. The fact that it did not meant the Court was changing the standards, toughening them up. However, the Court refrained from saying so, for quite a while. Its doctrinal reticence is perhaps explained by a dilemma.

In response to a thriving women's movement, officially launched with the formation of the National Organization for Women (NOW) in October 1966, Congress by late 1970 was indicating massive support for the Equal Rights Amendment (ERA) to the Constitution. By the time *Reed v. Reed* came along, the House of Representatives had voted for the ERA twice, first by a margin of 10 to 1 and the second time 20 to 1. One month later the Supreme Court handed down *Reed v. Reed.* Four months later the Senate passed the ERA, again with near unanimity, 84 to 8. Several states ratified immediately and the ERA looked as if it were on its way to easy passage. As it turned out, eventually the ratification process stalled with only 70 percent of the states having ratified by the ten-year deadline, not the required 75 percent, even though public opinion polls were showing majorities in every state in favor. That the ERA was widely popular but politically stalled became evident by late 1976. Meanwhile, many gender discrimination cases were being brought to the Supreme Court, posing challenges under the existing Fourteenth Amendment equal protection clause.[4]

The Equal Rights Amendment specifically prohibited denying "equality of rights under the law on account of sex," but the Fourteenth Amendment used only the general phrase "equal protection of the laws." The traditional reading of the latter allowed plenty of unequal treatment, as long as it had a rational basis. The Court's dilemma was that the ERA would do for gender discrimination what the Fourteenth Amendment had done for its historic target, race discrimination—make such discrimination all but forbidden (short of the rare instance of a "compelling government interest" necessitating a particular discrimination). The American public clearly, and by wide margins, favored this constitutional transformation; but the sentiment was just short of that overwhelming level needed for formal amendment to the Constitution. The Court at first coped with this dilemma by mouthing the words of the old rational basis test but producing case results that made sense only as viewed through the lens of some stricter test. The justices applied this approach in the years 1971 to 1976 to declare unconstitutional not only the preference for males as estate administrators but also (1) a law that gave spousal benefits to all army officers who had wives but denied them to officers who had "nondependent" husbands *(Frontiero v. Richardson)*; (2) a law automatically exempting all women from jury duty *(Taylor v. Louisiana)*; (3) a law giving social security benefits to the surviving spouse of male contributors who died leaving young children but not to the surviving spouse of female contributors who died in the same situation *(Weinberger v. Weisenfeld)*; and (4) a law establishing a younger age of majority for females (eighteen) than for males (twenty-one), which provided fewer years of divorced parental-support payments to daughters than to sons *(Stanton v. Stanton)*.

Eventually, once it became clear that the ERA was both widely popular and likely to die, the Supreme Court stepped in and unofficially amended the Constitution by producing a new rule of constitutional law for gender discrimination. The Court opted for language in between that of the ordinary, rational basis test and that of the compelling government interest test applied to racial classifications. Gender-based classifications, beginning in December 1976, officially had to meet the requirement of being "substantially related to" (not quite "necessary for," but not merely "rationally related to") an "important" (not merely a "legitimate," but not quite a "compelling") governmental interest *(Craig v. Boren).*

This "important governmental interest" test was then used to strike down more gender discrimination laws, starting with the *Craig v. Boren* case that initiated the test, where the Court voided a law that allowed eighteen- to twenty-year-old women but not eighteen- to twenty-year-old men to purchase light beer. The test was then used to void a law that gave social security benefits to all surviving wives of contributors who died but only to those surviving husbands who could prove economic dependency *(Califano v. Goldfarb);* one that allowed alimony awards only to wives, never to husbands *(Orr v. Orr);* one that required permission from all mothers and from married or divorced fathers but not from unwed fathers before their parental rights could be cut off in order to place their child for adoption *(Caban v. Mohammed);* one that gave welfare benefits to families with unemployed fathers but not to those with unemployed mothers *(Califano v. Westcott);* one that gave workmen's compensation to widows but not to widowers of protected workers *(Wengler v. Druggists Mutual Insurance);* one that gave husbands unilateral control over all marital property *(Kirchberg v. Feenstra);* and one that allowed women but not men to attend a particular state nursing college *(Mississippi University for Women v. Hogan).* After this last one in July 1982, the Supreme Court stopped declaring instances of gender discrimination unconstitutional until 1994.[5]

Statutory Extension

The Burger Court justices did not stop innovating on behalf of women's rights in 1982 when they turned away from declarations of unconstitutionality on behalf of gender equity. Instead, they moved into full gear for phase three, in which the Court embraced various feminist interpretations of existing federal law so as to extend them in ways probably unanticipated by the Congress that had passed the original law. The law in question was usually Title 7 of the 1964 Civil Rights Act, which prohibited employment practices that discriminate or tend to discriminate on the basis of race, sex, national origin, or religion absent a "bona fide occupational qualification" (such as religion in the case of clergy). Sometimes the law was Title 9 of the Education Amendments of 1972, which forbade most gender discrimination in schools that receive federal funds.[6]

Phase three actually began in 1978 and arguably was triggered by a specific incident: Congress' reaction to a Supreme Court interpretation of Title 7 handed down at the end of 1976. Employer exclusion of childbirth costs from employee health insurance benefit packages that covered all other medical disabilities, even elective plastic surgery, had been challenged as sex discrimination, with the argument that all of male workers' disabilities were covered but a woman-only disability was excluded *(G.E. v. Gilbert)*. The Supreme Court had reasoned that the exclusion discriminated not between men and women but between "pregnant [persons] and non-pregnant persons." Therefore it was not sex discrimination. The congressional rebuff was swift and emphatic. In 1977 the Senate voted 75 to 11 for the Pregnancy Discrimination Amendment (PDA) to Title 7, a bill that specifically defined employer discrimination on the basis of pregnancy as being included in the forbidden practice of sex discrimination. The bill became law by 1978.

Meanwhile, the Supreme Court promptly started more aggressive readings of Title 7. Even *before* the PDA became law, but after it had passed the Senate overwhelmingly, the Supreme Court said (in patent inconsistency with its *Gilbert* reasoning but refusing to overrule the decision) that it counted as illegal sex discrimination for employers to deny accrued seniority to workers returning after a maternity leave when the employers do not deny it to workers who take other medical disability leaves *(Nashville Gas v. Satty)*. In the years to follow, even though the PDA referred specifically only to maternity benefits for employees, the Supreme Court was to extend its reach to benefits for the spouses of employees *(Newport News Shipbuilding v. EEOC)*.

The lesson evidently inferred by the Court—viz., that Congress wanted aggressive readings of Title 7 on sex discrimination—extended to many other arenas besides pregnancy during this period. First, despite the fact that women have longer life expectancies on average than men, the justices interpreted Title 7 as forbidding sex discrimination in employee pension plans, whether by deducting bigger pension payments from female paychecks to put into the plan or by providing smaller monthly payments to female retirees *(Los Angeles Department of Water and Power v. Manhart, Arizona Governing Committee v. Norris)*. Second, despite the freedom of association arguments that were posed to the contrary, Title 7's reach was extended to promotion decisions labeled as entry into a partnership, such as those that are the norm in major law firms and accounting firms *(Hishon v. King & Spaulding)*. Third, the Supreme Court in 1986 (in *Meritor Savings v. Vinson*) unanimously accepted the idea that sexual harassment in the workplace is included in the category "discrimination on the basis of sex . . . in terms or conditions of employment," which Title 7 forbids (a view favored by scholar Catharine MacKinnon, who had nonetheless lamented in print in 1979 [at xi] that it was still "legally unthinkable"). Fourth, although the words of Title 7 forbid the making of employment decisions such as hiring or promotion "because of [an] individual's sex [or race, and so on]," the Supreme Court ruled that affirmative action programs to diversify the employees in a traditionally segregated job category are permitted, so that it is not illegal to pick a woman over a roughly equally qualified male simply on the grounds that she is female *(Johnson v. Transportation Agency)*. Fifth, also in the late 1980s, the Court ruled that penalizing a female for not conforming to her stereotypical gender role in personality, demeanor, and clothing style violated Title 7's ban on sex discrimination *(Price Waterhouse v. Hopkins)*.

It is remarkable that the Burger and then the Rehnquist Courts (Rehnquist moved up to chief justiceship in 1986), in the face of both expectations and general reputation to the contrary, have acted as liberal innovators on the women's rights front through aggressive interpretations of federal statutes at least from 1978 through 1988.[7] An apparent pause in this feminist momentum appeared to be in the wings in 1989; the Supreme Court introduced some rather technical interpretive narrowing of Title 7, mostly having to do with burdens of proof in racial discrimination cases (with similar negative implications for gender discrimination), and the Congress again moved to rebuff the Court with the 1990 (vetoed) and 1991 (enacted) Civil Rights Restoration Acts.[8]

As in 1978, the Supreme Court seemed to respond to Congress' push by again moving out ahead of it: in 1991, 1992, and 1993 the Court returned to its pattern of feminist extensions of Civil Rights statutes through interpretation. In 1991 the Court ruled in *UAW v. Johnson Controls* that an employer's fear of lawsuits from persons who had been damaged in the fetal state was not adequate (under Title 7) as a "bona fide occupational qualification" to justify eliminating all fertile women or even all pregnant women from jobs that endanger a fetus (11 S.Ct.1196). In 1992 the Court expanded the reach of Title 9 of the Education Amendments of 1972, contrary to the arguments of the solicitor general of the United States and to the rulings of lower courts; and it did so unanimously. Citing a related 1986 Congressional statute as offering implicit support for its position, the Court ruled that under Title 9 individual students who felt themselves to be victims of sex discrimination (in this case, sexual harassment) could sue school boards for damages *(Franklin v. Gwinnett County Schools)*.[9] And in fall 1993 the

Supreme Court reaffirmed and clarified its decision concerning sexual harassment in the workplace in such a way as to correct circuit court rulings that had narrowed the reach of its own 1986 precedent. Employees do not have to prove they have actually suffered some measurable psychological damage in order to bring a sexual harassment complaint; employers are obligated under Title 7 to maintain a workplace that is free of discriminatory intimidation or ridicule *(Harris v. Forklift Systems, Inc.)*.

Judicial Agenda Setting

To answer the question driving this study, it is helpful to think about the broader question: What factors can be identified as shaping the flow and ebb of Supreme Court policy leadership on a given topic? In light of the focus of this book on institutionalism as an explanatory variable, one should acknowledge that several scholars have pointed to the U.S. Supreme Court's discretionary control over its own docket (which has been a practical reality since 1925) as an important causal variable. This discretion makes it possible for changes in judicial interest to effect changes in the agenda the Court sets for itself (Epp 1996, 767–68 and citations therein).

It is indeed a commonplace among Court-watchers that Supreme Court interest in particular policy topics varies over time. Certain very broad shifts of topic are widely acknowledged: during the first several decades of the nineteenth century the Supreme Court's agenda dealt predominantly with issues presenting conflicts between state and national authority; from about 1876 to 1937 questions of governmental power to regulate the economy occupied the bulk of the Court's attention; and from 1938 to the present, questions of noneconomic civil liberties have been at the center of the Court's attention.[10]

H. W. Perry's recent study of cert-granting decisions provides some evidence that changes of policy topic are driven by the justices' own inclinations; he quotes an unidentified Supreme Court justice: "The Court was ready for [*Gideon v. Wainwright*], and a third-rate lawyer from Yonkers could have won it. To a degree, the Court was ready for *Brown v. Board,* [1954]— same way with one man, one vote" (1991, 210). That Supreme Court attention to particular topics varies over time is clear; what causes these risings and then fallings-off of Supreme Court attentiveness to particular policy subjects, however, has received relatively little attention.

Numerous scholars have looked at the side of the question that seeks to identify the attention-getting impetus from particular cases accepted for review. This body of scholarship, which can roughly be described as the "judicial agenda-setting" literature, turns out to be of only limited utility for the analyst who wants an explanation of shifts in judicial policy making over time. In this literature scholars generally have attempted to identify those attributes of individual cases that will cause either particular justices or the Court as a whole to vote to hear a given case, but the studies assume the constant salience of the topic involved in the case.[11]

There are a few exceptions to the general pattern; a small group of scholars have taken a look at the transformation of the judicial agenda over time and have searched for causal variables. Doris Provine's 1980 book on the agenda-setting process acknowledged as important shapers of the judicial agenda both litigation flow and concerted litigation strategies as well as the individual justices' own view of their proper role, their views of the law, and their policy concerns (see especially chapter 2 and conclusion). Greg Caldeira (1981) has confirmed that an individual Supreme Court justice's "ideology" was significantly related to his willingness to hear criminal procedure appeals in the time period from the 1930s to the 1970s. Caldeira also learned that news media coverage and changes in political control of Congress did not correlate significantly with Supreme Court agenda alterations on this topic. Roy Flemming et al. (1994) have explored the possibilities that expressions of the president's policy concerns, Congress' policy concerns, and media attention precipitate alteration of the Supreme Court's agenda. Like Caldeira, this group found no influence from the media. They also found no discernible impact from presidential speeches on judicial agenda topics. They did notice significant interaction between congressional legislation and the amount of judicial agenda space devoted to civil rights issues (I will return to congressional/Supreme Court interaction). In a counter, or at least supplement, to Provine's claim that an upsurge in litigation on a certain topic sometimes sparks an increase in Supreme Court attention, Joseph Kobylka (1991, chaps. 3, 5, 6) found in interviews with interest-group litigators that the Supreme Court sometimes shapes its own agenda by pronouncements of new judicial doctrine, which can sharply discourage or encourage future litigation.[12]

In sum, other scholars have identified two external forces on the evolution of the Supreme Court agenda: the flow of litigation and an interactive influence from the Congress. Forces on the agenda internal to the Court are judicial preferences about policy outcomes or for particular legal interpretations,[13] judicial beliefs about the proper judicial role, and judicially produced legal doctrine (both as shaper of litigation flow and as guide to judicial cert grants).[14] Even with the recognition that attention to a given policy topic (that is, space on the judicial agenda) is not the same dependent variable as willingness to alter policy on that topic (a recognition spotlighted by the abortion cases where extrajudicial politics was obviously driving them onto the Court's agenda in the 1978–1992 period even as the Court basically reiterated the same policy year after year), these five forces seemed the appropriate causal variables to investigate for understanding the sharp switch in the Court's approach to gender equity policy making in the early 1980s.

Of these variables, signals from Congress, reinforced evidently by judicial desire for outcome, whether on legal or on policy grounds, appear to have been critical as initiating both phase two and phase three. In August 1970 and again in October 1971 the House of Representatives produced near-unanimous votes for the Equal Rights Amendment ban on sex discrimination by government. In November 1971 for the first time in history the Supreme Court ruled (in *Reed v. Reed*) that a sex discriminatory statute violated the equal protection clause of the Fourteenth Amendment—thus beginning phase two, the constitutionalization of gender equity. In 1977 the Senate, again with near unanimity, voted for the Pregnancy Discrimination Act, a direct rebuff to the Supreme Court's December 1976 ruling (in *G.E. v. Gilbert*) that discrimination against pregnant women should not be viewed as unlawful sex discrimination. In December 1977 (in *Nashville Gas v. Satty*) the Supreme Court—initiating its statutory extension phase of gender equity policy making—immediately began to act as though the Pregnancy Discrimination Act had already been fully adopted by Congress (which did not happen until 1978).

However, the ending of phase two—that is, the limiting of gender equity promotion to the statutory-extension-techniques approach of phase three— can be tied to no obvious congressional signal.[15] Nor could the judicial policy desire variable explain this shift, since both phases moved policy in the same direction. This elimination process leaves one likely culprit for the explanatory variable: judicial role preference.

By the 1982 term, the Court consisted of only three holdovers from the Warren Court (Brennan, Marshall, and White), a court noted for liberal activism. Chief Justices Burger and Rehnquist, their post–Warren Court colleagues, and the presidents who appointed them openly espoused constitutional theories that emphasized the countermajoritarian difficulty in

declarations of unconstitutionality and the propriety of the Court's refrain-
ing from activist policy making. This rhetoric was compatible with a hypothesis that the shift away from declarations of unconstitutionality and toward
statute-based gender equity advancement evinced a conscious strategy of
the post–1982 Burger Court and the current Rehnquist Court. In this
hypothesis, the justices would be picking and choosing among available, suitable cases on the basis of a deliberate approach to the judicial role, a role in
which policy innovation on the basis of statute is preferred as more in keeping with a representative democracy. In this conception, if the unelected justices "get it wrong," the elected Congress is free to tell them so. With
legislative interpretation, Congress can override judicial "mistakes"; with
constitutional interpretation, such "correction" is not so readily available. If,
on the other hand, the justices manage to guess the future correctly (and
Congress silently accepts their reading of the law), then they, the justices, get
to be the heroes.

Alternatively, the policy-making shift might have taken place because of
a combination of judicial alterations of constitutional doctrine in the 1970s,
doctrine with which state and federal governments had complied by 1982,
a cleanup of the statute books that resulted in a drying up of the flow of litigation by that year. This alternative hypothesis, legislative cleanup, combining the first and fifth variables from the preceding list would lead one to
expect a sharp falling off in requests for cert from around 1980 to 1982 and
then virtually no requests since then. Hypothesis one, judicial role preference, would show up clearly if the number of Constitution-based requests
for cert remained more or less constant over time, with the justices themselves revealing their role preference when they began showing a marked
preference for statute-based gender equity appeals.

Data Analysis and Interpretation

My research assistant, Diana Stech (on the basis of a count derived from *U.S.
Law Week*) produced a chart showing the litigation pattern for gender equity
appeals to the Supreme Court in the period of the 1968 term through the
1993 term (see Fig. 10.1).

Figure 10.1 reveals that requests for cert claiming constitutional violations of gender equity were relatively few in the 1968–1972 period (fluctu-
ating between two and seven per term, from a total of several thousand), as
were requests for cert claiming statutory violations of gender equity in the

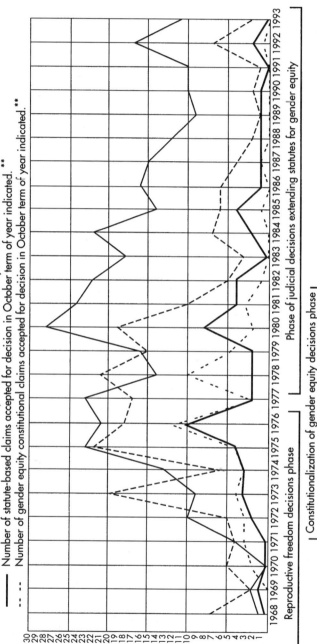

Legend (top):

— Statute-based gender discrimination claims presented in October term of year indicated.*

- - - Gender equity constitutional claims presented in October term of year indicated.*

━━ Number of statute-based claims accepted for decision in October term of year indicated.**

- ·- Number of gender equity constitutional claims accepted for decision in October term of year indicated.**

X-axis years: 1968 1969 1970 1971 1972 1973 1974 1975 1976 1977 1978 1979 1980 1981 1982 1983 1984 1985 1986 1987 1988 1989 1990 1991 1992 1993

Y-axis: 1 through 30

Phase labels (bottom):

| Reproductive freedom decisions phase | Constitutionalization of gender equity decisions phase | Phase of judicial decisions extending statutes for gender equity |

Note: For the years indicated the graph notes the number of requests for certiorari rather than the number of cases appealed. Thus if both sides on one case request certiorari, that is listed as two claims. The number of cases presenting such double claims is 1972, 1; 1973, 3; 1974, 4; 1977, 1#; 1978, 2; 1979, 1; 1980, 4; 1981, 1+; 1982, 1#+; 1988, 1. (The # indicates three requests of certiorari for one case; the + indicates a claim brought to the Court on a case for which another party requested certiorari in the previous year.) If certiorari is granted in such a case, it is listed as two grants; that happened in 1972, 1; 1973, 1; 1974, 1; 1975, 2; 1981, 1+.

*For the years indicated the graph includes the following number of cases presenting both types of claims: 1968, 1; 1972, 1; 1973, 2; 1975, 3; 1976, 5; 1977, 5; 1978, 1; 1980, 2; 1983, 1; 1984, 2; 1986, 1; 1987, 1; 1992, 2.

**For the years indicated the graph includes the following number of claims accepted for decision presenting both types of claims: 1976, 1; 1977, 2.

Figure 10.1. Litigation Pattern for Gender Equity Appeals, 1968–1993.

1968–1971 period (ranging from zero to four per term).[16] After the 1971 term, during which the ratio of grants of cert to requests for cert on constitutional gender equity claims was an astoundingly high 3:4 (the overall ratio of grants to requests in a term being approximately 1:40), both types of gender equity cert requests rose sharply. Constitution-based cert requests in the 1973–1980 terms numbered fifteen or more in seven of the eight years. Statute-based requests increased somewhat more gradually, but in the 1975, 1976, and 1977 terms numbered more than twenty per year; and beginning in the 1980 term they have dramatically outnumbered Constitution-based requests. This marked predominance of statute-based gender equity requests continued uninterrupted at least until 1994.

Thus, the fact that the Supreme Court decided virtually no Constitution-based gender equity claims after the 1982 term[17] is largely a function of litigation flow: the cert requests were not there to be decided. As in the pre-1973 period, the number of such requests fluctuated between one and seven. But unlike the earlier cases, these 1980s and 1990s claims did not present broad questions of law. The Constitution-based claims of this latter period virtually all presented custody-related claims of unwed fathers, claims that are heavily fact-specific[18]—just the sort of cases the justices routinely avoid, not as an exercise of policy preference but simply because they are not "good vehicles"—that is, not suitable for establishing or clarifying broad legal principles (Perry 1991). So the data do show that cert requests claiming constitutional violations of gender equity did essentially dry up after the 1981 term.

The pattern of cert requests uncovered here invites the conclusion that hypothesis two, legislative cleanup, is correct: the combination of Supreme Court decisions in the 1971–1976 period repeatedly striking down statutory gender discriminations as unconstitutional and then the clear constitutional doctrine after December 1976 (that is, the "important government interest" test of *Craig v. Boren*) served in the short term to stir up lots of litigation to clarify the contours of the doctrine and eventually pushed state and federal legislators to cleanse the statute books of those gender discriminations that lacked strong justification. After all, these legislators do take oaths to uphold the Constitution. Legislative cleanup is implicit in the Caldeira-Pacelle theory of judicial policy life-cycles, but my hypothesizing it here was also stimulated by a personal experience. In the late 1970s I participated, at the invitation of my state senator who organized and chaired it, on a state commission to study and reform the state legislative code in order to bring it into line with the *Craig* ruling.

The private behavior of 250 million Americans is not so easily brought into line, so the flow of litigation claiming statutory violations continues unabated. And the Supreme Court, still committed to a much stronger version of gender equity policy than prevailed prior to 1970, continues to hand down important policies protecting gender equity against statutory violations. One must conclude not that the justices were unwilling from 1983 to 1994 to base their decisions on constitutional grounds but that appropriate, "good vehicle" cases requiring such reasoning simply did not come forth from litigants.

Does this finding mean that the Supreme Court really is best conceptualized as the passive branch, which must wait quietly for issues to be brought to it? Not necessarily. First, even if the legislative cleanup hypothesis tells the essential story, it is worth noting that the Supreme Court decisions drove the cleanup campaign. Thus, the drying up of the litigation flow, while a response to legislative change, at root is responding to the Supreme Court moves that stimulated the legislative reform. In other words, the evolution of phase two appears to have followed the judicial policy innovation "life cycle" pattern suggested by the research of Caldeira and Pacelle.

Second, the data interpretation cannot stop here because logically hypotheses one and two are not mutually exclusive. It is possible both that gender-equity-offending statutes were eliminated at the state level and that the late Burger Court consciously preferred statute-based to Constitution-based jurisprudence. Indeed, the drying up of the stream of Constitution-based claims may in part reflect litigators' responsiveness to signals the Court was sending in its opinions. In other words, interest-group attorneys might have stopped bringing Constitution-based appeals in the fear of losing at the Supreme Court. They might have been calculating, on the basis of things said by the justices, that their chances of gender equity success were greater if they had a reinforcing statute to rely on than if they were relying simply on constitutionally mandated equal protection.

This last possibility emphasizes the interaction between judicial doctrine and litigation flow, and it combines elements of the first two hypotheses; to some degree the formulation of judicial doctrine reflects judicial role preference. It also suggests a more complete explanation for the data shown in Figure 10.1, specifically for the rise and fall of litigation flow on gender equity.

H. W. Perry (1991, 212–14) documents a belief held by at least some of the justices that they consciously issue veiled "invitations" in opinions they write, indicating which future litigation they would welcome; he refers to litigative responses to such invitations as "RSVP's." Joseph Kobylka (1991, chaps. 3 and 6) found that certain litigating groups also read particular doctrinal innovations as the opposite of invitations—as "stay away" messages—and they heed the messages.

Scholars familiar with the relevant cases can point to such possible signals: the *Dothard v. Rawlinson* Title 7 decision in June 1977, striking down a governmental employment policy neutral on its face but with a gender discriminatory impact, might have appeared to invite more Title 7 challenges of such policies; the *Personnel Administrator v. Feeney* decision in June 1979, rejecting an equal protection clause challenge to a state civil service rule that had a strongly disproportionate impact against females, might have discouraged Constitution-based challenges that focused on disparate impact. The combined import of these two decisions is that equal protection challenges to government policies with a gender discriminatory impact needed to prove the discrimination is intentional; Title 7-based challenges did not have that burden.

Moreover, in both 1977 *(Dothard)* and in April 1978 *(L.A. Water and Power v. Manhart,* declaring unlawful gender-based disparities in pension deductions), the Supreme Court decided solely on Title 7 grounds cases that had presented requests to review both Title 7 and equal protection challenges. Although it is an official judicial norm to dispose of cases by relying on statutory grounds and avoiding constitutional grounds whenever possible, the Court does not always stick closely to this rule. The fact that it did in these two prominent cases could have served as a signal to Court-attuned public-interest litigators that statutory claims for gender equity would have a better chance of success with these justices than constitutional claims would. And the litigators may have proceeded accordingly.

In order to test this hybrid hypothesis that Court signals shaped the litigation flow on this subject, which in turn shaped the judicial agenda, I interviewed attorneys who had been involved in the 1980s in organized litigation-strategizing for women's interest groups.[19] Attorneys from two of the three organizations consulted volunteered the information that the combination of the rules (concerning facially neutral practices with discriminatory impact) set forth in *Feeney* and in *Dothard* definitely pushed them toward litigating on statutory grounds. When I inquired about this possibility to the attorney from the third organization, she confirmed that it had been influential for her organization, too. Further, attorneys from the three organizations indicated that legislative cleanup was a big part of why they stopped bringing Supreme Court cases; by 1982 all the state laws of sizable impact that openly discriminated by sex had been either eliminated or upheld by the U.S. Supreme Court (with the exception of the male-only admissions policy of two state military colleges, Citadel and VMI, which were under Court challenge during the time of this research).

Whether the Court structures the litigation pattern by setting forth legal doctrine that indicates the kinds of claims that have a good chance of winning, or whether it controls that pattern by setting forth clear constitutional doctrine that causes laws to be eliminated so that they are no longer around to be litigated against, in either of these two situations the Court is structuring its own agenda. On the other hand, as the discussion of congressional-Court interaction highlighted, the Supreme Court often chooses to respond to congressional signals, and Congress not uncommonly alters statutes in order to control judicial interpretation of them. Although the pattern of cert requests naturally reflects the general political climate to a degree, it is also powerfully shaped by judicial as well as by congressional choices.

The data strongly indicated that approximately five years after the Court set forth clear constitutional doctrine in December 1976 *(Craig)* condemning all governmental gender discrimination that could not be proved "substantially related to an important governmental interest," litigation alleging such discrimination essentially stopped coming to the Supreme Court. This fact left a Supreme Court still sympathetic to gender equity with only statutory claims, for the most part, to adjudicate.

Interviews with the prominent litigating interest groups of the period revealed that this drying up of Constitution-based gender equity litigation was caused by a combination of two factors: the success of such litigation and consequent elimination of statutes that explicitly discriminated on the basis of sex, and judicial doctrine interpreting the language of Title 7 and of the constitutional equal protection clause, such that practices with a gender-disproportionate impact became much harder to challenge on constitutional grounds than on Title 7 grounds.

It would take further research to determine whether these findings on the federal judicial role in shaping gender policy over the past three decades have a wider applicability. This study suggests that the Burger Court and the pre-1994 Rehnquist Court exhibited a substantial degree of deference to Congress as a coequal branch of government; that Supreme Court decisions relatively quickly produced an impressive level of reform at the state legislative level; and that interest groups who use litigative lobbying strategies are closely attuned to pronouncements of judicial doctrine relevant to their goals and adjust their strategies accordingly. This study also confirmed that the five variables identified by other scholars as playing a role in altering the judicial agenda over time in fact had an impact on shaping the pattern of judicial policy innovation on women's rights in the past thirty years. Those variables are the flow of litigation, an interactive influence from the Congress, judicial preferences about policy outcomes or for particular legal interpretations, judicial beliefs about the proper judicial role, and judicially produced legal doctrine (both as shaper of litigation flow and as guide to judicial cert grants).

Notes

1. It is conceivable that the Court is at the point of a new period of innovation with the (summer 1993) accession of Justice Ruth Bader Ginsburg; for the decision in April 1994 in *J.E.B. v. T.B.*, which declared it unconstitutional to permit the gender-based use of peremptory strikes for jury composition, marked the first time in twelve years that the Supreme Court declared any gender discrimination unconstitutional. One should note, however, that the Court granted cert for that case during the 1992–1993 term, long before Justice Ginsburg was nominated. The Court followed the *JEB* decision with a second important constitution-based gender equity decision in 1996, *U.S. v. Virginia*. If my conclusions in this chapter are correct, these are best viewed as isolated incidents, not as the beginning of a major new period of innovation.

2. Greg Caldeira, in an examination of Supreme Court policy making on criminal procedure over a forty-year period, suggested that issues have a certain natural "life cycle" once the Supreme Court alters policy on them. After a while the policy becomes clear and stable, and political actors conform to it. At this point (barring other stimuli), the number of appeals brought would naturally decline. In proffering this suggestion, Caldeira was building on unpublished work by Thomas Likens (Caldeira 1981, 449, 466–68, nn. 2 and 44). Richard Pacelle (1990) has proposed a typology for the general pattern of Supreme Court policy making that seems to fit the specific abortion picture quite well. According to his scheme, from time to time a particular issue captures the attention of the Supreme Court on a repeated, annual basis; Pacelle suggests it should then be viewed as having its own doctrinal identity, and policy making on it will thenceforth go through four stages: (1) justices establish new policy; (2) they extend the policy to new and more complicated questions; (3) they confront the clashes between policy on this issue and policy on competing values (e.g., the clash between reproductive freedom and a desire by many taxpayers to refrain from subsidizing abortions); and (4) policy on the issue is then firmly enough established that the Court is free to turn to other matters. Though Pacelle's typology may not fit every topic perfectly, it certainly expresses

a plausible logic and does seem to resonate with the common observation that the Supreme Court devotes much more attention to some issues in some periods than in others. In a way, it expresses a kind of natural history of judicial policy-making phases; assuming Supreme Court legitimacy, it is only logical to expect that certain issues would eventually pass off the agenda, as state and federal legislators and policing agents adjusted their behavior to match what the Court explained to be the constitutional requirements on a given subject. (The politics of abortion has caused continuing litigation, but the Court stopped producing dramatic policy innovations after 1977 and may well start to refuse to hear these cases in the post-*Casey* era.)

3. These models, however, were developed to account not for chronologies of policy innovation but for patterns of judicial agenda setting. Space on the Supreme Court agenda continued to be occupied by abortion cases long after the Court ceased innovations on the subject. This fact is attributable to political factors external to the Court, specifically, the willingness of the solicitor general to bring cases at presidential behest and the general willingness by the Court to hear cases brought by the solicitor general of the United States (Salokar 1992).

4. For a more detailed account of the linkages between ERA politics and Supreme Court alterations of constitutional doctrine, see L. Goldstein (1987).

5. One should note that in this phase of constitutionalization of gender equity, the Supreme Court did not acquiesce in every feminist demand. Sometimes the Court ruled that there was an important enough governmental interest being served by the discrimination and they upheld it. Most salient of such interests has been the desire to compensate women for social discrimination they face. On that score, the Supreme Court, for example, upheld a couple of temporary social security adjustments that upped women's benefits as compared to like-earning men *(Califano v. Webster, Heckler v. Matthews)*. Another such interest has been the need to give Congress wide latitude in areas of foreign relations *(Fiallo v. Bell)* and national security *(Rostker v. Goldberg)*. (Thus the Supreme Court in this period permitted males-only draft registration, and implicitly the males-only combat rule.) Finally, the Court has acknowledged that there is an important governmental interest in taking into account actual physiological differences between the sexes. These have come into play both in the context of statutory rape laws, which the Court upheld, reminding us that girls can get pregnant; boys cannot *(Michael M. v. Sonoma County)*, and in the context of legal distinctions between unwed mothers and unwed fathers, which the Court generally seems to uphold as long as the unwed father is given a procedural option to put himself into the same legal category as the mother— that is, official parent, who then has the same rights as the mother *(Lehr v. Robertson, Quilloin v. Walcott, Caban v. Mohammed)*.

6. In the calendar year 1972, Congress adopted this antidiscrimination measure, formally sent the ERA to the states for ratification, and opened the national military academies to women. After 1972, Congress was not particularly active on the specific subject of gender equity; it adopted the Equal Credit Opportunity Act in 1975, but its other statutes that bear even indirectly on the subject (in the sense of expressing a congressional attitude toward interpreting its civil rights laws) were essentially congressional

rebuffs of narrow Supreme Court readings of Congress' earlier civil rights ordinances. A list of such statutes would include not only the instances described below but also the congressional alteration of section 2 of the Voting Rights Act (of 1965) in 1982, effectively overruling *Mobile v. Bolden,* and the congressional overruling of *Grove City v. Bell,* with the Civil Rights Restoration Act of 1988.

7. This conclusion is based on a qualitative, political analysis of the substantive policy impact of Court decisions in this decade. For a quantitative analysis that comes to the same conclusion, see George and Epstein (1991). The latter does not notice the shift from constitution-based decisions to statute-based ones.

8. For further details on these 1989 cases and their congressional aftermath, see L. Goldstein (1994, 227–31).

9. For details, see ibid., 256–57.

10. Richard Pacelle (1990; 1991; 1995) provides a detailed quantitative tracking of the Supreme Court's shift of attention from the broad category "economic issues" to the broad category "civil liberties."

11. See review of this literature in H. Perry (1991, 12–15 and chap. 5, especially 119). Several studies have confirmed that either of two "cues" in a request for certiorari will substantially increase the likelihood that cert will be granted: first, support for the request by the solicitor general of the United States—that is, by the executive branch of the federal government, or second, a conflict of opinion among the federal circuits on the legal question presented.

12. Specifically, he found that "purposive" (i.e., ideologically motivated) interest groups reacted to new judicial doctrine by increasing or decreasing the number of lawsuits they brought but that material-incentive groups, such as book publisher associations, litigated steadily whether doctrine made them optimistic or pessimistic.

13. For research purposes these two are, to some degree, inextricably intertwined. A justice may vote for gender equity because of a desire for the policy outcome or because it seems the most sensible way to read the equal protection clause. Either way, what the researcher sees is the vote. The justice will normally explain the vote as a response to honest legal interpretation, and some researchers choose not to believe that explanation.

14. Since presidents, with the Senate, appoint justices, these forces dubbed internal are themselves affected in the long run by politics external to the Court, but this impact is not easy to measure. Donald Songer (1979) did find such an impact with respect to grants of cert to economic policy cases for the presidencies of Franklin Roosevelt and Richard Nixon. However, twelve years of presidents actively committed to appointing justices who would reverse *Roe v. Wade,* presidents who appointed six new justices, failed to overturn the "essential holding" of that case. See *Planned Parenthood v. Casey* (1992).

15. Nonetheless, it is true that when the Supreme Court seemed to begin to turn away from aggressively progender-equity readings of civil rights statutes in 1989, Congress responded with an additional stimulus (see preceding discussion).

16. In the chart what counts as a term for cert requests ("claims presented") is approximately July 1 (the exact date being determined by the Court's adjournment for summer recess) to approximately June 30 of the following year. What counts as a term for accep-

tance of cases for decision ("claims accepted") is roughly October 1 to July 1, the period the Court is in session. For instance, the 1968 term for cert requests purposes began approximately July 1, 1968, but the 1968 term for cert-granted purposes began approximately October 1, 1968 (specifically, the first Monday of that October). The figures presented here differ from those in Provine (1980, 50); since we both used the same source for our count, I cannot explain the disparity.

17. They did decide one in the 1983 term but upheld the statute under challenge; see *Heckler v. Mathews,* for which cert had been granted in the 1982 term. The one cert request granted in the 1985 term involved a statute of limitations for requests for child support orders. The Court noted that since the case had been filed, the state in question had eliminated the law; and since the only issue left was retroactivity of the state's reform, the Court sent it back to the state for decision *(Paulussen v. Herion).* The one case granted review in the 1987 term involved an unwed father who had never lived with his child and who was challenging the state law that allowed unwed mothers but not unwed fathers to veto the adoption of an out-of-wedlock child. The Supreme Court did set the case for oral argument, but then after the case was argued, during the 1988 term, the Court dismissed the case for "want of a properly presented federal question" *(McNamara v. San Diego County,* docket 87-5840). The case accepted for decision in the 1992–1993 term is the one the Court decided on April 4, 1994, ending its twelve-year period of abstinence from such decisions (see *J.E.B. v. T.B.,* n.1).

18. Indeed, unless the facts reveal that the unwed fathers in question have lived with their children as a family in a relationship substantially identical to that of the children's mother, the Court treats these not as equal protection cases but as due process cases. Compare *Stanley v. Illinois* and *Caban v. Mohammed* (equal protection issue considered) with *Quilloin v. Walcott* and *Lehr v. Robertson* (equal protection issue as to fathers versus mothers not considered).

19. For a close look at this litigation campaign during the 1970s, see O'Connor (1980). O'Connor's work identified the relevant interest groups; the groups themselves supplied names of the attorneys involved in litigation-strategy decisions for the time period in question. Attorneys interviewed include Isabelle Katz Pinzler, in the 1980s director of the Women's Rights Project of the ACLU; Phyllis Segal and Sally Burns, two of the directors of the NOW Legal Defense and Education Fund during the 1980s; and Helen Norton of the Women's Legal Defense Fund. In addition to the turn toward statutory litigation, the NOW Legal Defense Fund people also indicated that their group turned during the 1980s to a conscious strategy of emphasizing congressional lobbying and to litigating at state courts on the basis of state ERAs, because some state supreme courts were interpreting those as having stronger gender equity requirements than prevailed at the national level. These litigating decisions were made not on the vague perception of some new "political climate" on the U.S. Supreme Court but on the basis of concrete doctrinal rulings from the Court and what those rulings foretold about the prospects for rulings in future cases.

Chapter 11

Queer New Institutionalism: Notes on the Naked Power Organ in Mainstream Constitutional Theory and Law

Susan Burgess

The considerable overlap between new institutionalism and queer theory has not yet been discussed by scholars of either theory. In this chapter, I discuss the common claims of queer theory and new institutionalism and suggest that a hybrid approach, which I refer to as queer new institutionalism, might offer a deeper understanding of the construction of meaning and authority in mainstream constitutional law and theory. I argue that queer new institutionalism holds great promise for understanding the structure and limitations of mainstream constitutional theory and law, particularly regarding its self-defined central problem, the lack of an objective or widely accepted standard of constitututional interpretation upon which judicial review might be grounded. Although space contraints prevent me from exploring the promise of queer new institutionalism fully or offering a full-blown alternative to the conceptual structures of mainstream constitutional theory, I do offer evidence that suggests that a fuller application or testing of queer new institutionalism would be quite desirable. This evidence comes from brief case studies of Herbert Wechsler's "Toward Neutral Principles of Constitutional Law" (1959) and *Griswold v. Connecticut* (1965). I begin by discussing the claims of queer theory in greater detail than those associated with new institutionalism, on the assumption that readers of this book will be less familiar with the claims and insights of the former. Queer theory and new institutionalism emerged in the academy at roughly the same time. The first level of scholarship in queer theory appeared in the mid-1980s and early 1990s when scholars such as Eve Sedgwick, Judith Butler, and Michael Warner laid out its main claims and methods.[1] A second level of queer scholarship emerged in the early to mid-1990s when several

199

scholars began applying queer theory to law, usually analyzing cases that directly address homosexuality, such as *Bowers v. Hardwick* (1986).[2] In this chapter I offer a third level of queer analysis that constructs a queer new institutionalism and suggest how it may be used to critique several concepts that structure mainstream constitutional theory and law. Although these concepts have little obvious relation to the legal regulation of homosexuality, I argue that queer new institutionalism can uncover the heterosexist constructions of sexuality and desire that are deeply embedded in mainstream conceptual structures. I then offer evidence from mainstream constitutional theory that suggests that the very visible surface conflict between advocates of judicial restraint and judicial activism acts as a facade masking a deep level of agreement that exists regarding the construction of sexuality, desire, marriage, and the family. I argue that the roots of this illusion may be found in the work of Herbert Wechsler (the father of modern judicial self-restraint, particularly in his seminal discussion of naked power organs and neutral principles). I also suggest the import of these findings for understanding leading cases in U.S. constitutional law, paying particular attention to *Griswold v. Connecticut.* Recognizing the space and scope limitations inherent here, I conclude by hoping that the provocations, challenges, and evidence presented will encourage a broader application of queer new institutionalism as well as a full-blown discussion of queer alternatives to mainstream constitutional theory and law in future scholarship.

Although queer theory and new institutionalism share a number of common claims and insights, queer theory contains several distinctive features to which I will attend first. I will next address the common features of queer theory and new institutionalism and construct a hybrid of the two, queer new institutionalism, which I will then employ in subsequent sections to analyze the dominant conceptual structures used in mainstream constitutional law and theory.

Queer Theory on the Construction of Meaning and Sexuality

Queer theorists argue that meaning in Western systems is typically constructed through a series of oppositional categories or binarisms (e.g., restrained/active; reason/desire; heterosexual/homosexual; male/female; black/white), in which each term is defined by distinguishing itself from the other term in the pair. Thus, the terms are mutually dependent for their meaning.

Although the terms in each binarism may appear natural (that is, before the law, as well as prepolitical or apolitical) and symmetrical due to their oppositional relation, queer theorists claim they are neither. Instead, queer theorists argue that the meaning of binaristic terms is a product, rather than a precursor, of legal, political, and social contestation. Meaning is produced within specific cultural contexts and entails specific political choices. These cultural contexts tend to reproduce themselves and their related conceptual systems, such that over time they appear to be given rather than chosen—prepolitical, natural, and universal—instead of being seen as products of political choices made within particular historical and cultural contexts.

Moreover, queer theorists claim that binaristic terms are asymmetrical; as long as the legitimacy of the second or minor term in each binarism is questioned or suspect, the first or major term gains a default legitimacy, remaining largely unquestioned. Thus, the major term in each binarism is valorized and centralized, and the minor term is demonized and marginalized. The surface conflict between the oppositional terms in each binarism conceals both the mutual dependence between the terms as well as the underlying mutual agreement between disputants regarding the appropriate parameters of debate. The surface opposition also obscures the rhetorical and material leverage of the major term and those who associate themselves with it. Thus, Halley (1993, 98) concludes that "definitional incoherence is the very mechanism of material dominance."

Queer theory distinguishes itself from other forms of postmodernism and poststructuralism by contending that major conceptual systems and their binarisms—even those that seemingly have nothing to do with sexuality—will necessarily be marked by the "modern crisis of homo/heterosexual definition."[3] Various queer theorists have argued that it would be difficult, if not impossible, to understand the meaning and function of major binarisms in Western culture without also analyzing how those concepts are inflected with sexuality. Sedgwick (1990, 1), for example, argues that "virtually any aspect of modern Western culture must be, not merely incomplete, but damaged in its central substance to the degree that it does not incorporate a critical analysis of modern homo/heterosexual definition." Warner (1993, xiii) argues that "the logic of the sexual order is deeply embedded by now in an indescribably wide range of social institutions, and is embedded in most standard accounts of the world." Sedgwick (1985, 9–10) adds that analyzing sexuality may require deconstruction of the obvious and visible, as well as the less obvious and more concealed constituents of established discourses.

Queer theorists also hold that since the major term of the binarism is defined by its relation to the minor term, the logic of the binarism often leads those who wish to establish their association with the major term more clearly to "out" putative "others"; that is, they hope to distinguish themselves from others identified with the minor term. Although outers seek to distinguish themselves from outees and thus establish association with the positive, major term, the irony is that the more an outer attempts to associate others with the minor term, the more likely he is to reveal his own dependence on and connection to the minor term and those associated with it. Thus, the dependence of the major and minor terms inevitably leads outers to visibly associate with the minor term, even as they attempt (often quite desperately) to distinguish themselves ever more clearly from the latter.[4] In due course, the specific meaning of the terms becomes rather incoherent or fuzzy, despite (or perhaps, ironically, due to) the outer's desire to separate and distinguish the meaning of the major and minor terms.

Queer Theory and New Institutionalism

Both queer theory and new institutionalism pay careful attention to how knowledge and practice are constructed and granted authoritative status within specific political and cultural systems.[5] Both tend to focus analysis on widely shared cultural assumptions rather than on surface variation of political preferences; both argue that widely accepted and frequently unexamined conceptual systems and cultural institutions may restrict the field of political choice. New institutionalists have argued, and I think queer theorists would agree, that contemporary political scientists' focus on variance, conflict, and individual preferences obscures the effects or even the existence of the shared conceptual systems and cultural institutions that structure more visible, surface-level political conflict. Both maintain that the construction and reproduction of these conceptual systems and cultural institutions are intensely political, arguing that scholars who ignore the deeper agreement on the parameters of the debate in which surface conflict occurs are themselves acting politically, by precluding a broader discussion of alternative conceptual systems and cultural institutions. In the words of March and Olsen (1984, 741), the sort of politics that "creates and confirms interpretations of life" matters deeply, largely dictating the shape of the debate about public policy. As Rogers Smith has argued: "Many economic currents and even political actors' own purposeful commitments are affected by relatively enduring legacies of past political choices" (1988, 96). As a consequence, independent variables should be located from among "relatively enduring structures of human conduct" that shape "the existing array of resources, rules, and values, instead of simply taking that array as given" (98).

Thus, queer theory and new institutionalism have much in common. However, new institutional scholars have largely failed to discuss the shared assumptions about sexuality that underlie their work and the import of such assumptions for understanding its focus: the construction of political authority and meaning. Yet it does not seem that new institutionalism and queer theory are necessarily antagonistic in this respect; rather, these bridges have not yet been built by leading new institutionalists or queer theorists. I therefore address this gap and describe the parameters of a queer new institutionalism.

Queer New Institutionalism and the Heterosexual Family

For a rough sketch of an application of a hybrid of queer theory and new institutionalism, let's consider the family. The family is a leading, if not the primary, social institution that transmits dominant concepts generally as well as values regarding sexuality and desire more specifically. Queer new institutionalism might address (heterosexual) marriage and the (patriarchal) family as relatively enduring social institutions, inflected with (often unnoticed or at least undiscussed hetero)sexuality, which emerged in their present form in historical and cultural contexts that are coincident with the rise of capitalism and the modern nation-state. As such, the adoption and maintenance of these institutions in their present forms are the product of significant political choices regarding the organization of sexuality and the family, even though the latter choices are left unanalyzed or are represented in a manner that suggests they are prepolitical in foundation and apolitical in the present. Queer new institutionalism allows us to examine the binary construction of sexuality and desire that is central to the formation and maintenance of heterosexual marriage and the patriarchal family and to challenge their apparent givenness, naturalness, and universality. In the modern nation-state, the heteropatriarchal family is represented as the private, prepolitical, noncontractual seat of desire and emotion, as distinguished from the public, political, and contractual realm of reason and sober thought. As Peterson and Parisi argue:

Heterosexism is "naturalized" by reifying "the family" . . . as "prepolitical"—as "sentiment based" and non-contractual. Liberal commitments are crucial to this depoliticization of the family insofar as they naturalize a categorical distinction between public and private spheres that relegates sex/affective relations to the latter. Human rights discourse and practice reproduce this naturalization of heterosexism and "the family" (including gender inequalities within the family) by upholding the distinction between public/state and private/family spheres and focusing exclusively on states as both protectors and violators of individual rights.[6]

Within the family, heterosexuality is constructed as benign, or asexual, or both, because of its higher purpose, procreation (rather than its lower, erotic purposes). This sets up women (within the family) "as virgins and mothers while men are cast as either phallic, erect, and strong (sons) or all brains (fathers)."[7] Homosexuals are either invisible within this arrangement, or, along with racial others and (sexual) women living outside the family, are characterized as threats to the established order and thus marginalized.

Queer New Institutionalism and the "Central Problem" of Mainstream Constitutional Theory

I identify the central binarism[8] of mainstream constitutional theory as judicial restraint/judicial activism, suggesting that judicial restraint gains a default legitimacy from its binaristic relationship to judicial activism. Although mainstream constitutional theorists have long admitted that an impasse exists between advocates of judicial restraint and judicial activism, their resistance to deeper analysis of the central problem has prevented them from fully considering leading theoretical alternatives, such as critical race theory and feminist legal theory, that might move them beyond the impasse. I also discuss the way in which the central concepts of mainstream constitutional theory are inflected with sexuality, a topic that remains largely undiscussed, even in the alternative literatures.

Judicial restraint/judicial activism is the central binarism that structures meaning in mainstream constitutional theory in the post–World War II period. The conflict between advocates of judicial restraint[9] and judicial activism[10] is widely accepted as the natural or given starting point of contemporary constitutional theorizing. Despite intense opposition between advocates of judicial restraint and judicial activism, constitutional theorists on both sides largely agree on the terms of the debate, or what has come to be known as the "central problem": that judicial review as practiced by electorally unaccountable judges is difficult, if not impossible, to reconcile with liberal democracy because there is no widely accepted standard or objective constitutional grounding upon which judges might base their decisions. In the oft-cited words of John Hart Ely (1980, 4), some version of which is referred to either directly or indirectly in most major modern constitutional decisions of the U.S. Supreme Court, "The central function is at the same time the central problem of judicial review: a body that is not elected or otherwise politically responsible in any significant way is telling the people's elected representatives that they cannot govern as they'd like."

Given the consensus on the central problem, it would seem that both restraintist and activist forms of judicial review would be difficult, if not impossible, to justify on liberal grounds. Yet the central problem creates a much greater burden for proponents of judicial activism. Its advocates must offer an objective or at least a widely acceptable grounding to make a broader practice of judicial review responsible or accountable; without this grounding, activist judicial review appears irresponsible on the grounds that it is antidemocratic as well as subjective and partisan. Advocates of judicial restraint are able to sidestep this dilemma at least somewhat, by highlighting judicial restraint's characteristic deference to democratic authority. However, advocates of judicial activism point out that restrained courts typically offer little protection from legislative abridgments of individual rights. Since neither side is willing to scrap judicial review altogether, judicial restraint appears to be the less risky and more responsible option—at least until an objective grounding can be found for a more active use of judicial review. This search has continued in vain and became particularly pronounced in the post–World War II era.[11] Throughout, judicial restraint has gained a default legitimacy from its binaristic relation to its more problematic alternative, judicial activism.

Despite all the attention given to the central problem by mainstream constitutional scholars, little, if any, attention has been paid to mainstream scholars' roles in constructing "the problem" and its central binarism, judicial restraint/judicial activism. Mainstream scholars focus on the relative merits of judicial restraint and judicial activism rather than on scholarly construction of these mutually dependent terms, thus leaving the impression that the terms existed before law and apart from political and social contestation. Moreover, the continuing conflict between advocates of judicial restraint and judicial activism obscures the fact that they share a desire to limit the terms of these debates to those conventionally associated with liberal democracy. Nearly a generation ago, Paul Brest (1981, 1105) argued that the central problem was "not susceptible to resolution within its own terms" and would not be resolved "until despair or hope impels us to explore alternatives to the [liberal democratic] world we currently inhabit." Despite Brest's injunction, the central problem still serves as the focal point of mainstream constitutional theory. Some scholars continue to advance "new" justifications for judicial activism; others continue to insist that such efforts fail to make the grade on both democratic and objective grounds, thus concluding that judicial restraint remains the only viable option.

The central problem and its central binarism shield mainstream conceptual theory from the sort of alternative for which Brest appeared to be hoping (or despairing of). Although there has been some call from within the mainstream to explore constitutional interpretation through the lens of performance,[12] literature,[13] or intellectual projection,[14] none of these scholars has offered an alternative conceptual framework or style of presentation that fully challenges the apparent givenness of the central problem and its central binarism, judicial restraint/judicial activism. Each seems to take the parameters of mainstream constitutional theory for granted and attempts to see how far its strictures can be expanded. As such, at its best, this work often appears as eccentric play, and at its worst, as unself-conscious support of status quo constitutional theory and its impasse.

Alternative theory that is more fully critical of the limits of mainstream constitutional theory can be found in critical legal studies,[15] critical race theory,[16] and feminist legal theory.[17] The theories advanced by these scholars have powerfully challenged mainstream constitutional theorists' purportedly neutral treatment of class, race, and gender and revealed various ways that mainstream claims of neutrality serve to uphold white, upper-class, male dominance in legal theory and political practice.

To the extent that mainstream scholars have discussed alternative work, they have often been quite critical, on the grounds that it is subjective, political, and partial and thus by (mainstream) definition, unauthoritative. Of course, alternative theorists are aware of the political nature of their work; they challenge the notion that constitutional theorizing takes place outside of, or before, legal and political conflict. Rather than trying to separate law from politics, they argue that apparent neutrality and objectivity typically mask the rhetorical and material dominance of the mainstream, which is based on biased representations of race, gender, and class. Nevertheless, central conceptual constructions of mainstream constitutional theory remain largely undiscussed even in the alternative literature. Further, both alternative and mainstream legal literatures fail to discuss the role that sexuality plays in constructing meaning in contemporary constitutional theory.

Sexuality and Mainstream Constitutional Theory

No commentators, mainstream or alternative, seem to have noticed, let alone addressed, seemingly obvious sexualized language in mainstream constitutional theory and its relation to the construction of categories such as judicial restraint and judicial activism. This silence is not due to a lack of material to analyze. For example, in what is undoubtedly one of the most cited and long-lasting passages in mainstream constitutional thought, Herbert Wechsler (1959, 12, 19) has characterized judicially active courts as "naked power organs." Despite the fact that this phrase appears in Wechsler's "Toward Neutral Principles of Law" only twice, contemporary defenders of judicial activism and advocates of judicial restraint have extended and reproduced his apparently catchy formulation. Thus, Cass Sunstein (1990) asserts that active courts force their "naked preferences" on to an unsuspecting public; and perhaps the most visible contemporary advocate of judicial restraint and neutral principles, Robert Bork, has chosen sexualized titles for both his books, *The Tempting of America: The Political Seduction of the Law* (1990), and *Slouching Towards Gomorrah: Modern Liberalism and American Decline* (1996). Moreover, in the wake of his failed confirmation hearings the phrase "he got Borked" is now heard with some frequency in scholarly and political commentary. This sexualized language has also been racialized by proponents of judicial restraint, as in Carl Cohen's book, *Naked Racial Preference: The Case Against Affirmative Action* (1995). Defenders of judicial activism have also used sexualized language while criticizing judicial restraint. Thus, Sanford Levinson (1992, 129) has said that adherence to judicial restraint and the written Constitution is characterized by a "very high confidence in the ability of language both to 'harden' and to control," and Richard Rorty has added that judicial restraint may amount to "beat[ing] the text into a shape which will serve his [i.e., the interpreter's] purpose."[18] As yet, no one has publicly discussed or deconstructed the openly sexualized terminology that seems as unselfconsciously accepted in mainstream constitutional theory as the judicial restraint/judicial activism binarism that it reproduces. Therefore, I offer a

closer exploration of sexuality in constitutional theory by returning to its
source—the naked power organ.

Herbert Wechsler: The Neutral Principle/ Naked Power Organ Binarism

In deconstructing Wechsler's "Toward Neutral Principles of Constitutional
Law," I argue that he creates a binarism between neutral principles/naked
power organs that serves as a basis for characterizing *Brown v. Board of Education* (1954) as a prototypical example of the Court acting as a naked power
organ. I also suggest that this neutral principle/naked power organ binarism
is inflected with (undiscussed hetero)sexuality and demonstrates the import
of the reason/desire binarism for Wechsler's understanding of judicial
restraint/judicial activism.

I focus here on Wechsler not only because he appears to have presented
the naked power organ most actively, but also because his seminal article,
"Toward Neutral Principles of Constitutional Law," was instrumental in setting the terms of the debate in modern constitutional theory for both re-
straintists and activists. My analysis of Wechsler exemplifies a queer new
institutionalist approach that reveals and challenges often unexamined
assumptions that underlie much of the debate in mainstream constitutional
theory. Supportive and critical scholarly discussions of the leading examples
of judicial activism in the modern era, *Brown* and *Roe v. Wade* (1973), follow the parameters that Wechsler set in "Neutral Principles" by explicitly
adopting naked power organ language or by embracing the central binarisms that structure his article, such as reason/desire and judicial restraint/
judicial activism. Although space constraints prevent making the latter argument here fully, I do identify other theorists who appear to adopt Wechsler's
conceptual framework. It is also worth noting that, regardless of their position in the judicial restraint/judicial activism debate, constitutional theorists
of various ideological stripes regard Wechsler as one of the most prominent
constitutional theorists of the modern era, if not the father of modern constitutional jurisprudence.[19]

Perhaps Wechsler's most enduring contribution to mainstream constitutional theory is his juxtaposition of reason and neutral principles on the
one hand and desire and naked power organs on the other. According to
Wechsler, justices (and scholars?) act as naked power organs when they evaluate cases on the basis of personal desire rather than on the basis of neutral

principles, which are said to be dictated by reason. Wechsler (1959, 15) argues that courts may establish their neutrality by issuing decisions that "transcend . . . the immediate result" and that can be applied to other cases, "preferably those involving an opposing interest." Similarly, scholars may establish neutrality by opposing a decision that furthers their personal desires or political preferences, thus demonstrating the ability to subordinate personal desire to reason and politics to law. Wechsler himself attempts to do so when he states that although he personally favors the outcome in *Brown,* he nevertheless opposes the decision on constitutional grounds because it lacks legitimate legal reasoning.

Wechsler represents himself as an older man who respects limitations, cares about reason, and is disdainful of personal desire or willfulness in judicial decision making, thus casting himself in the role of father and distinguishing himself from sons or younger men who will not accept a distinction between reason and desire and who therefore will be unable to subordinate their desire to reason, or political preferences to legal principle. By the time Wechsler makes his first direct reference to the naked power organ, the split between reason and desire appears complete: "The man who simply lets his judgment turn on the immediate result [i.e., on his desire] may not, however, realize that his position implies that the courts are free to function as a naked power organ" (12). Thus, the naked power organ, a (not very) euphemistic reference to the penis, emerges as the symbol of unmanageable personal desire and unlimited political preference, apparently embodied in an unwise younger man, a son.

Despite his disdain for judicial activism,[20] acting as a power organ (as opposed to a *naked* power organ) does not necessarily seem to be problematic for Wechsler; exercising power is both appropriate and necessary when power is clothed in neutral principles. Thus, in his second direct reference to the naked power organ, Wechsler juxtaposes the exercise of power clothed in law, on the one hand, with the use of naked and apparently political power on the other: "The courts have both the title and the duty when a case is properly before them to review the actions of the other branches in the light of constitutional provisions, even though the action involves value choices, as invariably action does. In doing so, however, they are bound to function otherwise than as a *naked* power organ; they participate as courts of law" (19). Thus, nakedness or exposure of the power organ, not the power organ itself, seems to be at the root of Wechsler's concern. To exercise power legitimately, judges (and scholars) must clothe their power organs with neutral principles.

Wechsler's theory contains a number of binarisms that are inflected with (undiscussed) sexuality. In his view, law does not desire, law reasons; politics is grounded in desire rather than reason. Although he concedes that interpretation involves discretion and thus power, power must not be exercised in an exposed fashion, lest it be associated with desire and politics. Neutral principles of law serve to conceal the politics of desire underlying law's seeming neutrality. Although desire, of course, need not necessarily refer to sexual desire, Wechsler's use of naked power organ language leaves little room for doubt in this case; the power organ represents the penis, traditionally understood as the embodiment of male (hetero)sexuality and reproductive power. It is, along with neutral principles, central to Wechsler's analysis. The clothing of neutral principles allows Wechsler to associate the power organ with valorized, major terms in the various binarisms he employs, namely, reason, law, and judicial restraint (and presumably heterosexuality); without the clothing of neutral principles, the naked power organ is exposed and associated with the minor, marginalized terms such as desire, politics, and judicial activism (and perhaps homosexuality).

Moreover, Wechsler has already begun to break through the limitations and boundaries that his binarisms are meant to create. Although he seems to desire the containment, if not the eradication, of desire and politics in constitutional law and theory, neutral principles seem unable to accomplish this feat. Indeed, neutral principles function to conceal, rather than to eradicate, desire and politics, thus creating a mere facade of reason and objectivity. To further understand what lies beneath this facade, and what the naked power organ represents, it is necessary to examine Wechsler's analysis of cases that address racial discrimination, particularly *Brown*.

Wechsler on *Brown*

Wechsler begins his discussion of *Brown* by arguing that racial segregation may have unexpected benefits, such as fostering security and reducing hostility, just as, in his view, the cotton gin had the unexpected effect of increasing, rather than decreasing, the need for slave labor; and "Japanese relocation" [*sic*] provided the unexpected effect of "breaking down forever the ghettos in which [Japanese Americans] had previously lived" (27). In what seems to be another attempt to establish his neutrality, Wechsler notes that despite his personal feelings that "Japanese relocation" was an abomination, as a government lawyer he defended the policy in Court. He adds that because "I still believe that decisions . . . dealing with the primary [*sic*], covenants [*sic*], and schools [*sic*] have the best chance of making an endur- ing contribution to the quality of our society of any that I know in recent years. . . , I ask how far they rest on neutral principles and are entitled to approval in the only terms that I acknowledge to be relevant to a decision of the courts" (27). Wechsler then analyzes various cases that invalidated (white) primaries and (race-restrictive) covenants and (racial segregation of blacks in public) schools, each time stating that although he supports the result, he finds that the Court failed to ground these cases in neutral principles. Concluding with a standard device of judicial restraint, defer- ence to the legislatures, he states: "I prefer to see the issues faced through legislation, where there is room for drawing lines that courts are not equipped to draw" (31).

In Wechsler's view, *Brown* is not constitutionally grounded and does not "really turn upon the facts" (33). He asserts that because *Brown* focuses on equality rather than on the associational freedom that he favors, it is neces- sarily based on subjective, and thus inappropriate, factors, such as percep- tions of harm to black children. He argues that discriminatory motivation cannot be properly inferred when "those who are affected by it" are those who will determine whether harm exists (33). For Wechsler, blacks' judg- ments of harm are necessarily laden with partiality and hence illegitimacy. Citing *Plessy*'s (infamous) assertion (1896) that segregation "stamps the col- ored race with a badge of inferiority" only if "they" choose "to put that con- struction upon it," Wechsler links subjectivity, race, gender, and sexuality in a manner anticipated by several queer theorists by posing certain questions, which for him are rhetorical: "Does enforced separation of the sexes dis- criminate against females merely because it may be the females who resent it and it is imposed by judgments predominantly male? Is a prohibition of miscegenation a discrimination against the colored member of the couple who would like to marry?" (33). Wechsler's desire to avoid partiality appears to make white, presumptively heterosexual men, such as himself, devoid of partial interests and personal desire in the outcome of such judgments and thus neutrally positioned to decide cases dealing with race, gender, and sex- uality on the basis of law and neutral principles (thus seemingly avoiding association with politics and the naked power organ). His rhetorical ques- tions seem to indicate that this will happen precisely at those moments when there is most at stake in terms of the politics and law of race, gender, and sexuality and most particularly where these categories intersect, as is the case with miscegenation policy.[21] In any case, following this logic, Wechsler offers his version of how *Brown* ought to have been decided.

According to Wechsler, the central constititutional question of *Brown* ought to have been freedom of association rather than equality. Asserting that claims of associational freedom create conflict between "those individuals who wish [desegregation] or imposing it on those who would avoid it," he states that he cannot find a neutral principle upon which to justify *Brown*. Thus, he concludes that desegregating public education would "force an association upon those for whom it is unpleasant or repugnant" (34). In Wechsler's view, *Brown* lacks a neutral, constitutional grounding because it unfairly favors the rights and liberties of blacks at the expense of the associational freedoms of whites.

Wechsler's interpretation ignores and deflects attention away from the historical context of race relations, particularly the unequal power positions occupied by whites and blacks.[22] Moreover, his interpretation attempts to disassociate white men (including himself) from desire, subjectivity, and political preference by locating these characteristics in others, such as blacks and women (and homosexuals).

Perhaps the most striking aspect of Wechsler's attempt to deflect attention away from the unequal distribution of power based on race occurs earlier in his essay. There, Wechsler seems to begin to acknowledge a power differential based on race while recounting a story about Charles Houston, a black lawyer who was forced to eat at a segregated lunch counter in Washington, D.C., while arguing a case to which Wechsler was also assigned. Yet Wechsler immediately draws back from fully acknowledging the extent of white power, and at the same time reveals his own subjectivity, by asserting that southern whites also "pay heavily" for segregation, suffering guilt and denial of the benefits that integration might offer. Thus, he concludes that Houston "did not suffer more than I" (34) when racist law and practice forced them to lunch apart, suggesting that Wechsler desires integration or at least greater association with blacks.

Wechsler's confession of suffering outs his own desire and political partiality; his contention that he was harmed by segregation equally as much as Houston and thus desires integration places Wechsler, on his own terms, in a rather partial position relative to the outcome of the case, at the very moment that he earlier had insisted that neutrality is most necessary—during the assessment of harm. Despite his best efforts, Wechsler fails to distance himself completely from the minor, demonized terms of the binarisms he creates, such as desire, politics, and judicial activism. Much as he would like to ascribe naked power to others, such as blacks and women (and homosexuals), without the clothing of neutrality and neutral principles, his own white heteropatriarchal power organ, along with its desires and preferences, becomes exposed. As suggested by queer theorists, the slippage between theoretical terms in any binarism inevitably emerges when those terms are applied in practice. Their argument, and mine, is not that Wechsler's (unmet) goal of closeting his desire is reachable or even desirable but that his goal is ill-conceived and unattainable.

In sum, Wechsler's juxtaposition of neutral principles and naked power organs is consistent with a queer new institutionalist understanding of how meaning and authority are typically constructed in our cultural system. Wechsler seeks to establish his own neutrality by distancing himself from *Brown* and by associating it and judicial activism with naked power, partiality, and politics. These moves allow the material and rhetorical dominance of the white heteropatriarchal perspective to remain largely undisturbed in his theory. Wechsler's work fosters definitional conflict and incoherence through the creation of the neutral principle/naked power organ binarism, the terms of which are mutually dependent; employs binarisms such as reason/desire and neutral principles/naked power organ that are deeply inflected with sexuality; allows the sexuality underlying his central binarisms to remain undiscussed; valorizes the major terms in each binarism by distinguishing them from demonized minor terms; uses definitional struggle and incoherence to deflect attention away from power relations to maintain or foster the material and rhetorical advantage of the dominant group; projects his repressed desire onto racialized and gendered others, thereby outing his own association with minor terms even as he attempts to out others.

Much as mainstream constitutional theory's persistent focus on "the central problem" and its central binarism (judicial restraint/judicial activism) shields mainstream scholars from critical race theory, feminist jurisprudence, and critical legal theory, Wechsler's neutral principle/naked power organ binarism deflects attention away from, and reproduces, the power inequities based on race and gender (and sexuality) that are embedded in mainstream constitutional theory and American politics. Wechsler's neutral principle/naked power organ binarism continues to influence the shape of mainstream constitutional theory's central debate about judicial restraint/judicial activism and the proper extent of judicial review. Scholars on both sides of the debate continue to attempt to delegitimize opponents' positions by characterizing them as exercises of shockingly naked power. For example, John Hart Ely made similar claims regarding neutrality and restraint to the next generation of constitutional scholars; and, like Wechsler, he did so in the context of questioning the legitimacy of his cohort's leading example of judicial activism, *Roe v. Wade*. Like Wechsler with *Brown,* Ely (1973, 920) claims to support the outcome of *Roe,* yet he cannot locate a principled, constitutional grounding for it. Cass Sunstein, who has discussed "naked preferences" at length,[23] recently offered an interesting variation on this theme by stating that although he supports homosexual rights and liberties and thinks there is a solid constitutional grounding for them, the Court should not move more quickly than the majority wishes on this issue, for fear of creating a powerful backlash.[24] Thus, the work of Ely and Sunstein suggests that Wechsler successfully transmitted his preferred conceptual positions to those scholars who came after him.

Queer new institutionalism posits that systems of meaning grounded in binaristic thinking, such as those found in mainstream constitutional theory, inevitably lead to conceptual incoherence and intellectual impasse, which in turn tend to reinforce the political status quo. However, it also maintains that the deconstruction of these conceptual structures will create opportunities for change by dismantling apparent impasses. Thus far I have offered two applications of queer new institutionalism, deconstructing contemporary constitutional theory's central problem and Herbert Wechsler's theory of neutral principles and naked power organs, as well as suggesting a linkage between the two. Of course, the conceptual structures of mainstream constitutional theory and constitutional adjudication in the United States overlap significantly. It is time, then, to discuss the implications of queer new institutionalism for better understanding U.S. constitutional law by briefly analyzing *Griswold v. Connecticut,*[25] a case that, at first glance, appears to address homosexuality only incidentally.

Implications of Queer New Institutionalism for Understanding Constitutional Adjudication

Much has been written about the institutionalization of heterosexist constructions of sexuality and desire that can be found in cases that deal directly with legal restrictions on homosexuality such as *Bowers v. Hardwick.*[26] The institutionalization of heterosexist constructions of sexuality and desire can also be found in cases that do not deal directly with the legal regulation of homosexuality, such as *Griswold*. *Griswold* embraces the central binarism of mainstream constitutional theory, judicial restraint/judicial activism, as well as the default legitimacy of judicial restraint. Thus, Justice Douglas's opinion begins by denying any association with *Lochner v. New York* (1905), the prototype of judicial activism gone awry for most liberal and conservative mainstream constitutional theorists, and adds that the Court does "not sit as a super-legislature to determine the wisdom, need, and propriety of laws that touch economic problems, business affairs, or social conditions."[27] Moreover, the discussion of restraint and activism serves as the focal point of the conflict between majority and dissenting justices, drawing attention away from the politics of support for the heteropatriarchal family unit that underlies every opinion in *Griswold*.

In each opinion in *Griswold*, the heterosexual, patriarchal family is represented as natural rather than historically situated, as prepolitically given rather than a result of political choice, as noncontractual or noneconomic rather than contractual and economically based, and as private rather than public. Justice Douglas asserts:

> We deal with a right of privacy older than the Bill of Rights—older than our political parties, older than our school system. Marriage is a coming together for better or for worse, hopefully enduring, and intimate to the degree of being sacred. It is an association that promotes a way of life, not causes; a harmony in living, not political faiths; a bilateral loyalty, not commercial or social projects. Yet it is an association for as noble a purpose as any involved in our prior decisions.[28]

Justice Goldberg is even more explicit, nearly intimating that he cannot imagine the Constitution without marriage.[29] Citing Justice Harlan in *Poe v. Ullman* (1961) he asserts that "the intimacy of husband and wife is necessarily an essential and accepted feature of the institution of marriage, an institution which the State not only must allow, but which always and in every age it has fostered and protected."[30]

Further, Douglas explicitly valorizes (heterosexual) marriage throughout his opinion, raising it to the level of sacred on several occasions.[31] This level of valorization and naturalization of heterosexual marriage is met with demonization and politicization of its binary opposite. Thus, Goldberg attempts to legitimize the zone of privacy for the heterosexual family by juxtaposing it against deviant relationships such as adultery, fornication, and homosexuality, which the state can restrict. Goldberg also conflates the concepts of marriage, home, family, and privacy, using heterosexuality to tie them together, stating that "the home derives its preeminence as the seat of family life. And the integrity of that life is something so fundamental that it has been found to draw to its protection the principles of more than one explicitly granted Constitutional right. . . . Of this whole 'private realm of family life' it is difficult to imagine what is more private or more intimate than a husband and wife's marital relations."[32]

Little attention has been paid to the importance of *Griswold* for the ruling in *Hardwick,* except that liberals generally characterize the latter as inconsistent with the ruling in *Griswold,* and conservatives inconsistently applaud the Court's decision in both cases, overlooking the obvious activism of *Griswold.* Instead of simply suggesting that the rather surface political preferences of these liberal and conservative constitutional theorists drive their analyses of the Court, I maintain that *Griswold* and *Hardwick* are quite consistent, both deeply grounded in the heterosexism that undergirds the dominant conceptual structures of mainstream constitutional theory and law, including judicial restraint/activism, reason/desire, and hetero/homosexuality. Rather than turning to alternative constitutional clauses (such as the equal protection clause) for deliverance,[33] I propose that liberals ought to better understand the heteropatriarchal roots of the cases they have long applauded, such as *Griswold,* before they devise alternative legal strategies. I also suggest that conservatives ought to better understand that their constitutional theories simply do not lead to support of activist cases like *Griswold* precisely because it is ultimately impossible for them to closet their political preferences and desires successfully, despite their best efforts to do so.

Queer new institutionalism leads beyond the facade of judicial restraint/judicial activism, opening up conservative (and liberal) closets along the way and indicating different strategic paths to well-meaning liberals (and conservatives)—even where, or perhaps especially where, legal restriction of homosexuals is not immediately and obviously at stake.

Acknowledgments

Thanks to Cornell Clayton, Howard Gillman, Harry Hirsch, Kate Leeman, Eleanor Miller, Spike Peterson, Shane Phelen, and Sylvia Schafer for their thoughtful and helpful comments on various drafts of this chapter. Earlier versions were presented at the American Political Science Association Meeting in San Francisco in March 1996 and the Western Political Science Association Meeting in Tucson in March 1997.

Notes

1. The section relies primarily on the discussion of queer theory in Butler (1990), Duggan (1992), Phalen (1993), Phelan (1994), Sedgwick (1985, 1990, and 1993), and Warner (1993).

2. See, e.g., Bower (1994, 1009); Duggan and Hunter (1995), Halley (1989, 915, and 1993, 82), Stychin (1995), and Thomas (1993, 33).

3. Sedgwick (1990, 11).

4. Sedgwick, for example, notes that it is "entirely within the experience of gay people to find that a homophobic figure in power has, if anything, a disproportionate likelihood of being gay and closeted" (1990, 242). See also P. Phalen (1993, 6–11).

5. This section draws primarily on the historical and interpretive strand of new institutionalism, as discussed in Burgess (1993, 445), Koebel (1995, 231), March and Olsen (1984, 735), Robertson (1993, 1), M. Shapiro (1989, 89), and R. Smith (1988, 93).

6. Peterson and Parisi (1997, 3). See also Peterson (1997, 185).

7. Nast (forthcoming).

8. Of course there are many other binarisms at work in mainstream constitutional theory, e.g., democratic authority/individual rights, law/politics, reason/desire. Although I discuss these and other binarisms in greater detail in the section on Herbert Wechsler, an even fuller investigation, I believe, would reveal that each of these binarisms in mainstream constitutional theory functions in a manner consistent with the claims of queer theory. I focus on judicial restraint/judicial activism here because, of the many binarisms that structure meaning in mainstream constitutional theory, it is the most extensively discussed.

9. See, e.g., Bork (1990 and 1996), Morgan (1984), and Nagel (1989 and 1994).

10. See, e.g., Barber (1984 and 1993), Dworkin (1978 and 1986), Perry (1982 and 1994), Richards (1986), Tribe (1987), and Tribe and Dorf (1991).

11. This brings to mind Mark Tushnet's insight that "despite the existence of competing grand [constitutional] theories, each one is in its essentials a revived and purified version of an earlier grand theory that invites comment on its timing" (Tushnet 1988, 1).

12. See, e.g., Carter (1985 and 1991).

13. See, e.g., Levinson (1992, 129), and White (1990 and 1984).

14. See, e.g, Harris (1993).

15. See, e.g, Karst (1993), Tushnet (1988), and Unger (1986).

16. See, e.g, Bell (1992 and 1987), Delgado (1995), and Williams (1991).

17. See, e.g., Becker, Bowman, and Torrey (1994), Fineman (1995), Frug (1992), and West (1994).

18. Richard Rorty, as cited in Levinson, 133.

19. For example, Ronald Kahn (1994) claims that Wechsler's jurisprudence "was the start of the search that continues today for a more principled theory of constitutional law" (89). David Richards (1986) characterizes Wechsler as one of five leading theorists of this century (chapter 1). John Hart Ely (1980, 54) and Leslie Goldstein (1991, 96) among others, characterize Wechsler's "neutral principles" as "widely heralded" and "influen-

tial." Cass Sunstein claims that Wechsler's article represents "the most famous use of the term *neutrality* in all of constitutional scholarship" (1993, 76). Many contemporary constitutional theorists continue to follow Wechsler's theory of neutral principles; according to Harry Wellington, Robert Bork is the most prominent torchbearer of Wechsler's theory (Wellington 1990, 43).

20. Actually, Wechsler characterizes both judicial activism and judicial restraint as definitionally incoherent, although he is particularly disdainful of the former. Only a cautionary call for judicial restraint can effectively limit power, if neutral principles or "a forceful analysis" is applied (Wechsler 1959, 25). Judicial activism, as exemplified by the "preferred position," is completely boundless and thus a wholly ineffective delimiter of power. Regarding the preferred position, Wechsler concludes that "it never has been really clear what is asserted or denied to have a preference and over what" (ibid.).

21. This should also serve as a reminder that "out" groups are not necessarily the source of so-called identity politics.

22. Sunstein (1993, 76) also makes this point.

23. See, e.g., Sunstein (1984, 1689).

24. Sunstein, (1994, 1).

25. 381 U.S. 479 (1965).

26. See note 2.

27. 381 U.S. 482.

28. 381 U.S. 486.

29. "To hold that a right so basic and fundamental and so deep-rooted in our society as the right of privacy in marriage because that right is not guaranteed in so many worlds by the first eight amendments to the Constitution is to ignore the Ninth Amendment and to give it no effect whatsoever" (381 U.S. 491). Or again: "The entire fabric of the Constitution and the purposes that clearly underlie its specific guarantees demonstrate that the rights to marital privacy and to marry and raise a family are of similar order and magnitude as the fundamental rights specifically protected" (381 U.S. 495). And "Although the Constitution does not speak in so many words of the right of privacy in marriage, I cannot believe that it offers these fundamental rights no protection . . . the traditional relation of the family—a relation as old and as fundamental as our entire civilization" (381 U.S. 496).

30. 381 U.S. 499.

31. 381 U.S. 484.

32. 381 U.S. 495, citing Justice Harlan in *Poe v. Ullman* 367 U.S. 497, 551–52.

33. See, e.g., West (1994, 137).

Chapter 12

Democratic Theory and Race-Conscious Redistricting: The Supreme Court Constructs the American Voter

Keith J. Bybee

Over 150 years ago Alexis de Tocqueville wrote, "There is hardly a political question in the United States which does not sooner or later turn into a judicial one" (Tocqueville 1966, 270). Although Tocqueville's observation clearly calls attention to the political role of the American judiciary, it leaves open the question of how judicial action ought to be studied. If it is true that our politics is frequently conducted in judicial terms, how should this fact of judicialization be understood?

Among political scientists, there is a strong tradition of assessing judicial activity relative to political practice, treating courts as policy-making bodies similar to any congressional committee or executive agency (M. Shapiro 1964; Murphy 1964). Such "political jurisprudence" has a tendency to downplay the importance of legal principles and ideas. Viewing judicial proceedings as simply the continuation of ordinary policy making, political jurisprudence often reduces legal doctrine to a rhetorical ploy designed to rationalize political preferences. In its strictest form, political jurisprudence suggests that there is little of intrinsic interest in judicial arguments themselves. To follow the interplay of political attitudes on the bench is to explain judicial decision making (Segal and Spaeth 1993).

There is an important element of truth in political jurisprudence. Legal criteria do not always point judges toward a singularly correct answer, especially at the level of the Supreme Court, where solid principles often exist on both sides of a dispute. The result is a significant degree of judicial discretion that permits justices to render the law consistent with their political preferences. Yet even if legal principles fail to provide clear answers in all cases, a more subtle form of influence may also be at work. The terms of judicial argument may not mechanically dictate outcomes, but the terms of legal reasoning may nonetheless shape the range of available options. The possibility of such constraint is a real one because issues must always be framed and interpreted in order to be deemed legally relevant. Legal disputes are not simply discovered lying about in the world and carted into court for resolution; the order of legal claims is fashioned rather than found. It is this rendering of issues as *legal* ones that may make a difference in how problems are perceived and solutions are proposed.

This point has received a substantial amount of theoretical articulation and empirical verification (Brigham 1978; Gillman 1993; Geertz 1983; Carter 1985; J. White 1985; Baum 1988 and 1992; Epstein and Kobylka 1992; George and Epstein 1992; and Lloyd 1995). Indeed, in spite of recent trends, advocates of political jurisprudence originally recognized the importance of legal framing. As one leading figure wrote, legal "doctrine is the halfway house between law, in the sense of statutes and precedents binding on the Justices, and policy, in the sense of political choice unhampered by such bonds. . . . [Thus, doctrines] are at the same time acknowledgments by the Court that they are limited by statutes and vehicles for effectuating one of the range of choices available within those legal limits" (M. Shapiro 1964, 47).

These observations suggest that the political role of the American judiciary cannot be completely captured by mapping attitudes, noting alliances, and tallying votes. Even though the law may be used instrumentally, legal reasoning amounts to more than the manipulation of rules to reach preferred ends. To understand the judicialization of American politics that Tocqueville famously noted, the meaning of judicial ideas and principles must also be the object of study. Without some attention to the history and structure of judicial arguments, the significance of framing political questions in legal terms cannot be grasped and, in turn, the impact of judicial decisions and the nature of judicial institutions cannot be fully explored.

The need for such analysis is nowhere greater than in the adjudication of race-conscious redistricting. Over the past few decades increasing numbers of electoral districts have been drawn to enhance minority representation. Such districts typically feature a majority of minority voters, thereby ensuring that minority groups have an opportunity to elect candidates of their choice. The creation of these "majority-minority" districts peaked following the 1990 census, when the number of congressional districts with African American majorities grew from seventeen to thirty-two, and the number of Latino-majority congressional districts increased from nine to nineteen. Although the Supreme Court initially fostered race-conscious redistricting (see Bybee forthcoming), it has reacted to the rising numbers of majority-minority districts with skepticism. In *Shaw v. Reno* (1993), the Court questioned a majority-minority district in North Carolina. The district followed a highway corridor for nearly 160 miles and, at points, was no wider than the highway itself. This unusual shape prompted one state legislator to remark that "if you drove down the interstate with both car doors open, you'd kill most of the people in the district" (*Shaw*, 636). District voters elected Melvin Watt, the first black member of Congress from North Carolina since Reconstruction, but the Court hardly saw Watt's election as a harbinger of racial progress. Instead, the five-member majority ruled that the district's amalgamation of geographically separated minority voters approached "political apartheid" (*Shaw*, 647).

Shaw marked a victory for the conservative justices who had come to dominate the high bench—a victory that was consolidated in subsequent rulings (*Miller v. Johnson* [1995]; *Bush v. Vera* [1996]; *Abrams v. Johnson* [1997]). Yet by establishing a framework in which majority-minority districts could be contested, *Shaw* did not merely provide a rationalization for political opposition to race-conscious redistricting. It also offered a new set of terms in which the problem of minority representation could be understood. The resulting framework made a difference in how representative institutions were conceptualized and structured. As Justice O'Connor observed, *Shaw* enacted a set of principles that altered the process of redistricting and, in doing so, played "an important role in defining the political identity of the American voter" (*Bush*, slip op., 58).

What is the vision of fair representation enforced by *Shaw*? What is the origin of this representational vision? What alternative conceptions of representation did *Shaw* displace? What do *Shaw*'s representational claims suggest about the Court as an institution? To ask these questions is not to deny the role of political preferences in judicial decision making. On the contrary, it is to insist that the form of judicial argument, as a means of envisioning the issues in question, remains a crucial part of judicial action. It is in this spirit that I examine the judicial treatment of race-conscious redistricting here. First, I consider the theory of representation at work in *Shaw*, demonstrating how the Court's opposition to majority-minority districts depends upon a particular conception of political identity. I then draw *Shaw*'s representational theory into sharper focus, by highlighting its commonalties with theories of interest-group pluralism and by outlining the representational alternatives that it superseded. Finally, I assess *Shaw*'s theory of representation in institutional terms, evaluating it against the representative role that the judiciary plays in our political system. My overall aim is to illuminate the framework in which the Court now situates minority representation and to examine this framework in view of the Court's own representative functions.

Political Representation in Theory and in Court

The study of representational theories should start with a definition of terms or, with what amounts to the same thing, a discussion of Hanna Pitkin's seminal work, *The Concept of Representation*. According to Pitkin, the word "representation" means to make present in some sense that which is itself not literally or fully present. Therefore, as Pitkin notes, representation is a matter of "*re-presentation,* a making present again" (Pitkin 1967, 8). Political representation, the "making present" of the people in the authoritative decisions of their government, can be conceived of in a number of ways. Political representation may be viewed as purely formal, with those who are merely "authorized" to act on the behalf of the people being labeled representatives. Or such representation may be defined as a matter of "standing for" the people, with only those who descriptively or symbolically resemble the people being designated as representatives. And political representation may be seen as a matter of "substantively acting for" the people, with only those whose actions are in some way guided by their constituents being deemed representatives.

Each of these views of political representation is, of course, open to some interpretation. These views together, along with their various interpretations, form a complex matrix of conceptual resources that can be used to fashion a political community. That is, political representation provides a means for generating a common political framework, a way of adjudicating disputes and developing consensus. Since representation can be interpreted in a wide range of ways, the *kind* of political community to be forged by representative government is itself open to debate. The result is that representational debates are always anchored in disputes over the nature of the political community. As Pitkin concludes in her analysis of political theory, "The position a writer adopts within the limits set by the concept of representation will depend on his *metapolitics*—his broad conception of human nature, human society, and political life. His views on representation will not be arbitrarily chosen, but embedded in and dependent on the pattern of his political thought" (Pitkin 1967, 167, emphasis added). The rendering of representation a theorist gives depends on the political purposes she seeks to serve; as a consequence, each treatment of political representation incorporates its own sense of what people and which interests are to count.

What Pitkin finds to be true in political theory holds as well in concrete political practice. At stake in actual representational controversies—conflicts over how the people ought to be made politically present—are "metapolitical" visions of who the people are, what their interests look like, and how their politics ought to be conducted. The basic terms of representational debates are thus invested with their own emphases and exclusions, comprising a distinct discourse that frames political thought and action. Political actors engaged in such a discourse of representation appeal to a limited set of assumptions and commitments, producing specific understandings of what counts as meaningful or important in the debate. Any given politics of representation, then, engenders a discrete repertoire of strategies for making sense of the political community. To identify and evaluate this repertoire is to understand the politics of representation.

How might Pitkin's approach be applied to the representational claims in *Shaw*? Writing for the *Shaw* majority, Justice O'Connor stated, "We believe that reapportionment is one area in which appearances do matter. A reapportionment plan that includes in one district individuals who belong to the same race, but who are otherwise widely separated by geographical and political boundaries, and who may have little in common with one another but the color of their skin bears an uncomfortable resemblance to political apartheid" (*Shaw*, 647). O'Connor was careful to argue that this claim did not hold the design of legislative districts to some strict criteria of shape. The constraints traditionally applied to district shape (e.g., compactness, contiguity, and respect for political subdivisions) *were not* constitutionally required (*Shaw*, 647). The goal was to avoid "political apartheid"—a goal that might well be advanced (although not necessarily secured) by paying attention to traditional districting criteria.

Political apartheid was not strictly a problem of district shape so much as a violation of fair representation. What conception of fair representation did O'Connor use to illuminate and criticize the pathology of political apartheid? Consistent with Pitkin's analysis, O'Connor offered a theory of representation backed by a metapolitical vision of who the people are and how their interests ought to be expressed. These metapolitical commitments surfaced in O'Connor's discussion of the harms engendered by political apartheid. O'Connor claimed that political apartheid reinforced impermissible stereotypes, strengthening the perception that all members of the segregated racial group "think alike, share the same political interests, and will prefer the same candidates at the polls" (*Shaw*, 647). She also contended that racially segregated districts sent a "pernicious" message to elected officials, encouraging them "to believe that their primary obligation is to represent only the members of [the segregated minority] rather than their constituency as a whole" (*Shaw*, 648).

The two harms O'Connor enumerated made sense only if one adopted an individualistic understanding of political identity. O'Connor's assertion that the North Carolina district could reinforce impermissible stereotypes (stereotypes that in turn distorted the responsiveness of elected officials) was essentially a claim that the government could impose restrictive "group" identities on the fluid assemblage of equal individuals constituting the electorate. In the absence of governmental intervention, political identities were not defined by membership in a single racial group. Diverse political alliances were free to form in such a context. Political apartheid froze the individuals into rigid political categories, manufacturing racialized political identities that obstructed the flow of political action.

O'Connor's individualistic understanding of the people was evident in her refusal to acknowledge the race of the voters contesting the North Carolina district. According to O'Connor, the appellants did not claim that North Carolina had diluted "white" voting strength, for the appellants "did not even claim to be white" (*Shaw*, 641). The appellants objected to the majority-minority district precisely because they believed it gave racial identities political meaning, erasing the "constitutional right to participate in a 'colorblind' electoral process" (*Shaw*, 642). There were no special racial identities to which the political system should respond; instead, the aim was to avoid the generation of such identities in the first place, invalidating districting plans that would "balkanize us into competing racial factions" (*Shaw*, 657).

Theoretical Background and Bypassed Alternatives

Shaw was not decided in a vacuum. The Court's first sustained encounter with issues of representation began in the 1960s, when it considered the constitutionality of large population disparities across legislative districts. In these early disputes over malapportionment, members of the Court opted for an individualistic understanding of "the people." As Justice Black wrote, "We hold that, construed in its historical context, the command of Art. I, sec. 2, that Representatives should be chosen 'by the People of the several States,' means that as nearly as practicable one man's vote in a congressional election is to be worth as much as another's. . . . The House of Representatives, the [Constitutional] Convention agreed, was to represent the people *as individuals,* and on a basis of *complete equality* for each voter" (*Wesberry v. Sanders,* 376 U.S. 1, 7–8, 14 [1964], emphasis added). Subsequent decisions generalized Black's claim, using his notion of the people as an assemblage of equal individuals to insist that electoral districts have equal populations (*Reynolds v. Sims* [1964]). Confronted with a national patchwork of lopsided districts, the Court simply responded with "one person, one vote"—equal numbers of legislative representatives for equal numbers of voters.

In a broad sense, the individualism of *Shaw* stemmed from the one-person-one-vote reasoning of the early reapportionment decisions. Yet *Shaw* was not a simple application of this rationale. According to O'Connor's opinion, North Carolina voters were not at risk of being counted unequally but of having a restrictive political identity imposed on them. The difficulty was not that some voters would enjoy undue representation but that certain voters would be represented on the wrong terms. The fear of such misrepresentation was not the result of the reapportionment decisions nor was it original to *Shaw.* In the years preceding *Shaw,* a highly contentious debate over minority representation had begun to emerge. Conservative participants in this debate repeatedly expressed concern over the invidious stereotypes inflicted by race-conscious redistricting. It was this conservative critique that provided the raw theoretical material for *Shaw's* brand of individualism.

The leading voice in the conservative camp was Abigail Thernstrom, who forcefully descried minority quotas in the electoral sphere (Thernstrom 1987; see also Alexander 1989; O'Rourke 1992; and K. Butler 1985). Though Thernstrom acknowledged an original need to end the political exclusion of southern blacks, she asserted that the proliferation of majority-minority districts had significantly distorted American politics. Ordinarily, our politics functioned well without granting race special relevance (Thernstrom 1987, 4–9, 23, 234). Once minorities could register and vote freely, their voting strength rivaled that of any other political participant. To speak of "vote dilution" or "meaningful representation" was to deflect attention away from conditions of equal political opportunity toward claims of special treatment.

The driving question behind the quest for greater minority representation thus became, "How much special protection from white competition are blacks entitled to?" (Thernstrom 1987, 5).

Thernstrom effectively drew her account of ordinary politics (or "politics as usual" as she called it) from older theories of interest-group pluralism (Truman 1951; Dahl 1956 and 1961). Interest-group pluralism envisioned society as consisting of a multiplicity of groups, each with its own narrow interest. Democratic rule within such a social context was not rule by a monolithic majority but rule by a coalition of groups. As long as participation was open, elections frequent, and political entrepreneurs plentiful, any group shut out of the majority on one decision could hope to join it in the next (Dahl 1956). The composition of the ruling coalition was therefore dynamic, with coalition membership shifting from decision to decision. This fluid process of political competition hinged on a particular understanding of political identity. Specifically, interest-group pluralism held that individual political identity was never solely defined by membership in a single group (Dahl 1956; Truman 1951). Individuals were assumed to identify with a broad range of groups and interests. The sheer number of competing political identities ensured that any given majority would be inherently unstable, forever threatened by potential majorities that could form along alternative group cleavages. The pluralist political market was flexible and dynamic, in other words, because the fungibility of political identity meant that every player was potentially open to new deals.

The free-wheeling bargaining process engendered by overlapping group membership must itself be somehow sustained. If individuals became unwilling or unable to step up to the bargaining table, the benefits of the political market could never be fully realized. Interest-group pluralism located the primary forces of market maintenance within a broad consensus on rules of the democratic game (Dahl 1961; Truman 1951). Social consensus kept individuals wedded to the bargaining process as the means to make and enforce decisions. The result was that groups in the minority need not fear that the majority coalition would use its strength to entrench itself, transforming the political victory of the moment into a position of lasting dominance.

Interest-group pluralism thus furnished a portrait of politics that could be easily pressed into service by Thernstrom and other conservatives. Where political identities were multiform and fungible, racial affiliation did not have any special political valence and there could be little reason to grant racial minorities electoral preferences. In the words of one conservative commentator: "As voters we are Democrats and Republicans, blacks and whites, males and females, but we are also hawks and doves, redistributionists and laissez-faire advocates. . . . The list of our voting-relevant divisions is virtually endless" (Alexander 1989, 575). In this context of enormous political diversity, judicial intervention typically inflicted political harm, for individual political identity was simply too protean to be captured in the judicial decision. Judicial efforts to ensure the election of minorities simply frustrated the political process and fostered racial balkanization. In the absence of judicial strictures, individuals would construct the political community on their own terms, relying on bargaining and coalition building to give different groups the political representation that the pluralist market could bear. Of course, in extreme cases of exclusion, the judiciary might help restore access to the political market. Beyond that, however, judicial action had little political use. As Thernstrom concluded, "If a community of citizens is an unattainable ideal, and if blacks and Hispanics are represented only by one of their own, then aggressive federal action to restructure methods of voting to promote minority officeholding is appropriate. But if the logic of politics works for inclusion (once basic enfranchisement has been assured), then a lighter touch, a more hesitant intervention, is possible" (Thernstrom 1987, 242).

With *Shaw*'s claim that race-conscious redistricting unconstitutionally froze the fluid political process, the Court essentially accepted the conservative critique of majority-minority districts and effectively endorsed the basic terms of interest-group pluralism. In doing so, the Court abandoned alternative approaches that past justices had used to understand minority representation. The alternatives deployed by past justices fell into distinct categories organized around notions of popular vigilance, abstract individualism, legislative learning, and group competition (see Bybee forthcoming). A detailed account of such alternatives is beyond the scope of this chapter. Even so, it is worth noting that even though these alternatives tolerated majority-minority districts to very different degrees, they were united in their rejection of interest-group pluralism. Without asserting the fungibility of political identities or the marketlike efficiency of political bargaining, each alternative approach offered its own particular conception of politics against which claims of minority representation could be assessed.

As an example, consider the appeal to legislative learning that characterized the Court's earliest interpretations of the Voting Rights Act of 1965.

The Voting Rights Act featured a number of provisions designed to protect the right to vote from denial or abridgment on the basis of race or color. The heart of the act was to be found in Sections 4 and 5, which not only suspended literacy tests in political communities with unusually low voter registration or turnout but also subjected these same communities to "preclearance," requiring each covered community to submit proposed changes in voting rules to the federal government for approval. Since 1965, Congress has renewed Sections 4 and 5 on three occasions, keeping preclearance central to the act's enforcement. In fact, it was the preclearance process that generated the majority-minority district at issue in *Shaw.*

Sections 4 and 5 were also the target of the first challenge to the act's constitutionality in *South Carolina v. Katzenbach* (1966). South Carolina's suit attacked the suspension of literacy tests, the coverage of selected communities, and the establishment of preclearance as unconstitutional exercises of congressional power. Chief Justice Earl Warren, writing for an eight-member majority, defended the act against South Carolina's charges, holding the contested provisions to be "valid means for carrying out the commands of the Fifteenth Amendment" (*South Carolina v. Katzenbach,* 337). In reaching this conclusion, Warren did not refer to the necessities of maintaining pluralist bargaining in the United States. On the contrary, he anchored his defense of the Voting Rights Act in an account of legislative deliberation. At the outset of his opinion, Warren noted that the act was introduced during eighteen days of committee hearings, featuring testimony from sixty-seven witnesses (*South Carolina v. Katzenbach,* 308). These hearings were followed by nearly thirty days of debate on the floors of both the House and Senate, resulting in a "voluminous legislative history" that exhaustively documented the denial of minority voting rights (*South Carolina v. Katzenbach,* 309). Warren credited the massive infusions of information with persuading Congress that voting discrimination was deeply entrenched and resistant to simple remedies. Through its deliberations, Congress had gained new knowledge that made the aggressive enforcement mechanisms of the act reasonable and, hence, constitutional (*South Carolina v. Katzenbach,* 324).

Warren arguably used the notion of legislative learning as a touchstone to explain more than the constitutionality of the act. He recognized that preclearance was perhaps the most formidable of the act's provisions (*South Carolina v. Katzenbach,* 334–35). Preclearance would prohibit covered communities from unilaterally determining the fundamental rules of political organization. Instead of fashioning the political practice as they wished, covered communities would be forced to justify changes in political rules to the federal government. Preclearance would thus compel covered subdivisions to perform a political task they had historically neglected—to deliberate on behalf of the entire people without discriminating on the basis of race or color. The implicit model of such deliberation was to be found in the creation of the Voting Rights Act itself. As Warren described it, the passage of the Voting Rights Act was virtually an archetype of fair deliberation undertaken in the name of ensuring fair political opportunities. By orchestrating his opinion around the admirable example of Congress, Warren seemed to suggest that for covered subdivisions to survive preclearance, proof of having conducted Congress-like deliberations ought to be required. The suggestion was, in other words, that preclearance required covered subdivisions to justify new political procedures much as Congress had—by demonstrating an understanding of what was in the interest of the people as a whole.

Warren's appeal to legislative learning was revisited and developed in subsequent cases, including *Allen v. State Board of Elections* (1969) and *United Jewish Organizations of Williamsburgh, Inc. v. Carey* (1977). For my purposes here, however, it is less important to trace the career of Warren's argument on the bench than it is to highlight its differences with the principles embraced by *Shaw*. Unlike O'Connor in her *Shaw* opinion, Warren was not worried that race-conscious reform would impose a false or invidiously rigid political identity onto a diverse electorate. By the same token, Warren did not defend the act by identifying discrete racial blocs that deserved their own representation. On the whole, Warren avoided a discussion of essential or prepolitical identities; his concern was less with what "the people" were (e.g., protean individuals or members of monolithic racial groups) than with what they could make themselves into. Although he clearly wished to remedy the political exclusion of racial minorities, his ultimate objective was not to construct a scheme of racial representation for its own sake. Racial redistricting was justified, not because it reflected the most salient cleavage among competing groups but because Congress had learned that racial districting was necessary to help move the entire polity toward the goal of effective political deliberation. The "people" for whom Warren sought representation were a people who could learn through deliberation. Thus, the Court was to enforce the act's provisions in an effort to help legislatures work through racial divisions, producing the conditions in which representatives might seek and serve common interests.

Evaluating Judicial Theories of Representation

In view of the preceding analysis, one can say that *Shaw* offered a distinct way of envisioning issues of minority representation, consistent with a broader account of interest-group pluralism. The terms endorsed by *Shaw* were not the only ones available; members of the Court had explored a variety of alternatives in the past, all of which situated minority representation within different political contexts. What can be made of the representational theory that the *Shaw* Court selected?

Like all theories of representation, the theory at the heart of *Shaw* depends on its own sense of "the people" to be represented. Since every representational theory possesses its own set of metapolitical claims, no theory of representation can be free of biases or exclusions and no view of fair representation can be beyond debate. To say that the claims about representation are inherently controversial, of course, is not to say that in every instance all such claims are equally valid. The absence of one final or universal theory of representation does not make it impossible to distinguish better theories from worse ones. The value of any given representational theory depends on the context in which it operates and the purposes it seeks to serve. Accounts of representation may be more or less appropriate for local circumstances, more or less suited for specific institutional settings and political environments.

The question of how the individualistic theory of representation in *Shaw* ought to be evaluated thus hinges on a prior question: What representational role does the Supreme Court play in our political system? In answer to this question, the first point to note is that the Supreme Court is a unique sort of representative institution. Appointed by the president and confirmed by the Senate, Supreme Court justices are constitutionally permitted to hold office "during good behavior," a term that has in practice allowed most justices to serve on the Court for life. Effective life tenure frees justices from the restraints of direct electoral accountability, creating a Court that can review and interpret legislation from an independent perspective. In this sense, the Court might be said to be unrepresentative by design. Yet if judicial independence distances the Court from the mass constituencies that underwrite and oversee representative government, the aim of such independence is *not* that the Court will forego the task of representing altogether. Instead, judicial independence permits the Court to represent the interests of the people as a whole.

Of course, if the Court is to represent the people as a whole, it must first be possible to think of the entire people as a coherent political actor capable of having interests. The claim that the entire people could express a political will emerged during the initial years of the republic. Many of the earliest state constitutions had been written by state legislatures, but in the 1780s states began to rely on constitutional conventions to write their political charters (Wood 1969, 306–43; Rogers 1987). Constitutional conventions provided an institutional context in which the political will of the people could be asserted independently from that of the legislature. State constitutions consequently represented something more than ordinary legislation; they were dictates of the whole people that not only provided the framework for ordinary legislation but that also remained unaltered unless changed by the people themselves. Framed and ratified by convention, the U.S. Constitution could be similarly viewed as a product of the whole people, making it unique among national charters.

This is not to say that the entire people literally participated in the production of the Constitution, as some scholars have suggested (Ackerman 1991). In fact, only a small proportion of eligible Americans were involved in the ratification process. The use of constitutional conventions nonetheless opened a new political possibility. The identification of the Constitution with the will of the people created an opportunity for political actors to claim to speak for the people by interpreting the constitutional text. Throughout our history the Supreme Court has been the institution that has most consistently exploited this opportunity (Bybee forthcoming).

On the whole, then, the Court can be said to be a representative institution—not in the sense that justices are directly accountable to electoral constituencies but in the sense that the Court usually justifies its political authority in terms of its capacity to speak for the people as a whole. That is, judicial representation is not a matter of *political agency* (responding to the demands of a preexisting constituency) so much as it is a matter of *political entrepreneurship* (organizing or creating the constituency on whose behalf the Court shall speak). To recognize the Court's political entrepreneurship is to call attention to the multiplicity of ways in which the judiciary may justify its authority. Judicial scholars who have assessed the Court in representational terms have sometimes denied its entrepreneurial flexibility, limiting the Court to a single understanding of "the people" and their interests (Ely 1980). Yet as the judicial treatment of minority representation shows, there are a variety of representational theories on which the Court may draw. The denial of such variety does not alter the fact of its existence.

Of course, judicial freedom is not total. If claims of judicial authority are to be consistent with democratic rule—if they are to engender government by the sovereign people rather than to erect government by an unaccountable judiciary—then the Court's political entrepreneurship must be exercised so that it can be reviewed and ultimately controlled by the people and their electoral representatives. In a word, the Court must not speak for the people in a way that prevents the people from finally speaking for themselves. This requirement takes on particular significance when the Court adjudicates cases concerning political representation. Like all legal controversies, disputes over the meaning of fair representation provide the Court with an opportunity to recast the parameters of its own authority. Even so, representational litigation (including litigation over minority representation) is uniquely important because it directly affects the electoral rules that dictate the terms of political power. The politics of representation thus places the judiciary in a critical position: in judging between different representational theories, members of the Court not only select a form of political community that they believe ought to obtain, but they also reconfigure the institutional environment and, in doing so, directly determine the sort of political community that will obtain. In such a context, where the Court simultaneously chooses the terms on which itself and the people exercise power, it is essential that judicial actions taken on behalf of the people ultimately preserve the people's capacity to act for themselves.

This account of judicial representativeness sheds light on the representational theory found in *Shaw.* O'Connor's individualistic claims provide a partial foundation for judicial entrepreneurship by forswearing racial quotas. The creation of strict racial quotas runs the risk of emphasizing the differences between racial groups while obscuring important cleavages within such groups. The deeper problem is that the consistent use of such categorical schemes finally subverts the American ideal of a whole people. The "whole people" may of course be characterized in a number of ways. But the establishment of proportional racial representation does not promise such an alternative characterization; on the contrary, it threatens to undermine the notion of a whole people by reducing political membership to discrete racial blocs. The harder that claims for fixed racial representation are pushed, the more the politics of minority representation becomes a struggle for preservation *apart* from the majority group rather than a struggle for meaningful membership *among* the people as a whole. The more stringently the political voice is coded by race and fixed by law, the more difficult it becomes to understand how the people as a whole can be a coherent political actor.

From the perspective of judicial entrepreneurship, then, the representational theory of *Shaw* is valuable because it guards the notion of the whole people and thereby helps ensure the capacity of the people to speak for themselves. Yet when the Court acts in the name of a strictly individualistic people, it ultimately hobbles democratic sovereignty. This is so because even though it is important to stress the tensions between group identity and the notion of a whole people, it still is wrong to dismiss the demands of group identity altogether. In attempting to circumvent divisive group politics, *Shaw* calls into question the very existence of politically relevant racial identities. The Court thus saves the citizenry from racial categorization by presupposing that racial identity is politically significant only when the government makes it so. The problem with such a claim is that minority groups have been and, in many instances, continue to be politically constituted on the basis of race. As comprehensive studies continue to show, minority groups make up distinct voting blocs in many regions of the country (Davidson and Grofman 1994). In these regions, the idea that members of the same race generally vote together and support the same political interests is not the stuff of pernicious political stereotype but a fact of political life. Moreover, this is a fact with important consequences: where racial groups constitute stable voting blocs, minority group voices can easily be dominated by majority group votes. Thus, in some towns and cities, the vision of politically protean individuals identifying with a large range of groups is belied by the persistence of racial cleavage and minority exclusion. To stress the need for color blindness in the face of such hierarchy and division is to prevent the government from helping the very groups that have been discriminated against on racial and ethnic grounds. Indeed, to permit majority *white* districts to persist, regardless of shape, while holding majority-minority districts to strict scrutiny is to do more than deny minority groups a potential remedy. It is to suggest that citizens and their representatives cannot grant minorities the same treatment already accorded to members of the majority.

The difficulties with *Shaw*'s approach do not mean that the judiciary has no part to play in the politics of minority representation. I have argued that the framework of judicial argument, as a particular mode of envisioning issues, makes an important difference in how problems are conceived and resolved. Moreover, I have argued that judicial frameworks employed in representational disputes must be evaluated against the representative role played by the Court itself. Tensions between any given representational framework and the Court's institutional requirements are not insurmountable because a variety of alternative frameworks remain. Thus, the study of judicial framing not only calls attention to the significance of legal terms adopted in the past but also holds out the promise of finding better ones in the future. In the on-going debate over race-conscious redistricting, it is important to understand how the Court currently constructs the American voter and to remain sensitive to the potential of alternative constructions. It is only in this way that we can fully appreciate what it means to render the question of minority representation as a *legal* one.

Chapter 13

Reconnecting the Modern
Supreme Court to the Historical Evolution
of American Capitalism

Howard Gillman

The judicial process is not, as a too mechanical view might hold, powerless in the clutch of capitalist circumstance. . . . [Still,] for an explanation of the main trend of constitutional decisions we may . . . look to the institutional and ideological elements that exercise their compulsive force on the minds of the judges, and to the changes wrought in these elements principally by economic developments. For an explanation of the groupings within the Court, we may look to the variations in outlook and belief as between individual members.
—Max Lerner, "The Supreme Court and American Capitalism"

Once we make the decision to supplement the very successful "attitudinal model" of Supreme Court decision making (see Segal and Spaeth 1993) with approaches that highlight the influences of institutional and political context, we are immediately faced with what might be called "the levels of analysis" problem. The problem arises because the very idea of "decision-making context" is, without further specification, almost infinitely complex, and this complexity forces scholars to decide which particular contexts deserve some attention and which are safely relegated to the background.

Within the new institutionalist literature on Supreme Court decision making, a few major levels of analysis have become prominent. Some have focused on the structures, rules, and norms that are distinctive to the Court, such as the "rule of four" for the granting of certiorari, the dynamics involved in constructing a decisional majority during the opinion-writing process, or the influence of particular precedents or broader jurisprudential traditions (Bussiere 1997; Gillman 1993; Kahn 1994; Maltzman and Wahlbeck 1996;

235

H. Perry 1991; Symposium 1996). Others have attempted to highlight the Court's position relative to a larger collection of policy-making institutions, such as its lateral relationship to the Congress and the executive branch or its hierarchical relationship to a system of federal courts (Epstein and Knight 1998; Murphy 1964; Songer et al. 1994; and other chapters in this book). Still others have moved beyond the influence of formal institutions of government to examine other aspects of the political regime, such as governing coalitions and social movements (Dahl 1957; M. Shapiro 1964; Clayton 1999; Epp 1999; Graber 1993 and 1995; McCann 1994; and other chapters in this book).

However, there is a tradition in Supreme Court scholarship that looks beyond these variables toward a more broadly constitutive feature of political life in the United States—the historical evolution of American capitalism. In fact, much of this scholarship is well-entrenched in our conventional understanding of Supreme Court politics. When we reflect on the Court's pre–New Deal history—from the Marshall and Taney eras through the Gilded Age to the "switch in time"—the principal way in which we set the stage for an explanation of the decisions of a given era is by referring to the structure of capitalism during that period.[1] Before we introduce students to the personal attitudes of the justices of the Marshall Court, or to the structure of the infant federal judiciary, it is not unusual to first discuss Federalist political economy and debates in the early republic about whether manufacturing should be actively promoted through an expansion of federal power (especially the establishment of a system of public finance and credit) and a vigorous judicial defense of vested rights of property and contract. These background debates about political economy routinely come before an examination of the Court and its political context because we assume that, at some level, these other explanatory variables are in large measure constituted by the circumstances of early American capitalism.

Similarly, the shifting patterns of decision making that distinguish the Marshall and Taney Courts are mostly explained (even by Taney himself; see his decision in *Charles River Bridge v. Warren Bridge* [1837]) with reference to the need to stimulate new investment opportunities by reducing constitutional protections for vested rights and other special "privileges that had their origin in acts of government" (Hofstadter 1974, 70; see Freyer 1994; Hurst 1956; Kutler 1971). Perhaps most conspicuously, the standard accounts of the Court's turn-of-the-century jurisprudence—even those offered by researchers who call into question whether this period is properly labeled an era of "laissez-faire constitutionalism" (Benedict 1985; Gillman 1993; Scheiber 1997; cf. Kens 1997; Mendelson 1960)—assume that the justices were deeply influenced by the interests and ideologies that emerged during postbellum industrialization. (For standard accounts of each of these periods, see McCloskey 1994; Kelly et al. 1991.)

In the 1920s John R. Commons expressed the view that the Supreme Court operated as "the first authoritative faculty of political economy in the world's history" (Commons 1924, 7; see also Miller 1968, 5 and Hovencamp 1991). Four years after Max Lerner's classic essay, "The Supreme Court and American Capitalism," Professor Felix Frankfurter proclaimed that "the history of American constitutional law in no small measure is the history of the impact of the modern corporation upon the American scene" (Frankfurter 1964, 63, originally published in 1937). As Edward S. Greenberg (1982, 22) put it more recently, "To claim that the U.S. Constitution is basically capitalistic . . . , when it is the constitutive document of the world's leading capitalist nation, is no radical statement. What would be far more surprising—and would require far more justification—would be to claim that the constitutional-legal order and the prevailing economic arrangements in the United States are different, unrelated, or hostile to each other."[2]

Still, despite the persistence of such observations, this long-standing commitment to interpreting Supreme Court politics within the context of the history of American capitalism began to wane in the decades following Frankfurter's proclamation. Part of this neglect may have been due to developments within the social sciences, in particular the behavioralist revolution, which focused the attention of researchers on individual attitudes and behavior and away from the task of interpreting the broader social context within which political attitudes are constituted. More important, the Court's decision to shift its agenda from the supervision of economic regulation to the protection of civil and political rights and liberties (see note 4, *U.S. v. Carolene Products* [1938]) led some observers to believe that it was no longer necessary to understand Supreme Court decision making with reference to this traditional context.[3] This sensibility is reflected in Hovencamp's (1992) essay on capitalism in *The Oxford Companion to the Supreme Court of the United States,* which focuses exclusively on the pre–New Deal Court's decisions regarding property, contract, corporations, antitrust, the commerce clause, and the new takings jurisprudence. Apparently, the assumption is that capitalism was a relevant factor in understanding the Supreme Court when the justices addressed economic policy making but not after they abandoned that agenda.[4] Although decisions about the Bank of the United States or "liberty of contract" are obviously related to capitalism, could the same really be said for *Brown v. Board of Education* (1954) or *Roe v. Wade* (1973)?

Despite the temptation to answer that question in the negative, there have been scholars since the New Deal who have attempted to draw attention to the continued relevance of the context of capitalism for an understanding of the modern Court. In this chapter I will summarize and expand upon some of this work in order to make a case for why the historical evolution of capitalism—as an economic, social, and cultural system—is still an important level of analysis to incorporate into an adequate understanding of modern Supreme Court decision making. The point will be illustrated with reference to four areas of modern constitutional law: federalism, separation of powers, equal protection, and civil liberties. Some of these topics are more obviously related to issues of economic policy making, but others were chosen to illustrate how the influence of capitalism extends to other areas as well.

A few caveats are in order. First, it is not my intent to review all lines of Supreme Court decision making that may be usefully connected to capitalism; I am also not claiming that I have identified the most important or provocative areas. Capitalism is constitutive of virtually every aspect of life in the United States, and thus it may be implicated in almost every aspect of American law. By drawing out these relationships in a few familiar topics I hope to raise the question of whether it would be productive to follow the lead of other scholars and extend the analysis more systematically to these and other areas. Second, although not the focus of this chapter, it is important to recognize that capitalism's influence on Supreme Court politics extends beyond the evolution of case-law ideology. To the extent that Court politics is affected, for example, by the structure of interest-group activity around the judiciary we would expect that the evolution of different social interests and movements in the course of capitalist development would impact the Court as well.

Third, there is the question of how best to conceptualize the relationship between capitalism and Supreme Court decision making and to demonstrate its existence. The question implicates long-standing and still unresolved debates within and between Marxist and non-Marxist scholarship on the nature of the capitalist state and the relationship between law and the social power of dominant groups or classes (see Beirne and Quinney 1982; Greenberg 1982; Kairys 1982; McCann 1989; Thompson 1975; for a recent overview of the state theory debate, see Barrow 1993). The analysis that I have in mind attempts to isolate some of the distinctive influences of capitalist systems while avoiding mechanistic arguments about how political institutions serve the structural "needs" of the system or act as the instrument of dominant classes.[5]

What are some of the features of capitalist society that we may want to incorporate into explanations of Supreme Court decision making? Among other things capitalist societies are characterized by (a) the existence of a class of wage earners whose well-being is mostly a function of their ability to sell their labor to those who own productive property, (b) the existence of owners of productive property whose well-being is primarily a function of their ability to transform capital investments into profitable enterprises, and (c) the existence of a market in which the exchange value of capital, labor, commodities, and services is largely a by-product of not-always-equal bargaining among and between owners and wage earners. It is also assumed that this system generates (a) a set of social relationships that are structured around participation in this market, (b) a set of interests for these participants that is largely a function of their experiences as participants in the market, (c) a set of political arrangements that is designed to ensure that owners make profits and that the system is otherwise stable and free from serious disruption, and (d) a set of beliefs (more or less widely accepted) about negative liberties (freedom from government coercion, rather than the sorts of freedoms that might be dependent upon control over certain resources), equal opportunity (but not equality of social conditions), individual initiative and social mobility, efficiency in the allocation of resources, and limited government—each of which is designed to convince owners and others that this method of organizing social life is legitimate, natural, or at least better than any imagined alternative.

It is important to add that the sort of analysis I have in mind also assumes that societies that share these basic features have generated a wide variety of political arrangements and legal forms, depending on distinctive historical experiences and the local dynamics of class or group conflict (see Gordon 1984; Thompson 1975). This means that the relationship between capitalism and the law is not usefully asserted a priori except at the level that is necessary to establish the existence of the system (in the same sense that feudalism exists as a system only if the law protects land tenures). This is just another way of repeating the well-worn adage that law should be considered "relatively autonomous" from the social structures it purports to regulate and that discussions about law's relationship to society should be mindful of mitigating and intervening variables, such as the reality of legal ideology as a (relatively) independent factor in shaping the judicial mind (see Cushman 1998; Gillman 1993). This account depicts actors such as Supreme Court justices as having to cope with the contemporaneous context of capitalism but also as having a certain amount of agency in determining their preferred course of conduct. The upshot is that different decisions (such as whether or not to allow the federal government to regulate manufacturing) might each reflect the influence of its distinctive context (e.g., the rise of trusts, which was a development that made possible the formulation of the dispute in *U.S. v. E.C. Knight*) (see Gillman 1996), but because other factors mediate debates about context it cannot be the case that the situation *determines* outcomes. As McCann (1989, 237) put it:

> The Marxist model of economic causality tends to depoliticize and overdetermine law in much the same way as do traditional formalist or interpretivist theories. The structural relationships between legal ideology and capitalist social relations are important matters of analysis, yet they should be approached as variable, dynamic, and dialectical interactions between relatively independent and internally complex spheres of creative endeavor rather than reduced to simple terms of inevitability.

Yet although complex and contingent, patterns are still possible to discern. As Lerner (1933, 668) noted, "It is no historical accident but a matter of cultural logic that a Field should grow where a Morgan does; and a Brandeis is none the less organic a product of capitalist society than is a Debs."[6]

As for the question of how to demonstrate the significance of capitalist social structures for modern constitutional law, it should be clear that if we apply the standards of proof that dominate work in judicial behavioralism, then it may be that this relationship could never be established; and we may be left with the absurd conclusion that, from a social science perspective, capitalism has no discernible impact on the Supreme Court. These standards of proof must be rejected so long as one also rejects the view that capitalism takes distinct, predictable forms (or generates a set of objective interests) in favor of the view that it is an evolving social and ideological system with historically contingent configurations. In other words, capitalism does not lend itself to the generation of a fixed set of reliable predictions (such as "the law will give owners complete control over the organization of the workplace" or "courts will mimic the preferences of the

Business Roundtable"); and to this extent it becomes extremely difficult to imagine how we would construct a determinative hypothesis to test this relationship. For this work to go forward there must be a willingness to value scholarship that replaces the aspiration for reliable measurement with a commitment to advancing persuasive interpretive accounts of the relationship between social context and the "bounded subjectivity" or "grammar" of legal ideology (McCann 1989, 235–37).

To be persuasive, such accounts must often combine a thorough review of the prevailing structures of capitalism with a comprehensive summary of the perspectives of historical subjects and a careful analysis of the relevant jurisprudential traditions. For present purposes it is possible to sketch out only the broad outlines of what such an analysis may look like in a few select areas.

The Transformation of Federalism and Separation of Powers: Industrial Capitalism and the Rise of the Central Regulatory State

Although some scholars still hold the view that the Supreme Court's post-1937 accommodation of national power merely represented the principled reassertion of a more legitimate Marshallian tradition of nationalism against corrupt laissez-faire ideologues (Clinton 1994; Mendelson 1996), it is more generally accepted that the so-called "switch in time" ushered in an unprecedented expansion of federal governing authority (see Ackerman 1991; Cushman 1998; Griffin 1996; G. White 1997). Moreover, in seeking a satisfactory explanation for this shift, few scholars find it adequate merely to refer to changing policy preferences on the Court, since such an explanation begs the question of why this extraordinary shift in judicial preferences began to emerge at that particular time in the country's history. Instead, there seems to be general agreement that these developments were in response to a series of protracted battles over how best to cope with the distinctive challenges of production, distribution, and social conflict that emerged when American capitalism metamorphosed from a system of small-scale production for local markets to a system of large-scale industrial production for national and international markets (for standard accounts, see Kelly et al. 1991; Keller 1990).

This transformation affected the Court's decision making in at least three major ways. First, and most obviously, large-scale production put pressure on the assumption in traditional federalism jurisprudence that manufacturing and agriculture were primarily matters of local concern and jurisdiction. The Court had always recognized that the national government had authority to regulate the interstate movement of goods. But throughout the nineteenth century it consistently maintained that the act of production was a purely local matter that occurred prior to the introduction of an item into "commerce" (Gillman 1996). This was uncontroversial enough in an era when most production was by small-scale producers and growers for local markets and when (consequently) there was virtually no interest in establishing federal regulation of production. But with the rise of mass production and enhanced abilities to ship commodities across the country there was a developing consensus that manufacturing affected people across state lines; previously isolated communities had turned into a national market (Berk 1994; Wiebe 1967). If governmental oversight of this activity was called for, it would have to be accomplished at the federal level.

Arguments to this effect were first expressed—albeit tentatively, and not without some concerns about their constitutionality—in support of the passage of the Sherman Anti-Trust Act in 1890; they intensified two decades later during the debates over the appropriateness of federal child-labor legislation; and they reached a more fevered pitch after the Great Depression (which, we should keep in mind, was triggered by a crisis of overproduction). There was, perhaps, nothing inevitable about the Court finally accepting the view that manufacturing impacts on interstate commerce and that congressional authority may be exerted "no matter what the source of the dangers which threaten it" (*NLRB v. Jones & Laughlin Steel Corp.* [1937]); but there is also little doubt that this view is a direct result of changes in the structure of capitalist production, which transformed an activity of merely local consequence into one that directly affected the well-being of the nation as a whole.[7] This point is reflected in a series of memorandums written by Justice Jackson as he considered his decision in *Wickard v. Filburn* (1941) (raising the question of whether the federal commerce power extended to the regulation of surplus wheat for home consumption). The transformation of the economy made it so that "economic effects are exceedingly difficult to trace beyond immediate effects," and the "same economic forces which made the political pattern of a subdivided nation inept for regulatory purposes made all boundaries based on economic facts [e.g, distinguishing purely "local" activities from activities that affected interstate commerce] vague and blurred." Although "the federal compact [would be] pretty meaningless if Congress is to be sole judge of the extent of its own commerce power," he also reluctantly concluded that, unlike the nineteenth-century Court, "we have no legal judgment upon economic effects which we can oppose to the policy judgment made by Congress," since the complexity of an integrated economy made it impossible to state as a constitutional principle that certain economic activities had purely local consequences. As a result, "I don't see how we can ever sustain states' rights again as against a Congressional exercise of the commerce power" (cited in Cushman 1998, 215, 217–18).

In addition to shaping the modern Court's federalism jurisprudence, there is also a second, and less familiar, way in which industrialization fundamentally shaped the Court's post–New Deal decision making on matters relating to regulatory authority. It has to do with the impact that intensified class conflict had on the long-standing distinction between legitimate public-welfare legislation and illegitimate "class" legislation.[8]

At least since the era of Jacksonian democracy, federal and state courts had attempted to prohibit legislatures from using public power to impose special burdens or benefits on favored or despised groups or classes (Cushman 1998, 47ff; Gillman 1993; Olken 1997; Rosen 1997; Saunders 1997; Scheiber 1997).[9] This prohibition was premised on the assumption that capitalist markets were not creating dependent classes, which meant that unfettered (and unaided) participation in the market economy was consistent with republican independence and personal autonomy. So long as this was considered an essentially accurate description of capitalist social relations it would be deemed unnecessary for classes to receive special government favors in order to ensure their well-being. Thus, "class" or "unequal" legislation was considered corrupt, arbitrary, and fundamentally different from legislation that was designed to promote the health, safety, or morality of the community as a whole.

However, as industrialization transformed small producers into simple wage earners, and as it strengthened the social power of corporations over their market competitors (including workers and farmers), it also expanded the experience of social dependency. This in turn led increasing numbers of people to question whether the baseline of a common-law constructed "free" market should be the measure of fairness and neutrality (see Sunstein 1993). After all, if this market was now creating privileged and vulnerable social groups, then the government's continued commitment to "classless" legislation actually had the effect of advancing the interests of some classes at the expense of others. Indeed, the government's decision not to interfere in the "natural" social relations of industrial capitalism was increasingly considered as an instance of promoting the special interests of favored classes in precisely the same way as with traditional "class" legislation. As Seidman and Tushnet (1996, 29–31) put it, government action and government inaction had both become political "choices," and once there is no longer an agreed-upon base-line of neutrality and fairness in the structure and operation of the market, then there is no longer a basis upon which to maintain a distinction between legitimate public-welfare legislation and illegitimate class legislation.[10]

It took some time for this scenario to unfold (Gillman 1993)—that is, for "economic development and integration" to convince enough people that "certain of the system's premises ceased to be persuasive descriptive accounts of the world" (Cushman 1998, 42)—but by the time the Court handed down *West Coast Hotel v. Parrish* (1937) it was willing to acknowledge a legitimate role for the government to correct "serious social and economic maladjust-ments growing out of inequality in bargaining power." It was a role that had been rejected by the framers in the context of infant, small-producer capi-talism when they warned of the dangers of "factional" politics; but with the rise of a new system of industrial capitalism the legitimacy of interest-group liberalism would be viewed as a fundamental tenet of the new regime—a regime that Lowi (1969; 1985) referred to as the Second American Republic.

Concurrent with this dramatic expansion of the scope of regulatory power over market relations and practices, this new constitutional regime required a third major shift in jurisprudence: a reconfiguration of traditional divisions of governing responsibilities in the system of separation of pow-ers. One important reconfiguration that has been the subject of Karen Orren's (1991) important work involved a shift from judicial to legislative authority. This occurred when the collapse of traditional "common law" ordering of personal and labor relations (which involved judges supervising these relationships with an eye on protecting "natural" rights against unrea-sonable political manipulation) was replaced with a more modern commit-ment to considering these relationships to be a proper object of legislative policy making (see also Skowronek 1982 on the nineteenth-century state of "courts and parties").

Related to this was a shift from legislative to executive authority when the Court abandoned long-standing restrictions on the delegation of leg-islative authority to administrative agencies. By the end of the nineteenth century Lord Bryce could comment that while the "reader who has followed the description of Federal authorities, state authorities, county and city or township authorities, may think there is a great deal of administration," this observation needs to be seen in the context of a system where "the powers of each authority are so carefully and closely restricted" by law (see Lowi 1969, 131). As late as 1935 the Supreme Court, in *Schechter Poultry Corp. v. U.S.*, attempted to prevent the administrative accommodation of interest-group politics by prohibiting the Congress from delegating "legislative authority to trade or industrial associations or groups so as to empower them to enact the laws they deem to be wise and beneficent for the rehabilitation and expansion of their trade or industries." However, as Lowi discussed in *The End of Liberalism* (1969, 128, 132), the delegation of governing powers to administrative agencies that work closely with affected interests became a "widespread practice" once the "government began to take on regulatory functions" that required expanded capacities to monitor and intervene in economic activity. And by the 1940s the question of whether there were constitutional limits on Congress' authority to delegate its powers had become "a dead issue" (see Woll 1977, 156; Landis 1938; Horwitz 1992; on the general constitutional issues associated with the rise of the administrative state, see Kelly et al. 1991).

These shifts from judicial to legislative power and from legislative to executive power did not lead to "an end of economic supervision" by courts (McCloskey 1994, 123–26), although it did shift the terrain of that supervision from constitutional law to administrative law and statutory interpretation (see Peritz 1996; M. Shapiro 1986 and 1988; Carter and Harrington 1991). As Peritz (1996, 179) put it, throughout the prewar years the Court's opinions on a range of topics "oscillated between the rhetorics of conspiracy and market analysis, between consumerist and producerist images of the public interest." Moreover, the rise of the welfare state also imposed upon the Court a new set of monitoring responsibilities over questions such as whether government was required to supply some resources to the poor, whether welfare-eligibility decisions were governed by due process concerns, whether there were limits on the government's ability to impose restrictions on behavior as a condition of receiving benefits (so-called "unconstitutional conditions"), and how much freedom states had in determining who may receive certain benefits (McCloskey 1994, chap. 9). To one extent or another, these questions implicate core issues of political economy and the nature of state-society relations during this era in the historical development of American capitalism.

Keith Whittington has recently raised the question of whether our shift to a postindustrial global economy, along with other developments in post-1960s national politics, has set the stage for a new reconfiguration of federalism (and perhaps the separation-of-powers foundations of the administrative state). He suggests that the New Deal industrial model of national, hierarchical corporations operating under the wing of a corporate-liberal centralized federal bureaucracy may be giving way to economic structures that are simultaneously more global (thus transcending nation-state bureaucracies) and more decentralized (thus complicating the task of political management). Top-down corporate hierarchies are giving way to more entrepreneurial models of production and information processing, so much so that even government bureaucracies are being "reinvented" in order to mimic this trend toward decentralized decision making. It is still unclear whether one can make a persuasive case linking these developments to the Rehnquist Court's "new federalism" jurisprudence, and more specifically to decisions such as *U.S. v. Lopez* (1995), in which the justices decided for the first time in almost sixty years that Congress had exceeded the scope of its regulatory authority under the commerce clause. While that argument still waits to be systematically explored, we can nevertheless agree that the history of industrialization demonstrates that "long-term transformations in the objective condition of the economy, the social and political understanding of those conditions, and dominant political ideologies have significant implications for the trajectory of federalism" (Whittington 1998).

Equality and Liberty in the Context of Contemporary Capitalist Social Relations

It may be axiomatic that we can understand the modern Court's decision making on the authority of the administrative state only if we bring to the fore of the analysis the historical development of industrial capitalism. What is less widely accepted is the importance of this context for an understanding of modern civil rights and civil liberties jurisprudence.

There are at least two ways in which twentieth-century capitalism is related to contemporary decision making on equal protection.[11] First, the collapse of the "public welfare/class legislation" distinction forced a shift in the way that the Court conceptualized equal protection. During the time when that distinction was still efficacious, the justices treated all legislation that imposed special burdens or benefits on particular groups or classes (and not just "suspect" classifications) as a potential violation of the requirement that legislatures govern through general legislation. "Partial" or "unequal" legislation would withstand judicial scrutiny only if it could be justified on some class-neutral grounds relating to the health, safety, or morality of the community as a whole. This is what Sunstein (1982) refers to as the "public value" interpretation of orthodox equal protection jurisprudence, and it applied as much to legislation that imposed a special burden on Chinese laundry owners (*Yick Wo v. Hopkins* [1885]) as it did to legislation that singled out the railroads (*Gulf, Colorado and Santa Fe Railway Co. v. Ellis* [1896]) (see Gillman 1993; Kay 1980; Yudof 1990).[12] But this approach to equal protection analysis—which in essence amounts to a commitment to formal legal equality (political equality) rather than to equality of conditions (social equality)—collapses once there is an acceptance of the legitimacy of "special" legislation to assist some market competitors but not others. In other words, a government commitment to promote greater social equality through targeted legislation (such as minimum wage laws, price support schemes, or protections for union organizing) forced the Court to conclude that equal protection must mean something besides formal legal equality. How else could "interest-group liberalism" emerge as the governing ideology of the post–New Deal state?

Thus, one of the most important implications of allowing the government to mitigate the social inequalities of industrial capitalism was the transformation of equal protection from a prohibition against almost any kind of partial legislation to a prohibition against only certain specified forms of invidious discrimination: those rooted in "prejudice against discrete and insular minorities" (*U.S. v. Carolene Products Co.* [1938], note 4). The difference between these two sensibilities can be clearly seen when we contrast Justice Brown's emphasis in *Plessy v. Ferguson* (1896) on the formal equality of segregation statutes against Chief Justice Warren's focus in *Brown v. Board of Education* (1954) on the "feeling of inferiority" that was one of the intended consequences of racial separation. The modern approach is given an even clearer articulation in *Washington v. Davis* (1976), when the Court ruled that the equal protection clause was not violated when a state policy has a racially disproportionate impact but was not motivated by any discernible discriminatory purpose.[13] Like the nineteenth-century justices' approach, the Court is focusing on the inappropriate use of government power rather than on the problem of unequal social circumstances; but with "class legislation" no longer a constitutional epithet, the Court is now on guard against a much more limited set of inappropriate legislative motivations.

The *Davis* case provides a good illustration of a second way in which the logic of contemporary capitalist social relations informs the Court's civil rights jurisprudence. In upholding the District of Columbia's personnel test, the justices embraced a competitive "meritocratic marketplace logic of entitlement" as a legitimate form of social differentiation even in those circumstances where "ostensibly neutral performance tests" reproduce historically racialized social divisions (McCann 1989, 246–47). In other words, notwithstanding the Court's willingness to allow government to mitigate the effects of market inequalities, it is still the case that the logic of an individualistic, competitive marketplace represents the baseline standard of fairness for purposes of determining whether resources are being allocated in ways that raise equal protection concerns. This sensibility is at the core of the Court's heightened aversion to the use of race-conscious affirmative action programs as a way of mitigating the racially disproportionate results of individualistic competitive processes (see *Adarand Construction v. Pena* [1995]), which means that the modern judiciary's special hostility to "suspect classifications" imposes (ironically?) one of the few limits on the government's otherwise general authority to interfere with allocative inequalities in the market.[14]

Thus, "the evolved logic of constitutional equality discourse, like that of older property rights discourse, parallels and supports an individualistic, competitive logic of marketplace exchange relations that is profoundly inegalitarian at its core" (McCann 1989, 248). This continued commitment to incorporating into constitutional law arguments about the legitimacy of capitalist structures is also evident in the Court's unwillingness to extend equal protection scrutiny to discrimination based on poverty or to find some constitutional basis for welfare rights (see Bussiere 1997; Graber 1997; Loffredo 1993; Tushnet 1974).[15] Poverty is not treated as a suspect classification because it represents (in prevailing capitalist ideology) the inevitable result of an otherwise legitimate system of individual merit-based competition rather than a form of invidious discrimination. I make this point, not necessarily as a precursor to a critique of this jurisprudence, but just to emphasize that Supreme Court decision making on civil rights issues is almost literally incomprehensible without some explicit attention to the central role that modern capitalist structures and ideologies play in shaping the Court's rulings and doctrines. It is axiomatic that capitalism was central to the late-nineteenth-century Court's "liberty of contract" decisions, but we should also be clear about how "recent Fourteenth Amendment jurisprudence parallels the older [*Lochner* era] judicial activism not only in its substantive and economic character but also in its fundamental, if more subtle, embrace of ideas supporting uniquely capitalist forms of social organization against substantive egalitarian challenge" (McCann 1989, 232).[16]

Capitalist social relations have also had direct and indirect influences on the shape of post-*Lochner* civil liberties jurisprudence. Recall that the principal method by which civil liberty was protected throughout the nineteenth century was through a requirement that the government could interfere with liberty (economic or otherwise) only if its regulations promoted the health, safety, or morality of the community as a whole. Liberty was thus the residuum of a government of limited powers, and no cognizable liberty interest could be the basis for trumping a legitimate exercise of those powers. At issue, then, was not the importance of the liberty but the legitimacy of the government's purpose: if the ends were legitimate, as with community health (*The Slaughterhouse Cases* [1873]), the protection of women against physically demanding working conditions (*Muller v. Oregon* [1908]), or preventing obstruction of the draft (*Schenck v. U.S.* [1919]) then the liberty had to give way to the general welfare. If the ends were considered unrelated to the well-being of the community, as with limiting working hours in trades that were not unhealthy (*Lochner v. N.Y.* [1905]), prohibiting the teaching of modern languages other than English (*Meyer v. Nebraska* [1923]), or requiring parents to send their children to public schools (*Pierce v. Society of Sisters* [1925]), then the background condition of negative liberty would remain undisturbed (see Gillman 1994).

The New Deal decision to expand the government's regulatory authority so that it might more effectively manage an industrial social order put an end to the Court's traditional commitment to ensuring that only the promotion of the public good could justify the disruption of negative liberty. But how would civil liberty be protected if the Court was no longer willing to make decisions about legitimate public purposes? The answer was to single out certain liberties as particularly important and then to extend special protections to them against the near plenary regulatory authority of the state. The need to expand government powers in the wake of industrialization triggered the transformation of traditional libertarian tradition into the modern search for "preferred freedoms" (Gillman 1994; Graber 1991; G. White 1996).

There was only one question remaining: Which freedoms were to be preferred? Not surprisingly, the first preferred freedom was one that was considered essential for the maintenance of social order at a time when industrialization had produced disorder (Wiebe 1967). The same year that the Court abandoned the public-purpose limit on legislation, it declared that "the greater the importance of safeguarding the community from incitements of our institutions by force and violence, the more imperative is the need to preserve inviolate the constitutional rights of free speech, free press and free assembly in order to maintain the opportunity for free political discussion, to the end that government may be responsive to the will of the people and that changes, if desired, may be obtained by peaceful means" (*De Jonge v. Oregon* [1937]). By 1938 this conception of fundamental rights, representing what Ely (1980) would later call the "representation-reinforcing" model of judicial review, expanded and gelled into Justice Stone's footnote no. 4 in *U.S. v. Carolene Products* (1938), along with the suggestion that such rights might deserve "more exacting judicial scrutiny." Among other things this meant that the promotion of traditionally recognized community interests would not necessarily be enough to justify interferences with these liberties. And so, when the Court in *Schneider v. State* (1939) struck down a collection of ordinances forbidding the distribution of handbills on public streets and highways, Justice Roberts dismissed the government's asserted interest in preventing litter on the grounds that "mere legislative preferences or beliefs respecting matters of public convenience may well support regulation directed at other personal activities, but be insufficient to justify such as diminishes the exercise of rights so vital to the maintenance of democratic institutions." Of particular interest—at this time, anyway (and not during the reign of common-law ordering of work relations)—was the freedom to disseminate "information concerning the facts of a labor dispute," which was a topic that had just recently become a legitimate object of public policy making (*Thornhill v. Alabama* [1940]; see also Peritz 1996). It took only a few more years before these rights to free expression would formally receive the title "preferred freedoms" (see Stone's dissent in *Jones v. Opelika* [1942]).[17]

Still, in making decisions about the nature of these preferred freedoms, the Court often took its cue from those progressives who were primarily interested in the promotion of social order; and though this community often recognized "the social value of broadly dispersed powers of critical inquiry throughout society," they also "ignored and occasionally condemned dissent that did not contribute to this goal" (Rabban 1996, 959). The need to manage an industrial society was thus the impetus behind the creation of preferred freedoms; it also provided the logic by which those freedoms would frequently be curtailed, particularly when dissent arose from individuals who offered more radical critiques of capitalist America during World War I, the postwar red scare, and the cold war (see *Schenck v. U.S.* [1919]; *Whitney v. California* [1927]; *Dennis v. U.S.* [1951]; Kessler 1993).

Similarly, as Orren (1995) has pointed out, much of the Court's contemporary "substantive due process" jurisprudence is designed to build upon capitalist notions of work by "implement[ing] the decline of the family as a system of obligatory labor." This is particularly evident in cases involving childbearing and child rearing wherein women were attempting to be liberated from obligations imposed on them by common law. Justice Blackmun made this explicit when he wrote in *Planned Parenthood v. Casey* (1992) that "by restricting the right to terminate pregnancies, the State conscripts women's bodies into its service" without compensating women for that service. In drawing the connection between this mindset and more modern (postfeudal) conceptions of work associated with mature capitalism, Orren observes:

> In its rejection of common law ordering, the "activism" of the post-Warren Court in *Roe* is united with the "deference" of the New Deal Court in *Jones & Laughlin Steel.* As in *Brown,* the constitutional doctrine contemplates a change in the employment prospects of citizens most directly affected. In *Casey,* Justice O'Connor's majority opinion supports the adherence to *Roe* by the fact that the "ability to participate equally in the economic and social life of the Nation has been facilitated by [women's] ability to control their reproductive life."[18]

The final set of connections to draw between civil liberties jurisprudence and capitalism emerges when commentators investigate whether the justices' decisions might reflect a class bias. In his recent analysis of the "Clintonification" of constitutional law, Graber (1997) points out that scholars such as Loffredo (1993, 1364) complain that the justices have "displayed exceptional sensitivity toward elite communicative modes such as corporate campaign financing, corporate speech, large scale political expenditures, and, to a lesser extent, prerogatives of the mass media"; they "have also been markedly inhospitable toward distinctive plebeian modes of political expression and participation, like the public display of posters, picketing, residential distribution of handbills and demonstrations in public parks." There is hardly an issue in modern free speech jurisprudence (involving, of course, "the marketplace of ideas") that does not have to wrestle with marketplace practices or metaphors, including viewing the public as speech "consumers" (particularly of commercial speech), or deciding whether the "fragile ethos of consumerism" should trump the free speech inclinations of those who use shopping malls, or addressing the question of how to reconcile the editorial and profit-making privileges of being a cable company owner against the desire to create a public forum for the dissemination of ideas, or (to reiterate) announcing that money is equivalent to speech, at least when it comes to trying to influence elections (Peritz 1996, 247–49).

Privacy protections also seem to "end at the boundary . . . of their social class" and lifestyle (Tushnet 1974, 80). Heterosexual marital intimacy is protected (*Griswold v. Conn.* [1965]) but not sexual intimacy for gay men (*Bowers v. Hardwick* [1986]); abortion is legalized (*Roe v. Wade* [1973]), but there is no right to a state-funded abortion (*Harris v. McRae* [1980]). Graber (1997, 805) points out that even if the Court becomes more accommodating of gay rights and affirmative action, "the main beneficiaries [will be] minority business owners and a relatively affluent homosexual community. . . . The poor are likely to remain unwanted orphans in the American constitutional universe," and liberal constitutional theory will continue to "reproduce more progressive variations on the constitutional rights of the well-to-do." At the present time, "The only constitutional right to welfare that many liberals are presently willing to defend at any length seems to be the right to a state-financed abortion" (ibid., 736).

Graber makes it clear that he believes that affirmative action, abortion rights, and gay rights should be protected; he is simply objecting to the preoccupation among judges and law professors with elite interests and to the almost complete lack of concern for the well-being of the poor, especially among liberal theorists who refuse to take advantage of those features of our constitutional history that might provide support for welfare rights of some kind. As he puts it (809–10, 813):

> The more basic issue underlying debates between constitutional proponents and opponents is whether American constitutional institutions can be structured in ways that insure that elites in power act on the basis of their public values rather than on the basis of their class interests. . . . Judicial review cannot be justified if legal elites are merely advancing their class interests. . . . No theory of judicial review purports to justify an institution that declares laws unconstitutional only when government policies too severely trench on the interests of the most fortunate Americans.

This search for class bias may be, as in Graber's case, part of a normative critique of Supreme Court decision making, but it may also inform empirical projects designed to explore the relationship between the context of capitalism and legal ideology, even in doctrinal areas that, at first glance, may suggest no relationship worth mentioning.

The question of what features of the Court's context deserve to be placed in the foreground of an analysis depends ultimately on the ability of researchers to demonstrate that we are in a better position to understand certain aspects of Supreme Court politics if we pay more attention to heretofore neglected or underappreciated structural variables. As we move away from the attitudinal model, we have considered and debated the significance of a number of such variables, some of which may seem only occasionally relevant while others seem to illuminate more general features of the Court's behavior (for an overview see Epstein and Knight 1998). In this chapter I suggest that there are good reasons to think that we have much to learn by paying more attention to the ways in which the structure of contemporary capitalism influences the Court. But we will know if this is true only if more scholars consider possible relationships and become more willing to marshal the historical evidence that will lend support to claims about specific linkages.

It is tempting to view areas involving economic decision making as potentially more fruitful and to focus attention on the new takings jurisprudence, reviews of environmental regulations, the new federalism, administrative review of agency decision making, or case-law constructions of regulatory statutes or labor law (see Klare 1978; Peritz 1996). But capitalism's constitutive power extends beyond matters of economic policy making (narrowly defined), and interested scholars should be encouraged to find relationships in unexpected places. In what ways did the transformation of capitalism facilitate the decoupling of Fourth Amendment jurisprudence from its traditional property rights foundations? Is there a "liberty of contract" component to the way the Court envisions the decision of a suspect to waive his *Miranda* rights? Was there anything about the Warren Court's 1960s' due process revolution in criminal procedure that exhibits a concern about maintaining order or legitimacy in the inner cities (and do these developments parallel the New Deal's "search for order" at the national level)? Would we be making too much of the influence of capitalism (in the context of debates about the Great Society) by exploring Chief Justice

Burger's emphasis in *Wisconsin v. Yoder* (1972) on "Amish qualities of relia-bility, self-reliance, and dedication to work"—and how "its members are productive and very law-abiding members of society; they reject public wel-fare in any of its usual modern forms"—in the course of a ruling that extended special protections to their religious liberty? These topics may or may not be productive avenues of inquiry, but I hope they at least illustrate the range of possibilities that scholars may want to keep in mind as we con-sider the advantages of reconnecting the modern Supreme Court to the his-torical evolution of American capitalism.

Notes

1. The Court's motivation from 1787 to 1937 was "to construct a protective legal umbrella under which business enterprise could and did flourish" within changing cir-cumstances (Miller 1968, 24).

2. For an almost identical statement from a different part of the political spectrum, see Siegan 1982, 106: "The U.S. Constitution provides for and secures a capitalist econ-omy." I hope that my discussion makes it clear, though, that my claim is not simply that capitalism is "built into" the very interpretive logic of American constitutionalism (even though it was a central component of the original constitutional design). This would be misleading to the extent that it fails to take into account how capitalist development is a process that originates outside of these specialized interpretive practices (even though the course of development is sometimes influenced by these practices). At the same time, once new structures and relationships are forged in society they exert an influence on courts and law and, inevitably, work their way back into the activity of interpretation.

3. In 1960 Wallace Mendelson ended his *Capitalism, Democracy, and the Supreme Court* by celebrating how the post–New Deal justices no longer saw themselves respon-sible for nurturing, regulating, or protecting capitalism. The only remaining question was whether the justices would "permit the American Dream to develop its own demo-cratic devices of responsibility and self-confidence" (Mendelson 1960, 128).

4. While I take issue with this assumption, I should add that this point should not be considered a criticism of Hovencamp's work. For an excellent discussion of how changes in theories of political economy (which paralleled changes in economic structures) impacted the development of legal doctrine, see Hovencamp (1991).

5. Structural-functionalist explanations are useful in drawing attention to the influ-ences that are built into certain contexts (see n. 6), but unless modified they may also leave little room for human agency and for the contingencies of class or group conflict. Instrumentalist conceptions are useful in pointing out that certain groups or classes exert disproportionate power, but they may also understate the extent of intraclass conflict and the opportunities for nondominant classes or interests to exert influence over law and policy making.

6. Moreover, as we work to take the mechanistic sting out of structural analysis we should also keep in mind that, as some pluralist theorists are willing to admit (see Lindblom 1977), the social structure of capitalism puts owners in a "privileged position" by virtue of their control of resources that translate into strong political influence (such as campaign contributions or the ability to make investment decisions that can have serious public implications) and by virtue of the fact that ensuring profits for owners (but not, for example, full employment and a living wage for workers) is a precondition of the healthy operation of the system. Thus, it is reasonable to expect that, as a general rule, the law will tend to reflect the perspectives of dominant classes or groups in privileged positions as compared to those of competing interests.

7. In his *Jones & Laughlin* opinion Hughes also wrote that "undoubtedly the scope of [Congress' power to regulate production] must be considered in the light of our dual system of government and may not be extended to embrace effects upon interstate commerce so indirect and remote that to embrace them . . . would effectually obliterate the distinction between what is national and what is local and create a completely centralized government." But it soon became clear that this gesture in the direction of maintaining dual federalism was insincere: by 1941 a unanimous Court was prepared formally to overrule those decisions that had used the distinction between intra- and interstate commerce to limit the scope of congressional power and to declare instead that the "power of Congress over interstate commerce is not confined to the regulation of commerce among the states." As for the Tenth Amendment, the Court announced that it "states but a truism that all is retained which has not been surrendered" (*United States v. Darby,* 1941). The next year, the Court ruled that Congress' power to regulate commerce included the power to regulate agricultural "production not intended in any part for commerce but wholly for consumption on the farm" (*Wickard v. Filburn* [1942], upholding the Agricultural Adjustment Act of 1938). Cushman (1998) agrees that changes in the economy led to the breakdown of the traditional distinction between production (local) and distribution (national), but he argues that the distinction was not really jettisoned until *Wickard.*

8. A related, and maybe more familiar, distinction was between "businesses affected with a public interest" and those that were not; see *Munn v. Illinois* (1877). Both sets of distinctions attempted to identify a limited category of "public" space that was a proper object of state action and to treat legislation outside this category as arbitrary or otherwise unacceptable. As Cushman (1998) points out, these categories paralleled the concern in commerce clause jurisprudence to draw distinctions between activities that were a legitimate object of federal regulation (such as the movement of goods across state lines) from those that were not (manufacturing and production).

9. Saunders (1997, 255) suggests that "the nineteenth-century judicial hostility to partial or special laws had deep roots in Anglo-American legal and political thought. Since the early seventeenth century, the English common law courts had been invalidating royal grants of monopolies and other special privileges in domestic and foreign trade, on the ground that government should use its power only to advance the general welfare of the community as a whole, rather than the special interests of a favored few."

10. For similar reasons, the traditional distinction between a public sphere (which includes activities that are the proper object of community concern) and a private sphere (which should not be regulated by the state) also begins to unravel, as in the case of the "businesses affecting a public interest" doctrine; see Cushman 1998. This breakdown of what Cushman refers to as the traditional "public/private matrix" also leads to a dramatic reconceptualization of the nature of property rights.

11. A third connection relates to my colleague Mary Dudziak's (1988 and 1997) extremely provocative and well-documented thesis that desegregation was considered a "Cold War imperative."

12. While the actual legislation in *Yick Wo* did not single out Chinese business people for different treatment, the record did indicate that the law was being enforced in a way to have that intended effect, and for the Court this was enough to conclude that the principle of formal legal equality had been violated.

13. Seidman and Tushnet (1996, 105) suggest that *Brown* was premised on the assumption that a formally equal policy of segregation "had a disproportionate impact on blacks"; "there is not a word about intent in Chief Justice Warren's *Brown* opinion." They make this point as part of an effort to show that *Washington v. Davis* is incompatible with *Brown*. Although I am sympathetic to their efforts, it seems to me a stretch to characterize *Brown* as establishing the principle that the equal protection clause has been violated when a law has a discriminatory result even if it did not have a discriminatory intent. I would suggest that *Brown* is best read in light of the Court's post–*Carolene Products* emphasis on prohibiting legislatures from indulging invidious discrimination. And these authors even point out, in the very next paragraph, that "there are important differences between *Washington v. Davis* and *Brown,*" most notably that "the *intent* [my emphasis] behind the system of segregation was patent—to maintain the subordination of African-Americans."

14. Seidman and Tushnet (1996, 102) write: "Once it is conceded that it is permissible for the government to make generalizations about individuals along a whole range of dimensions, some observers might question why we should retain a special rule prohibiting such generalizations on the basis of race."

15. For what it is worth, I should clarify that I agree with Graber that these decisions are not inevitable by-products of our constitutional history or economic system (cf. Bussiere 1997).

16. At the same time, McCann (1989, 248) is correct to point out that "the deference extended to meritocratic justifications for differentiation is highly protective of status quo inequalities" including "inequalities of citizens' social backgrounds and capacities for basic needs fulfillment."

17. The "preferred freedoms" language was reiterated in *Thomas v Collins* (1945). Frankfurter launched an attack on the phrase in *Kovacs v. Cooper* (1949).

18. Orren (1995) adds that "it should be emphasized that 'modern substantive due process' in this reading does not present an analogy to labor but labor proper, albeit performed in a family setting, without compensation in the usual sense, and for which non-family persons are often hired without affectionate ties attached."

BIBLIOGRAPHY

Ackerman, Bruce. 1991. *We the People: Foundations*. Cambridge: Harvard University Press.

Adamany, David. 1980. "The Supreme Court's Role in Critical Elections." In *Realignment in American Politics*, ed. B. Campbell and R. Trilling, 229–59. Austin: University of Texas Press.

_____. 1973. "Legitimacy, Realigning Elections, and the Supreme Court." *Wisconsin Law Review* 3:790–846.

Adams, Greg D. 1997. "Abortion: Evidence of Issue Evolution." *American Journal of Political Science* 41:718–37.

Adler, David Gray. 1989. "Foreign Policy and Separation of Powers: The Influence of the Judiciary." In *Judging the Constitution: Critical Essays on Judicial Lawmaking*, ed. Michael W. McCann and Gerald L. Houseman, 154–84. Glenview, IL: Scott Foresman.

Alexander, Larry. 1989. "Lost in the Political Thicket." *Florida Law Review* 41:563–79.

Armstrong, Virginia C., and Charles A. Johnson. 1982. "Certiorari Decisions by the Warren and Burger Courts: Is Cue Theory Time Bound?" *Polity* 15:141–50.

Barber, Sotirios. 1993. *The Constitution of Judicial Power*. Baltimore: Johns Hopkins University Press.

_____. 1984. *On What the Constitution Means*. Baltimore: Johns Hopkins University Press.

Barker, Ernest. 1962. *The Politics of Aristotle*. New York: Oxford University Press.

Barrow, Clyde W. 1993. *Critical Theories of the State: Marxist, Neo-Marxist, Post-Marxist*. Madison: University of Wisconsin Press

Baum, Lawrence. 1992. "Membership Change and Collective Voting Change in the United States Supreme Court." *Journal of Politics* 54:3–24.

_____. 1988. "Measuring Policy Change in the U.S. Supreme Court." *American Political Science Review* 82:905–12.

_____. 1985. *The Supreme Court*. 2d ed. Washington, DC: CQ Press.

Beck, Paul Allen. 1976. "Communication—Critical Elections and the Supreme Court: Putting the Cart After the Horse." *American Political Science Review* 70:930–32.

Becker, Mary, Cynthia Grant Bowman, and Morrison Torrey. 1994. *Feminist Jurisprudence: Taking Women Seriously*. St. Paul. MN: West Publishing Company.

Becker, Theodore L., and Malcolm M. Feeley, eds. 1973. *The Impact of Supreme Court Decisions.* 2d ed. New York: Oxford University Press.

Beirne, Piers, and Richard Quinney, eds. 1982. *Marxism and Law.* New York: John Wiley and Sons.

Bell, Derrick. 1992. *Faces at the Bottom of the Well: The Permanence of Racism.* New York: Basic Books.

————. 1987. *And We Are Not Saved: The Elusive Quest for Racial Justice.* New York: Basic Books.

Benedict, Michael Les. 1985. "Laissez-Faire and Liberty: A Reevaluation of the Meaning and Origin of Laissez-Faire Constitutionalism." *Law and History Review* 3:243–331.

Bennett, W. Lance. 1980. "The Paradox of Public Discourse: A Framework for the Analysis of Political Accounts." *Journal of Politics* 42:792–817.

Berger, Margaret A. 1980. *Litigation on Behalf of Women.* New York: Ford Foundation.

Berk, Gerald. 1994. *Alternative Tracks: The Constitution of American Industrial Order, 1865–1917.* Baltimore: Johns Hopkins University Press.

Berry, Jeffrey M. 1989. *The Interest Group Society.* Boston: Little, Brown.

Beveridge, Albert J. 1919. *The Life of John Marshall.* Vol. 4. Boston and New York: Houghton Mifflin Company.

Bickel, Alexander M. 1962. *The Least Dangerous Branch: The Supreme Court at the Bar of Politics.* Indianapolis and New York: Bobbs-Merrill Company.

Blasi, Vincent, ed. 1983. *The Burger Court: The Counter-Revolution That Wasn't.* New York: Alfred A. Knopf.

Bork, Robert H. 1996. *Slouching Towards Gomorrah: Modern Liberalism and American Decline.* New York: Free Press.

————. 1990. *The Tempting of America: The Political Seduction of Law.* New York: Simon and Schuster.

Bower, Lisa. 1994. "Queer Acts and the Politics of 'Direct Address': Rethinking Law, Culture, and Community." *Law and Society Review* 28:1009–33.

Brady, David W., and Joseph Stewart Jr. 1982. "Congressional Party Realignment and Transformations of Public Policy in Three Realigning Eras." *American Journal of Political Science* 26:333–60.

Brest, Paul. 1981. "The Fundamental Rights Controversy: The Essential Contradictions of Normative Constitutional Scholarship." *Yale Law Journal* 90:63–1109.

Brigham, John. 1996. *The Constitution of Interests: Beyond the Politics of Rights.* New York: New York University Press.

————. 1987a. *The Cult of the Court.* Philadelphia: Temple University Press.

————. 1987b. "Right, Rage and Remedy: Forms of Law in Political Discourse." *Studies in American Political Development* 2:303–16.

————. 1978. *Constitutional Language: An Interpretation of Judicial Decision.* Westport, CT.: Greenwood Press.

Bright, Stephen B. 1997. "Political Attacks on the Judiciary." *Judicature* 80:165–73.

Brisbin, Richard. 1993. "Antonin Scalia, William Brennan, and the Politics of Expression:

A Study of Legal Violence and Repression." *American Political Science Review* 87:912–27.

Bullock, Charles S. III, and Charles M. Lamb. 1989. "Toward a Theory of Civil Rights Implementation." In *American Court Systems: Readings in Judicial Process and Behavior,* ed. Sheldon Goldman and Austin Sarat. 2d ed., 559–68. New York: Longman.

Bumiller, Kristin. 1988. *The Civil Rights Society: The Social Construction of Victims.* Baltimore: Johns Hopkins University Press.

Burgess, Susan R. 1993. "Beyond Instrumental Politics: The New Institutionalism, Legal Rhetoric, and Judicial Supremacy." *Polity* 25:445–59.

_____. 1992. *Contest for Constitutional Authority: The Abortion and War Powers Debates.* Lawrence: University Press of Kansas.

Burnham, Walter Dean. 1995. "Politics in the 1990s." In *The American Prospect Reader in American Politics,* ed. Walter Dean Burnham, 187–203. Chatham, NJ: Chatham House.

_____. 1982. "The Constitution, Capitalism, and the Need for Rationalized Regulation." In *How Capitalistic Is the Constitution?* ed. Robert A. Goldwin and William A. Schambra, 75–105. Washington, DC: American Enterprise Institute for Public Policy Research.

Burstein, Paul. 1991. "Legal Mobilization as a Social Movement Tactic: The Struggle for Equal Employment Opportunity." *American Journal of Sociology* 96:1201–25.

Bussiere, Elizabeth. 1997. *(Dis)Entitling the Poor: The Warren Court, Welfare Rights, and the American Political Tradition.* University Park: Pennsylvania State University Press.

Butler, Judith. 1990. *Gender Trouble: Feminism and the Subversion of Identity.* New York: Routledge.

Butler, Katherine. 1985. "Denial or Abridgment of the Right to Vote: What Does It Mean?" In *The Voting Rights Act: Consequences and Implications,* ed. Lorn Foster, 44–59. New York: Praeger.

Bybee, Keith J. Forthcoming. *Mistaken Identity: The Supreme Court and the Politics of Minority Representation.* Princeton: Princeton University Press.

Caldeira, Greg. 1981. "The United States Supreme Court and Criminal Cases: Alternative Models of Agenda-Building." *British Journal of Political Science* 11:449–70.

Caldeira, Gregory A., and John R. Wright. 1990. "Amici Curiae Before the Supreme Court: Who Participates, When, and How Much?" *Journal of Politics* 52:782–806.

_____. 1988. "Organized Interests and Agenda Setting in the U.S. Supreme Court." *American Political Science Review* 82:1109–27.

Canon, Bradley. 1977. "Testing the Effectiveness of Civil Liberties at the State and Federal Levels: The Case of the Exclusionary Rule." *American Politics Quarterly* 5:57–82.

Canon, Bradley, and S. Sidney Ulmer. 1976. "Communication—The Supreme Court and Critical Elections: A Dissent." *American Political Science Review* 70:1215–18.

Caplan, Lincoln. 1987. *The Tenth Justice: The Solicitor General and the Rule of Law.* New York: Alfred A. Knopf.

Carelli, Richard. 1997. "Chief Justice Says Independent Judiciary Is Vital." *News & Reports* (April 11, 1996); "Scalia Calls Move to Impeach Liberal Judges a Nonstarter." *News & Reports* (May 20, 1997). AP Wire Service, http://www.sddt.com/files/library/96W.

Carmines, Edward G., and James A. Stimson. 1989. *Issue Evolution: Race and the Transformation of American Politics.* Princeton: Princeton University Press.

Carney, Dan. 1997. "Battle Looms Between Clinton, GOP Over Court Nominees." *CQ Weekly Report,* February 8.

Carter, Lief. 1991. *An Introduction to Constitutional Interpretation.* New York: Longman.

———. 1988. *Reason in Law.* 3d ed. Glenview, IL: Scott Foresman.

———. 1985. *Contemporary Constitutional Lawmaking: The Supreme Court and the Art of Politics.* New York: Pergamon Press.

Carter, Lief H., and Christine B. Harrington. 1991. *Administrative Law and Politics: Cases and Comments.* New York: HarperCollins.

Casper, Jonathan. 1976. "The Supreme Court and National Policy Making," *American Political Science Review* 70:50–63.

Cavell, Stanley. 1984. *Themes Out of School.* San Francisco: North Point Press.

Clayton, Cornell. 1995. *Government Lawyers: The Federal Legal Bureaucracy and Presidential Politics.* Lawrence: University Press of Kansas.

———. 1994. "Separate Branches—Separate Politics: Judicial Enforcement of Congressional Intent." *Political Science Quarterly* 109:843–72.

———. 1992. *The Politics of Justice: The Attorney General and the Making of Legal Policy.* New York: M. E. Sharpe.

Clayton, Cornell, and Howard Gillman. 1999. *Institutional Approaches to Supreme Court Decision-Making.* Chicago: University of Chicago Press.

———. Forthcoming. "New-Institutionalist Analyses of Supreme Court Politics." In *The Supreme Court in American Politics: New Institutionalist Interpretations,* ed. Howard Gillman and Cornell W. Clayton. Lawrence: University Press of Kansas.

Clayton, Cornell, and James Giordano, 1998. "The Supreme Court and the Constitution." In *Developments in American Politics,* vol. 3, ed. Gillian Peele, Christopher Bailey, Bruce Cain, and B. Guy Peters, 71–96. London: Macmillan.

Clinton, Robert Lowry. 1994. "Judicial Review, Nationalism, and the Commerce Clause: Contrasting Antebellum and Postbellum Supreme Court Decision Making." *Political Research Quarterly* 47:857–76.

———. 1989. *Marbury v. Madison and Judicial Review.* Lawrence: University Press of Kansas.

Cohen, Carl. 1995. *Naked Racial Preference: The Case Against Affirmative Action.* Lapham, MD: Rowman and Littlefield.

Coleman, Peter J. 1974. *Debtors and Creditors in America: Insolvency, Imprisonment for Debt, and Bankruptcy, 1607–1900.* Madison: State Historical Society of Wisconsin.

Commager, Henry Steele. 1943. *Majority Rule and Minority Rights.* New York: Oxford University Press.

Commons, John R. 1924. *Legal Foundations of Capitalism.* Madison: University of Wisconsin Press.

Cook, Elizabeth Adell, Ted G. Jelen, and Clyde Wilcox. 1992. *Between Two Absolutes: Public Opinion and the Politics of Abortion.* Boulder, CO: Westview Press.

Cornell, Drucilla. 1991. *Beyond Accommodation: Ethical Feminism, Deconstruction, and Law.* New York: Routledge.

Corwin, Edward S. 1938. *Court Over Constitution: A Study of Judicial Review as an Instrument of Popular Government.* Princeton: Princeton University Press.

_____. 1928. *The "Higher Law" Backgrounds of American Constitutional Law.* Ithaca, NY: Cornell University Press.

Cover, Robert. 1986. "Violence and the Word." *Yale Law Journal* 95:1601–29.

Cox, Archibald. 1976. *The Role of the Supreme Court in American Government.* London: Oxford University Press.

Cox, Gary, and Samuel Kernell, eds. 1991. *The Politics of Divided Government.* Boulder, CO: Westview Press.

Coyle, Marcia. 1997. "Hat Tricks for These Two High Court Lawyers." *National Law Journal,* August 11, A10.

Crenshaw, Kimberle Williams. 1988. "Race, Reform, and Retrenchment: Transformation and Legitimation in Antidiscrimination Law," *Harvard Law Review* 101:1331–87.

Curran, Barbara A., Katherine J. Rosich, Clara N. Carson, and Mark C. Puccetti. 1986. *Supplement to the Lawyer Statistical Report: The U.S. Legal Profession in 1985.* Chicago: American Bar Foundation.

Curtis, Charles P. 1947. *Lions Under the Throne.* Boston: Little, Brown.

Cushman, Barry. 1998. *Rethinking the New Deal Court: The Structure of a Constitutional Revolution.* New York and Oxford: Oxford University Press.

Dahl, Robert A. 1969. "The Concept of Power." In *Political Power: A Reader in Theory and Research,* ed. Roderick Bell, David V. Edwards, and R. Harrison Wagner, 79–93. New York: Free Press.

_____. 1961. *Who Governs?* New Haven: Yale University Press.

_____. 1957. "Decision-Making in a Democracy: The Supreme Court as a National Policy-Maker." *Journal of Public Law* 6:279–95.

_____. 1956. *A Preface to Democratic Theory.* Chicago: University of Chicago Press.

Daily National Intelligencer. 1814. "The Supreme Court." February 24.

_____. 1819. "State Insolvency Laws." March 16.

Davidson, Chandler, and Bernard Grofman. 1994. *Quiet Revolution in the South.* Princeton: Princeton University Press.

Delgado, Richard. 1995. *Critical Race Theory: The Cutting Edge.* Philadelphia: Temple University Press.

"Developments in the Law—Class Actions." 1976. *Harvard Law Review* 89:1318–1644.

Dolbeare, Kenneth M. 1967. "The Public Views the Supreme Court." In *Law, Politics and the Federal Courts,* ed. H. Jacob, 194–212. Boston: Little, Brown.

Dolbeare, Kenneth, and Phillip E. Hammond. 1971. *The School Prayer Decisions: From Court Policy to Local Practice.* Chicago: University of Chicago Press.

Downs, Donald A. 1989. *The New Politics of Pornography.* Chicago: University of Chicago Press.

Dudziak, Mary L. 1997. "The Little Rock Crisis and Foreign Affairs: Race, Resistance, and the Image of American Democracy." *Southern California Law Review* 70:1641–1716.

———. 1988. "Desegregation as a Cold War Imperative." *Stanford Law Review* 41:61–120.

Duggan, Lisa.1992. "Making It Perfectly Queer." *Socialist Review* 22:11–31.

Duggan, Lisa, and Nan D. Hunter. 1995. *Sex Wars: Sexual Dissent and Political Culture.* New York: Routledge.

Dworkin, Ronald. 1986. *Law's Empire.* Cambridge: Harvard University Press.

———. 1978. *Taking Rights Seriously.* Cambridge: Harvard University Press.

Edelman, Lauren. 1990. "Legal Environments and Organizational Governance: The Expansion of Due Process in the American Workplace." *American Journal of Sociology.* 97:1531–76.

Eisgruber, Christopher L. 1992. "Is the Supreme Court an Educative Institution?" *New York University Law Review* 67:962–1032.

Ellis, Richard E. 1971. *The Jeffersonian Crisis: Courts and Politics in the Young Republic.* New York: Oxford University Press.

Ely, John Hart. 1980. *Democracy and Distrust: A Theory of Judicial Review.* Cambridge: Harvard University Press.

———. 1973. "The Wages of Crying Wolf: A Comment on *Roe v. Wade.*" *Yale Law Journal* 82 (3):920–49.

Epp, Charles. 1999. "External Pressure and the Supreme Court's Agenda." In *Supreme Court Decision-Making: New Institutional Approaches,* ed. Cornell W. Clayton and Howard Gillman, 255–79. Chicago and London: University of Chicago Press.

———. 1996. "Do Bills of Rights Matter? The Canadian Charter of Rights and Freedom." *American Political Science Review* 90:765–79.

———. 1990. "Connecting Litigation Levels and Legal Mobilization: Explaining Interstate Variation in Employment Civil Rights Litigation." *Law and Society Review* 24:145–63.

Epstein, Lee. 1994. "Exploring the Participation of Organized Interests in State Court Litigation." *Political Research Quarterly* 47:335–51.

———. 1986. *Conservatives in Court.* Knoxville: University of Tennessee Press.

Epstein, Lee, and Jack Knight. 1998. *The Choices Justices Make.* Washington DC: CQ Press.

———. 1997. "The New Institutionalism, Part 2." *Law and Courts* 7 (spring):4–9.

Epstein, Lee, and Thomas G. Walker. 1995a. *Constitutional Law for a Changing America: Institutional Powers and Constraints.* 2d ed. Washington DC: CQ Press.

———. 1995b. "The Role of the Supreme Court in American Society: Playing the Reconstruction Game." In *Contemplating Courts,* ed. Lee Epstein, 315–46. Washington, DC: CQ Press.

Epstein, Lee, Jeffrey A. Segal, Harold J. Spaeth, and Thomas G. Walker. 1994. *The Supreme Court Compendium: Data, Decisions and Developments.* Washington, DC: CQ Press.

Epstein, Lee, and Joseph F. Kobylka. 1992. *The Supreme Court and Legal Change.* Chapel Hill: University of North Carolina Press.

Eskridge, William N. Jr. 1994. *Dynamic Statutory Interpretation.* Cambridge: Harvard University Press.

_____. 1991. "Overriding Supreme Court Statutory Interpretation Decisions." *Yale Law Journal* 101:331–455.

Ethridge, Marcus E. 1985. "A Political-Institutional Interpretation of Legislative Oversight Mechanisms and Behaviors." *Polity* 17:340–60.

Farber, Daniel A., and Philip P. Frickey. 1991. *Law and Public Choice.* Chicago: University of Chicago Press.

Feeley, Malcolm M. 1973. "Power, Impact, and the Supreme Court." In *The Impact of Supreme Court Decisions,* ed. Theodore L. Becker and Malcolm M. Feeley, 218–29. New York: Oxford University Press.

Fehrenbacher, Don E. 1978. *The Dred Scott Case: Its Significance in American Law and Politics.* New York: Oxford University Press.

Fineman, Martha. 1995. *The Neutered Mother, the Sexual Family, and Other Twentieth-Century Tragedies.* New York: Routledge.

Fink, Leon. 1987. "Labor, Liberty and the Law: Trade Unionism and the Problem of the American Constitutional Order." *Journal of American History* 74:904–25.

Finnemore, Martha. 1996. *National Interests in International Society.* Ithaca, NY: Cornell University Press.

Fiorina, Morris P. 1992. *Divided Government.* New York: Macmillan.

Fish, Stanley. 1980. *Is There a Text in This Class?* Cambridge: Harvard University Press.

Fisher, Louis. 1985. "Constitutional Interpretation by Members of Congress." *North Carolina Law Review* 63:707–47.

Fiss, Owen. 1982. "Objectivity and Interpretation." *Stanford Law Review* 34: 739–63.

Flathman, Richard. 1976. *The Practice of Rights.* New York: Cambridge University Press.

Flemming, Roy B., John Bohte, and B. Ban Wood. 1997. "One Voice Among Many: The Supreme Court's Influence on Attentiveness to Issues in the United States, 1947–1992." *American Journal of Political Science* 41:1224–50.

Flemming, Roy, et al. 1994. "Attention, Agendas, and America's Constitutional Dialogues: A Preliminary Inquiry." Paper presented at meeting of the American Political Science Association, September 1–4, New York.

Forbath, William E. 1991. *Law and the Shaping of the American Labor Movement.* Cambridge: Harvard University Press.

Frank, John Paul. 1958. *Marble Palace: The Supreme Court in American Life.* New York: Alfred A. Knopf.

Frankfurter, Felix. 1964. *The Commerce Clause Under Marshall, Taney and Waite.* First published in 1937. Chicago: Quandrangle Paperbacks.

Frankfurter, Felix, and James Landis. 1928. *The Business of the Supreme Court.* New York: Macmillan.

Freeman, Alan. 1982. "Antidiscrimination Law: A Critical Review." In *The Politics of Law: A Progressive Critique,* ed. David Kairys, 96–116. New York: Pantheon.

Freyer, Tony A. 1994. *Producers versus Capitalists: Constitutional Conflict in Antebellum America.* Charlottesville and London: University Press of Virginia.

Fried, Charles. 1995. "Forward: Revolutions?" *Harvard Law Review* 109:13–77.

_____. 1988. "Jurisprudential Responses to Legal Realism." *Cornell Law Review* 73:331–67.

Frug, Mary Jo. 1992. *Women and the Law.* Mineola, NY: Foundation Press.

Fulwood, Sam. 1992. "Clinton Sees Cuomo as Potential Justice." *Los Angeles Times,* June 17, A12.

Funston, Richard. 1975. "The Supreme Court and Critical Elections." *American Political Science Review* 69:795–811.

Galanter, Marc. 1983. "The Radiating Effects of Courts." In *Empirical Theories of Courts,* ed. Keith D. Boyum and Lynn Mather, 117–42. New York: Longman.

———. 1974. "Why the 'Haves' Come Out Ahead: Speculations on the Limits of Legal Change." *Law and Society Review* 9:95–160.

Garth, Bryant, et al. 1988. "The Institution of the Private Attorney General: Perspectives from an Empirical Study of Class Action Litigation." *Southern California Law Review* 61:353–98.

Gates, John B. 1992. *The Supreme Court and Partisan Realignment: A Macro- and Microlevel Perspective.* Boulder, CO: Westview Press.

———. 1991. "Theory, Methods, and the New Institutionalism in Judicial Research." In *The American Courts: A Critical Assessment,* ed. J. Gates and C. Johnson, 469–90. Washington, DC: Congressional Quarterly Press.

———. 1989. "Supreme Court Voting and Realigning Issues: A Microlevel Analysis of Supreme Court Policy Making and Electoral Realignment." *Social Science History* 13:255–84.

———. 1987. "Partisan Realignment, Unconstitutional State Policies, and the U.S. Supreme Court: 1837–1964." *American Journal of Political Science* 31:259–80.

Gaventa, John. 1980. *Power and Powerlessness: Quiescence and Rebellion in an Appalachian Valley.* Urbana: University of Illinois Press.

Geertz, Clifford. 1983. *Local Knowledge.* New York: Basic Books.

———. 1973. *The Interpretation of Cultures.* New York: Basic Books.

George, Tracey E., and Lee Epstein. 1992. "On the Nature of Supreme Court Decision Making." *American Political Science Review* 86:323–37.

———. 1991. "Women's Rights Litigation in the 1980s: More of the Same?" *Judicature* 74:314–21.

Gillman, Howard. 1999. "The Court Is an Idea, Not a Building (or a Game): Interpretive Institutionalism and the Analysis of Supreme Court Decisionmaking." In *Supreme Court Decision-Making: New Institutionalist Approaches,* ed. Cornell W. Clayton and Howard Gillman, 65–87. Chicago and London: University of Chicago Press.

———. 1997. "The Collapse of Constitutional Originalism and the Rise of the Notion of the 'Living Constitution' in the Course of American State-Building." *Studies in American Political Development* 11:191–247.

———. 1996–1997. "The New Institutionalism, Part 1, More and Less Than Strategy: Some Advantages to Interpretive Institutionalism in the Analysis of Judicial Politics." *Law and Courts* 7 (winter):6–11.

———. 1996. "More on the Origins of the Fuller Court's Jurisprudence: The Scope of Federal Power over Commerce and Manufacturing in Nineteenth-Century Constitutional Law." *Political Research Quarterly* 49:415–37.

_____. 1995a. "Judicial Behavioralism's Problematic Jurisprudence: Post-Positivist Legal Theory and Social Science Investigations of the Legal Model." Paper, Annual Meeting of the American Political Science Association, Chicago.

_____. 1995b. "Sociological Jurisprudence Revisited, or Why Facts Can't Serve as Foundations for Constitutional Theory." *Law and Courts* 5:7–9.

_____. 1994. "Preferred Freedoms: The Progressive Expansion of State Power and the Rise of Modern Civil Liberties Jurisprudence." *Political Research Quarterly* 47:623–53.

_____. 1993. *The Constitution Besieged: The Rise and Demise of Lochner Era Police Powers Jurisprudence.* Durham, NC: Duke University Press.

Ginsberg, Benjamin. 1986. *The Captive Public: How Mass Opinion Promotes State Power.* New York: Basic Books.

Ginsburg, Benjamin, and Martin Shefter. 1990. *Politics by Other Means.* New York: Free Press.

Ginsburg, Ruth Bader. 1992. "Speaking in a Judicial Voice." *New York University Law Review* 67:1885–1904.

Gitenstein, Mark. 1992. *Matters of Principle: An Insider's Account of America's Rejection of Robert Bork's Nomination to the Supreme Court.* New York: Simon and Schuster.

Gold, David A., Clarence Y. H. Lo, and Erik Olin Wright. 1975. "Recent Developments in Marxist Theories of the Capitalist State." *Monthly Review* 27:29–43.

Goldman, Sheldon, and Elliot Slotnick. 1997. "Clinton's First Term Judiciary: Many Bridges to Cross." *Judicature* 80:254–73.

Goldstein, Judith. 1986. "The Political Economy of Trade: Institutions of Protection." *American Political Science Review* 80:161–84.

Goldstein, Leslie. 1997. "State Resistance to Authority in Federal Unions: The Early United States (1790–1860) and the European Community (1958–1994)." *Studies in American Political Development* 11:149–89.

_____. 1994. *Contemporary Cases in Women's Rights.* Madison: University of Wisconsin Press.

_____. 1991. *In Defense of the Text: Democracy and Constitutional Theory.* Totowa, NJ: Rowman and Littlefield, 1991.

_____. 1987. "The EPA and the U.S. Supreme Court." *Research in Law and Policy Studies* 1:145–61.

Goldwin, Robert A., and William A. Schambra, eds. 1982. *How Capitalistic Is the Constitution?* Washington, DC: American Enterprise Institute for Public Policy Research.

Goodrich, Peter. 1986. *Reading the Law.* Oxford: Basil Blackwell.

_____. 1984. "Rhetoric as Jurisprudence." *Oxford Journal of Legal Studies* 4:88–122.

Gordon, Robert W. 1984. "Critical Legal Histories." *Stanford Law Review* 36:57–125.

Graber, Mark. 1998a. "Establishing Judicial Review? *Schooner Peggy* and the Early Marshall Court." *Political Research Quarterly* 51: 7–25.

_____. 1998b. "Federalist or Friends of Adams: The Marshall Court and Party Politics." *Studies in American Political Development* (forthcoming).

_____. 1997. "The Clintonification of American Law: Abortion, Welfare, and Liberal Constitutional Theory." *Ohio State Law Journal* 58:731–818.

_____. 1996. *Rethinking Abortion: Equal Choice, the Constitution, and Reproductive Choice.* Princeton: Princeton University Press.

_____. 1995. "The Passive-Aggressive Virtues: *Cohens v. Virginia* and the Problematic Establishment of Judicial Power." *Constitutional Commentary* 12:67–92.

_____. 1993. "The Non-Majoritarian Difficulty: Legislative Deference to the Judiciary." *Studies in American Political Development* 7:35–73.

_____. 1991. *Transforming Free Speech: The Ambiguous Legacy of Civil Libertarianism.* Berkeley: University of California Press.

Greenberg, Edward S. 1982. "Class Rule Under the Constitution." In *How Capitalistic Is the Constitution?* ed. Robert A. Goldwin and William A. Schambra, 22–48. Washington, DC: American Enterprise Institute for Public Policy Research.

Greenhouse, Carol J. 1988. "Courting Difference: Issues of Interpretation and Comparison in the Study of Legal Ideologies." *Law and Society Review* 22:687–707.

Greenstone, J. David. 1988. "Against Simplicity: The Cultural Dimensions of the Constitution." *University of Chicago Law Review* 55:428–49.

Griffin, Stephen. 1996. *American Constitutionalism: From Theory to Politics.* Princeton: Princeton University Press.

Grogan, Susan E. 1991. "Judicial Apprentices? Law Clerks in the United States." Paper presented at the annual meeting of the American Political Science Association, Washington, DC.

Hall, Melinda Gann, and Paul Brace. 1993. "Integrated Models of Judicial Dissent." *Journal of Politics* 55:914–35.

Hall, Richard L., and Frank W. Wayman. 1990. "Buying Time: Moneyed Interests and the Mobilization of Bias in Congressional Committees." *American Political Science Review* 84:797–820.

Halley, Janet. 1993. "The Construction of Heterosexuality." In *Fear of a Queer Planet: Queer Politics and Social Theory,* ed. Michael Warner, 82–102. Minneapolis: University of Minnesota Press.

_____. 1989. "The Politics of the Closet: Toward Equal Protection for Gay, Lesbian, and Bisexual Identity." *UCLA Law Review* 36:915–76.

Haltom, William. 1995. "Facts of Political Life." *Law and Courts* 5:4–7.

Handler, Joel F. 1978. *Social Movements and the Legal System: A Theory of Law Reform and Social Change.* New York: Academic Press.

Hansen, John Mark. 1991. *Gaining Access.* Chicago: University of Chicago Press.

Harrington, Christine B. 1988. "Moving from Integrative to Constitutive Theories of Law: Comment on Itzkowitz." *Law and Society Review* 22:963–67.

Harrington, Christine B., and Daniel Ward. 1995. "Rethinking Litigation: The Role of Courts in Producing Litigation." In *Contemplating Courts,* ed. Lee Epstein, 206–26. Washington, DC: CQ Press.

Harrington, Christine B., and Barbara Yngvesson. 1990. "Interpretive Sociolegal Research." *Law and Social Inquiry* 15:135–48.

Harris, William. 1993. *The Interpretable Constitution.* Baltimore: Johns Hopkins University Press.

_____. 1982. "Binding Word and Polity." *American Political Science Review* 76:34–45.

Hart, Henry. 1959. "The Time Chart of the Justices." *Harvard Law Review* 73:84–129.

Haskins, George L., and Johnson, Herbert. 1981. *Foundations of Power: John Marshall, 1801–1815.* New York: Macmillan.

Hattam, Victoria C. 1993. *Labor Visions and State Power: The Origins of Business Unionism in the United States.* Princeton: Princeton University Press.

Heinz, John P., and Edward O. Laumann. 1982. *Chicago Lawyers: The Social Structure of the Bar.* New York: Russell Sage Foundation.

Heinz, John P., Edward O. Laumann, Robert L. Nelson, and Robert H. Salisbury. 1993. *The Hollow Core: Private Interests in National Policy Making.* Cambridge: Harvard University Press.

Hinkson-Craig, Barbara, and David M. O'Brien. 1993. *Abortion and American Politics.* Chatham, NJ: Chatham House.

Hirsch, H. N. 1992. *A Theory of Liberty: The Constitution and Minorities.* New York: Routledge Press.

Hofstadter, Richard. 1974. *The American Political Tradition.* 1948. Reprint, New York: Vintage Books.

Horowitz, Donald L. 1977. *The Courts and Social Policy.* Washington, DC.: Brookings Institute.

Horwitz, Morton J. 1992. *The Transformation of American Law, 1870–1960: The Crisis of Legal Orthodoxy.* New York and Oxford: Oxford University Press.

Hovencamp, Herbert. 1992. "Capitalism." In *The Oxford Companion to the Supreme Court of the United States,* Kermit L. Hall, editor in chief, 117–25. New York and Oxford: Oxford University Press.

_____. 1991. *Enterprise and American Law, 1836–1937.* Cambridge and London: Harvard University Press.

Hunt, Alan. 1993. *Explorations in Law and Society: Toward a Constitutive Theory of Law.* New York: Routledge.

Hurst, James Willard. 1956. *Law and the Conditions of Freedom in the Nineteenth-Century United States.* Madison: University of Wisconsin Press.

Husserl, Edmund. 1965. *Phenomenology and the Crisis of Philosophy.* New York: Harper and Row.

Ireland, Robert M. 1986. *The Legal Career of William Pinkney: 1764–1822.* New York: Garland Publishing.

Inter-university Consortium for Political and Social Research (ICPSR). 1996. American National Election Studies, 1948–1994. Ann Arbor, MI.

Ivers, Gregg, and Karen O'Connor. 1987. "Friends as Foes: The Amicus Curiae Participation and Effectiveness of the American Civil Liberties Union and the Americans for Effective Law Enforcement in Criminal Cases, 1969–1982." *Law and Policy* 9:161–78.

Jacobson, Gary C. 1990. *The Electoral Origins of Divided Government.* Boulder, CO: Westview Press.

Jessup, Dwight Wiley. 1987. *Reaction and Accommodation: The United States Supreme Court and Political Conflict, 1809–1835.* New York: Garland Publishing.

Johnson, Charles A., and Bradley C. Canon. 1984. *Judicial Policies: Implementation and Impact.* Washington, DC: Congressional Quarterly Press.

Johnson, James D. 1991. *Symbol and Strategy: On the Cultural Analysis of Politics.* Ph.D. dissertation, University of Chicago.

Jones, Charles O. 1990. "The Separated Presidency: Making It Work in Contemporary Politics." In *The New American Political System,* ed. Anthony King, 1–28. Washington, DC: AEI Press.

Kahn, Ronald. 1996. "Liberalism and the Rights of Subordinated Groups: Constitutional Theory and Practice at a Crossroads." Paper, Conference on the Liberal Tradition in American Politics: Consensus, Polarity, or Multiple Traditions? University of Chicago, November 23, 1996.

———. 1994. *The Supreme Court and Constitutional Theory, 1953–1993.* Lawrence: University Press of Kansas.

Kairys, David, ed. 1982. *The Politics of Law: A Progressive Critique.* New York: Pantheon.

Karst, Kenneth. 1993. *Law's Promise, Law's Expression: Visions of Power in the Politics of Race, Gender, and Religion.* New Haven: Yale University Press.

Katzmann, Robert A. 1997. *Courts and Congress.* Washington, DC: Brookings Institute.

Kay, Richard S. 1980. "The Equal Protection Clause in the Supreme Court: 1873–1903." *Buffalo Law Review* 29:667–725.

Keller, Morton. 1990. *Regulating a New Economy: Public Policy and Economic Change in America, 1900–1933.* Cambridge and London: Harvard University Press.

Kelly, Alfred J., Winfred A. Harbison, and Herman Belz. 1991. *The American Constitution: Its Origins and Development,* 7th ed., 2 vols. New York and London: W. W. Norton.

Kelman, Mark. 1987. *A Guide to Critical Legal Studies.* Cambridge: Harvard University Press.

Kens, Paul. 1997. *Justice Stephen Field: Shaping Liberty from the Gold Rush to the Gilded Age.* Lawrence: University Press of Kansas.

Kessler, Mark. 1993. "Legal Discourse and Political Intolerance: The Ideology of Clear and Present Danger." *Law & Society Review* 27:559–97.

Key, V. O. 1959. "Secular Realignment and the Party System." *Journal of Politics* 21:198–210.

———. 1955. "A Theory of Critical Elections." *Journal of Politics* 17:3–18.

King, Gary. 1987. "Presidential Appointments to the Supreme Court: Adding Systematic Explanation to Probabilistic Description." *American Politics Quarterly* 15:373–86.

Klaidman, Daniel. 1993. "Just Like Old Times? Liberals Challenge President on Some Judgeships." *Legal Times,* October 25, p. 1.

Klare, Karl E. 1979. "Law-Making as Praxis." *Telos* 40:122–35.

———. 1978. "The Judicial Deradicalization of the Wagner Act and the Origins of Modern Legal Consciousness, 1937–1941." *University of Minnesota Law Review* 62:265–339.

Klotz, Audie. 1995. *Norms in International Relations: The Struggle Against Apartheid.* Ithaca, NY: Cornell University Press.

Kluger, Richard. 1976. *Simple Justice.* New York: Alfred A. Knopf.

Knight, Jack, and Lee Epstein. 1996. "On the Struggle for Judicial Supremacy." *Law and Society Review* 30:87–120.

Kobylka, Joseph. 1991. *The Politics of Obscenity: Group Litigation in a Time of Legal Change.* Westport, CT: Greenwood Press.

Koelble, Thomas A. 1995. "The New Institutionalism in Political Science and Sociology." *Comparative Politics* 27:231–43

Kommers, Donald. 1989. *The Constitutional Jurisprudence of the Federal Republic of Germany.* Durham: Duke University Press.

Korn, Jessica. 1996. *The Power of Separation: American Constitutionalism and the Myth of the Legislative Veto.* Princeton: Princeton University Press.

Krislov, Samuel. 1965. *The Supreme Court in the Political Process.* New York: Macmillan.

Kutler, Stanley I. 1971. *Privilege and Creative Destruction: The Charles River Bridge Case.* New York: Norton.

Lamb, Charles M. 1976. "Judicial Policy-Making and Information Flow to the Supreme Court." *Vanderbilt Law Review* 29:45–124.

Landis, James M. 1938. *The Administrative Process.* New Haven: Yale University Press.

Lasser, William. 1988. *The Limits of Judicial Power: The Supreme Court in American Politics.* Chapel Hill: University of North Carolina Press.

———. 1985. "The Supreme Court in Periods of Critical Realignment." *Journal of Politics* 47:1174–87.

Lears, T. J. Jackson. 1985. "The Concept of Cultural Hegemony: Problems and Possibilities." *American Historical Review* 90:567–93.

Leo, Richard A. 1996. "Miranda's Revenge: Police Interrogation as a Confidence Game," *Law and Society Review* 30:259–88.

Lerner, Max. 1933. "The Supreme Court and American Capitalism." *Yale Law Journal* 42:668–701.

Lerner, Ralph. 1987. *The Thinking Revolutionary: Principle and Practice in the New Republic.* Ithaca, NY: Cornell University Press.

Leuchtenburg, William E. 1995. *The Supreme Court Reborn: The Constitutional Revolution in the Age of Roosevelt.* Oxford: Oxford University Press.

Levi, Edward. 1949. *An Introduction to Legal Reasoning.* Chicago: University of Chicago Press.

Levinson, Sanford. 1992. "Law as Literature." In *Modern Constitutional Theory*, ed. John Garvey and T. Alexander Aleinikoff, 129–35. 3d ed. St. Paul, MN: West Publishing.

Lewis, Anthony. 1964. *Gideon's Trumpet.* New York: Vintage.

Lindblom, Charles E. 1977. *Politics and Markets: The World's Political-Economic Systems.* New York: Basic Books.

Llewellyn, Karl N. 1931. "A Realistic Jurisprudence—The Next Step." *Columbia Law Review* 30:431–65.

Lloyd, Randall. 1995. "Separating Partisanship from Party in Judicial Research: Reapportionment in the U.S. District Courts." *American Political Science Review* 89:413–20.

Loffredo, Stephen. 1993. "Poverty, Democracy, and Constitutional Law." *University of Pennsylvania Law Review* 141:1277–1389.

Lowi, Theodore J. 1985. *The Personal President: Power Invested, Promise Unfulfilled.* Ithaca, NY, and London: Cornell University Press.

_____. 1969. *The End of Liberalism: Ideology, Policy, and the Crisis of Public Authority.* New York: W. W. Norton.

Lukes, Steven. 1974. *Power: A Radical View.* London: Macmillan.

MacKinnon, Catharine. 1979. *Sexual Harassment of Working Women.* New Haven: Yale University Press.

Madison, James. 1896. "Eighth Annual Message." In *A Compilation of the Messages and Papers of the Presidents, 1789–1897,* ed. James D. Richardson. Vol. 1. Washington, DC: Government Printing Office.

_____. 1910. *The Writings of James Madison,* ed. Gaillard Hunt. Vol. 9. New York: G. P. Putnam's Sons.

Malinowski, Bronislaw. 1944. *Freedom and Civilization.* New York: Roy Publishers.

Maltzman, Forrest, and Paul J. Wahlbeck. 1996. "Strategic Policy Considerations and Voting Fluidity on the Burger Court." *American Political Science Review* 90:581–92.

March, James G., and Johan P. Olsen. 1989. *Rediscovering Institutions: The Organizational Basis of Politics.* New York: Free Press.

_____. "The New Institutionalism: Organizational Factors in Political Life." *American Political Science Review* 78:734–49.

Marcus, Maeva. 1996. "Judicial Review in the Early Republic." In *Launching the "Extended Republic": The Federalist Era,* ed. Ronald Hoffman and Peter J. Albert, 25–53. Charlottesville: University Press of Virginia.

Marshall, John. 1990. *The Papers of John Marshall,* ed. Charles F. Hobson. Vol. 6. Chapel Hill: University of North Carolina Press.

Marvell, Thomas B. 1978. *Appellate Court and Lawyers: Information Gathering in the Adversary System.* Westport, CT: Greenwood Press.

Mather, Lynn. 1997. "Theorizing About Trial Courts: Lawyers, Policymaking, and Tobacco Litigation." Paper, annual meeting, American Political Science Association, Washington, DC.

Matthews, Donald. 1960. *U.S. Senators and Their World.* Chapel Hill: University of North Carolina Press.

McAdam, Doug. 1982. *Political Process and the Development of Black Insurgency, 1930–1970.* Chicago: University of Chicago Press.

McCann, Michael W. 1996. "Causal versus Constitutive Explanations (or, On the Difficulty of Being So Positive)," *Law and Social Inquiry* 21:457–82.

_____. 1995. "As a Matter of ('Social') Fact." *Law and Courts* 5:7–9.

_____. 1994. *Rights at Work: Pay Equity Reform and the Politics of Legal Mobilization.* Chicago: University of Chicago Press.

_____. 1993. "Reform Litigation on Trial," *Law and Social Inquiry* 17:715–43.

_____. 1989. "Equal Protection for Social Inequality: Race and Class in Constitutional Ideology." In *Judging the Constitution: Critical Essays on Judicial Lawmaking,* ed. Michael W. McCann and Gerald L. Houseman, 231–64. Glenview, IL: Scott Foresman/Little, Brown series in political science.

_____. 1986. *Taking Reform Seriously: Perspectives on Public Interest Liberalism.* Ithaca, NY: Cornell University Press.

McCann, Michael W., and Tracey March. 1996. "Law and Everyday Forms of Resistance: A Socio-Political Assessment." *Studies in Law, Politics and Society* 15:207–36.

McCloskey, Robert G. 1994. *The American Supreme Court.* 2d ed., rev. Sanford Levinson. Chicago: University of Chicago Press.

McGlen, Nancy E., and Karen O'Connor. 1980. "An Analysis of the U.S. Women's Rights Movement." *Women and Politics* 1:65–85.

McGuire, Kevin T. 1998. "Lobbyists, Revolving Doors, and the U.S. Supreme Court." Paper, annual meeting, Midwest Political Science Association, Chicago.

_____. 1995. "Capital Investments in the U.S. Supreme Court: Winning with Washington Representation." In *Contemplating Courts,* ed. Lee Epstein, 72–92. Washington: Congressional Quarterly Press.

_____. 1993. *The Supreme Court Bar: Legal Elites in the Washington Community.* Charlottesville: University Press of Virginia.

McGuire, Kevin T., and Gregory A. Caldeira. 1993. "Lawyers, Organized Interests, and the Law of Obscenity: Agenda Setting in the Supreme Court." *American Political Science Review* 87:717–26.

McGuire, Kevin T., and Barbara Palmer. 1996. "Issues, Agendas, and Decision Making on the Supreme Court." *American Political Science Review* 90:853–65.

McMichael, Lawrence G., and Richard Trilling. 1980. "The Structure and Meaning of Critical Realignment." In *Realignment in American Politics,* ed. B. Campbell and R. Trilling, 21–51. Austin: University of Texas Press.

Melnick, R. Shep. 1983. *Regulation and the Courts: The Case of Clean Air.* Washington DC: Brookings Institute.

Mendelson, Wallace. 1996. "John Marshall and the Sugar Trust: A Reply to Professor Gillman." *Political Research Quarterly* 49:405–13.

_____. 1960. *Capitalism, Democracy, and the Supreme Court.* New York: Appleton-Century-Crofts.

Merry, Sally Engle. 1986. "Everyday Understandings of the Law in Working-Class America." *American Ethnologist* 12:253–70.

_____. 1985. "Concepts of Law and Justice Among Working-Class Americans: Ideology as Culture." *Legal Studies Forum* 9:59–69.

Milbrath, Lester W. 1963. *The Washington Lobbyists.* Chicago: Rand McNally.

Miller, Arthur S. 1979. "Of Frankenstein, Monsters and Shining Knights: Myth, Reality and the Class Action Problem." *Harvard Law Review* 92:664–94.

_____. 1968. *The Supreme Court and American Capitalism.* New York: Free Press.

Milner, Neal. 1986. "The Dilemmas of Legal Mobilization: Ideologies and Strategies of Mental Patient Liberation." *Law and Policy* 8:105–29.

Minow, Martha. 1987. "Interpreting Rights: An Essay for Robert Cover." *Yale Law Journal* 96:1860–1915.

Mnookin, Robert H., and Lewis Kornhauser. 1979. "Bargaining in the Shadow of Law: The Case of Divorce." *Yale Law Journal* 88:950–97.

Monroe, James. 1896. "Eighth Annual Message." In *A Compilation of the Messages and Papers of the Presidents, 1789–1897* ed. James D. Richardson. Vol. 2. Washington, DC: Government Printing Office.

Morgan, Richard E. 1984. *Disabling America: The "Rights Industry" in Our Time.* New York: Basic Books.

Morris, Aldon. 1984. *The Origins of the Civil Rights Movement.* New York: Free Press.

Murphy, Paul L. 1972. *The Constitution in Crisis Times, 1918–1969.* New York: Harper and Row.

Murphy, Walter F. 1986. "Who Shall Interpret the Constitution?" *Review of Politics* 48:401–23.

_____. 1964. *Elements of Judicial Strategy.* Chicago: University of Chicago Press.

Nagel, Robert. 1994. *Judicial Power and American Character: Censoring Ourselves in an Anxious Age.* New York: Oxford University Press, 1994.

_____. 1989. *Constitutional Cultures: The Mentality and Consequences of Judicial Review.* Berkeley: University of California Press.

Nast, Heidi J. 1998. "Unsexy Geographies." *Gender, Place and Culture: A Journal of Feminist Geography* 5:191–206.

Nedelsky, Jennifer. 1990. *Private Property and the Limits of American Constitutionalism: The Madisonian Framework and Its Legacy.* Chicago and London: University of Chicago Press.

Newman, Jon 0. 1997. "The Judge Baer Controversy." *Judicature* 80:156–64.

Newmyer, R. Kent. 1968. *The Supreme Court Under Marshall and Taney.* New York: Thomas Y. Crowell Company.

Norpoth, Helmut, Jeffrey A. Segal, William Mishler, and Reginald S. Sheehan. 1994. "Popular Influence on Supreme Court Decisions." *American Political Science Review* 3:711–24.

O'Brien, David. 1999. "Institutional Norms and Supreme Court Opinions." In *Supreme Court Decision-Making: New Institutionalist Approaches,* ed. Cornell Clayton and Howard Gillman, 91–113. Chicago: University of Chicago Press.

_____. 1996. *Storm Center.* 4th ed. New York: Norton.

_____. 1988. "The Reagan Judges: His Most Enduring Legacy?" In *The Reagan Legacy,* ed. Charles Jones, 60–101. Chatham, NJ: Chatham House.

O'Connor, Karen. 1980. *Women's Organizations' Use of the Courts.* Lexington, MA: Lexington Books.

O'Connor, Karen, and Lee Epstein. 1989. *Public Interest Law Groups.* New York: Greenwood Press.

O'Fallon, James M. 1993. "The Case of Benjamin More: A Lost Episode in the Struggle over Repeal of the 1801 Judiciary Act." *Law and History Review* 11:43–57.

_____. 1992. "*Marbury.*" *Stanford Law Review* 44:219–60.

O'Neill, Timothy. 1981. "The Language of Equality." *American Political Science Review* 75:59–75.

O'Rourke, Timothy G. 1992. "The 1982 Amendments and the Voting Rights Paradox." In *Controversies in Minority Voting,* ed. Bernard Grofman and Chandler Davidson, 85–113. Washington, DC: Brookings Institute.

Olken, Samuel R. 1997. "Justice George Sutherland and Economic Liberty: Constitutional Conservativism and the Problem of Factions." *William and Mary Bill of Rights Journal* 6:1–88.

Olson, Susan M. 1984. *Clients and Lawyers: Securing the Rights of Disabled Persons.* Westport, CT: Greenwood Press.

Ornstein, Norman J., Thomas E. Mann, and Michael J. Malbin. 1996. *Vital Statistics on Congress, 1995–1996.* 1996. Washington, DC: CQ Press.

Orren, Karen. 1995. "The Primacy of Labor in American Constitutional Development." *American Political Science Review* 89:377–88.

———. 1991. *Belated Feudalism: Labor, the Law, and Liberal Development in the United States.* New York: Cambridge University Press.

Pacelle, Richard. 1995. "The Dynamics and Determinants of Agenda Change in the Rehnquist Court." In *Contemplating Courts,* ed. Lee Epstein, 251–74. Washington, DC: CQ Press.

———. 1991. *The Transformation of the Supreme Court's Agenda.* Boulder, CO: Westview Press.

———. 1990. "The Supreme Court's Agenda and the Dynamics of Policy Evolution." Paper, American Political Science Association, August 30–September 2, San Francisco.

Peltason, Jack W. 1971. *Fifty-eight Lonely Men.* Urbana: University of Illinois Press.

Peritz, Rudolph J. R. 1996. *Competition Policy in America, 1888–1992: History, Rhetoric, Law.* New York: Oxford University Press.

Perry, H. W. Jr. 1991. *Deciding to Decide: Agenda Setting in the United States Supreme Court.* Cambridge: Harvard University Press.

Perry, Michael. 1994. *The Constitution and the Courts: Law or Politics?* Oxford: Oxford University Press.

———. 1982. *The Constitution, the Courts, and Human Rights: An Inquiry into the Legitimacy of Constitutional Policymaking by the Judiciary.* New Haven: Yale University Press.

Peterson, V. Spike. 1997. "Whose Crisis? Early and Post-modern Masculinism." In *Innovation and Transformation in International Studies,* ed. Stephen Gill and James H. Mittelman, 97–185. Cambridge and New York: Cambridge University Press.

Peterson, V. Spike, and Laura Parisi. 1997. "Are Women Human? It's Not an Academic Question." Paper, International Studies Association, Toronto.

Phalen, Shane. 1994. *Getting Specific: Postmodern Lesbian Politics.* Minneapolis: University of Minnesota Press.

Phelan, Peggy. 1993. *Unmarked: The Politics of Performance.* New York: Routledge.

Phelps, Timothy. 1992. "Campaign '92—High Court." *New York Newsday,* October 30, A17.

Pitkin, Hanna. 1967. *The Concept of Representation.* Berkeley and Los Angeles: University of California Press.

Pomper, Gerald M. 1993. "The Presidential Election." In *The Election of 1992,* ed. G. Pomper, 132–56. Chatham, NJ: Chatham House.

Poole, Keith T., and Howard Rosenthal. 1997. *Congress: A Political-Economic History of Roll Call Voting.* New York: Oxford University Press.

Posner, Richard. 1990. *The Problems of Jurisprudence.* Cambridge: Harvard University Press.

Pound, Roscoe. 1917. "The Limits of Effective Legal Action." *International Journal of Ethics* 27:150–67.

Potter, David M. 1976. *The Impending Crisis, 1848–1861.* New York: Harper and Row.

Powell, Walter W., and Paul J. DiMaggio, eds. 1991. *The New Institutionalism in Organizational Analysis.* Chicago: University of Chicago Press.

Pritchett, C. Herman. 1948. *The Roosevelt Court.* Chicago: University of Chicago Press.

Provine, Doris Marie. 1980. *Case Selection in the United States Supreme Court.* Chicago: University of Chicago Press.

Rabban, David M. 1996. "Free Speech in Progressive Social Thought." *Texas Law Review* 74:951–1038.

Ragsdale, Lyn. 1996. *Vital Statistics on the Presidency.* Washington, DC: CQ Press.

Rakove, Jack N. 1997. "The Origins of Judicial Review: A Plea for New Contexts." *Stanford Law Review* 49:1031–64.

Rawls, John. 1971. *A Theory of Justice.* Cambridge: Harvard University Press.

Reps, John W. 1991. *Washington on View: The Nation's Capital Since 1790.* Chapel Hill: University of North Carolina Press.

Rhode, David W., and Harold Spaeth. 1976. *Supreme Court Decision Making.* San Francisco: Freeman and Company.

Richards, David A. J. 1986. *Toleration and the Constitution.* Oxford: Oxford University Press.

Robertson, David Brian. 1993. "The Return to History and the New Institutionalism in American Political Science." *Social Science History* 17:1–36.

Rockman, Bert A. 1994. "The New Institutionalism and the Old Institutions." In *New Perspectives on American Politics,* ed. Lawrence C. Dodd and Calvin Jillson, 143–61. Washington, DC: Congressional Quarterly Press.

Rodgers, Harrell R. Jr., and Charles S. Bullock III. 1972. *Law and Social Change: Civil Rights Laws and Their Consequences.* New York: McGraw-Hill.

Rogers, Daniel T. 1987. *Contested Truths: Keywords in American Politics Since Independence.* New York: Basic Books.

Rosen, Jeffrey. 1997. "Class Legislation, Public Choice, and the Structural Constitution." *Harvard Journal of Law and Public Policy* 21:181–93.

Rosenberg, Gerald N. 1992. "Judicial Independence and the Reality of Political Power." *Review of Politics* 54:369–98.

———. 1991. *The Hollow Hope: Can Courts Bring About Social Change?* Chicago: University of Chicago Press.

Salokar, Rebecca Mae. 1992. *The Solicitor General: The Politics of Law.* Philadelphia: Temple University Press.

Sarat, Austin, ed. 1997. *Race, Law, and Culture: Reflections on Brown v. Board of Education.* New York: Oxford University Press.

———. 1990. "The Law Is All Over: Power, Resistance, and the Legal Consciousness of the Welfare Poor." *Yale Journal of Law and the Humanities* 2:343–79.

———. 1985. "Legal Effectiveness and Social Studies of Law." *Legal Studies Forum* 9:23–31.

Saunders, Melissa. 1997. "Equal Protection, Class Legislation, and Color Blindness." *Michigan Law Review* 96:245–337.

Sax, Joseph L. 1971. *Defending the Environment: A Strategy for Citizen Action.* New York: Knopf.

Schattschneider, E. E. 1975. *The Semisovereign People: A Realist's View of Democracy in America.* Himsdale, IL: Dryden Press.

Scheiber, Harry N. 1997. "Private Rights and Public Power: American Law, Capitalism, and the Republican Polity in Nineteenth-Century America." *Yale Law Journal* 107:823–61.

Scheingold, Stuart A. 1989. "Constitutional Rights and Social Change." In *Judging the Constitution,* ed. Michael W. McCann and Gerald L. Houseman, 73–91. Glenview, IL: Scott, Foresman/Little, Brown.

———. 1974. *The Politics of Rights: Lawyers, Public Policy, and Political Change.* New Haven: Yale University Press.

Schlozman, Kay L., and John T. Tierney. 1986. *Organized Interests and American Democracy.* New York: Harper and Row.

Schmidhauser, John. 1960. *The Supreme Court: Its Politics, Personalities, and Procedures.* New York: Holt, Rinehart and Winston.

Schneider, Elizabeth M. 1986. "The Dialectic of Rights and Politics: Perspectives from the Women's Movement," *New York University Law Review* 61:589–652.

Schubert, Glendon. 1974. *The Judicial Mind Revisited: Psychometric Analysis of Supreme Court Ideology.* New York: Oxford University Press.

———. 1965. *The Judicial Mind: Attitudes and Ideology of Supreme Court Justices, 1946–1963.* Evanston, IL: Northwestern University Press.

Sedgwick, Eve Kosofsky. 1993. *Tendencies.* Durham, NC: Duke University Press.

———. 1990. *Epistemology of the Closet.* Berkeley: University of California Press.

———. 1985. *Between Men: English Literature and Homosocial Desire.* New York: Columbia University Press.

Segal, Jeffery A., and Harold J. Spaeth. 1993. *The Supreme Court and the Attitudinal Model.* Cambridge: Cambridge University Press.

Seidman, Louis Michael, and Mark V. Tushnet. 1996. *Remnants of Belief: Contemporary Constitutional Issues.* New York: Oxford University Press.

Selznick, Philip. 1996. "Institutionalism 'Old' and 'New'." *Administrative Science Quarterly* 41:270–77.

Shafer, Byron E., ed. 1991. *The End of Realignment: Interpreting American Electoral Eras.* Madison: University of Wisconsin Press.

Shapiro, Martin. 1989. "Political Jurisprudence, Public Law, and Post-Consequentialist Ethics: Comment on Professors Barber and Smith." *Studies in American Political Development* 3:88–102.

———. 1988. *Who Guards the Guardians? Judicial Control of Administration.* Athens: University of Georgia Press.

———. 1986. "The Supreme Court's 'Return' to Economic Regulation." *Studies in American Political Development* 1:91–141.

———. 1983. "Fathers and Sons: The Court, the Commentators, and the Search for Values." In *The Burger Court: The Counter-Revolution That Wasn't,* ed. Vincent Blasi, 218–33. New Haven: Yale University Press.

———. 1981. *Courts: A Comparative and Political Analysis.* Chicago and London: University of Chicago Press.

———. 1964. *Law and Politics in the Supreme Court.* New York: Free Press.

Shapiro, Stephen M. 1984. "Oral Argument in the Supreme Court of the United States." *Catholic University Law Review* 33:529–53.

Shiffrin, Steven H. 1993. *The First Amendment, Democracy, and Romance.* Princeton: Princeton University Press.

Shockley, John S. 1989. "All the Free Speech Money Can Buy? The Supreme Court Constricts Campaign Finance Reform." In *Judging the Constitution: Critical Essays on Judicial Lawmaking,* ed. Michael W. McCann and Gerald L. Houseman, 378–408. Glenview, IL: Scott Foresman.

Siegan, Bernard H. 1982. "The Constitution and the Protection of Capitalism." In *How Capitalistic Is the Constitution?* ed. Robert A. Goldwin and William A. Schambra, 106–26. Washington, DC: American Enterprise Institute for Public Policy Research.

Silverstein, Helena. 1996. *Unleashing Rights: Law, Meaning, and the Animal Rights Movement.* Ann Arbor: University of Michigan Press.

Silverstein, Mark, 1994. *Judicious Choices: The New Politics of Supreme Court Confirmations.* New York: Norton.

Silverstein, Mark, and Benjamin Ginsberg. 1987. "The Supreme Court and the New Politics of Judicial Power." *Political Science Quarterly* 102:371–88.

Silverstein, Mark and William Haltom. 1996. "You Can't Always Get What You Want: Reflections on the Ginsburg and Breyer Nominations." *Journal of Law and Politics* 12:459–79.

Simon, James F. 1972. *In His Own Image: The Supreme Court in Richard Nixon's America.* New York: David McKay Company.

Sinclair, Barbara. 1995. "Trying to Govern Positively in a Negative Era." In *The Clinton Presidency: First Appraisals,* ed. Colin Campbell and Bert A. Rockman, 88–125. Chatham, NJ: Chatham House.

———. 1989. *The Transformation of the U.S. Senate.* Baltimore: Johns Hopkins University Press.

Skinner, Quentin. 1974. "Some Problems in the Analysis of Political Thought and Action." Political Theory 2:277–303.

Skolnick, Jerome H., and James Fyfe. 1994. *Above the Law: Police and the Excessive Use of Force.* New York: Free Press.

Skowronek, Stephen. 1982. *Building a New American State: The Expansion of National Administrative Capacities, 1877–1920.* New York: Cambridge University Press.

Smith, Jean Edward. 1996. *John Marshall: Definer of a Nation.* New York: Henry Holt and Company.

Smith, Rogers M. 1992. "If Politics Matters: Implications for a New Institutionalism." *Studies in American Political Development* 6:1–36.

_____. 1988. "Political Jurisprudence, the 'New Institutionalism,' and the Future of Public Law." *American Political Science Review* 82: 89–108.

Songer, Donald R. 1979. "Concern for Policy Outputs as a Cue for Supreme Court Decisions on Certiorari." *Journal of Politics* 41:1185–94.

Songer, Donald R., Jeffrey A. Segal, and Charles M. Cameron. 1994. "The Hierarchy of Justice: Testing a Principal-Agent Model of Supreme Court–Circuit Court Interactions." *American Journal of Political Science* 38:673–96.

Spiller, Pablo T., and Emerson H. Tiller. 1996. "Invitations to Override: Congressional Reversals of Supreme Court Decisions." *International Review of Law and Economics* 16:503–21.

Spriggs, James F. II, and Paul J. Wahlbeck. 1997. "Amicus Curiae and the Role of Information at the Supreme Court." *Political Research Quarterly* 50:365–86.

"Statistics on the 1995 Term." 1996. *Harvard Law Review* 110:367–76.

Steinmo, Sven, Kathleen Thelen, and Frank Longstreth, eds. 1992. *Structuring Politics: Historical Institutionalism in Comparative Analysis.* New York: Cambridge University Press.

Stern, Gerald. 1976. *The Buffalo Creek Disaster.* New York: Vintage.

Stern, Robert H., Eugene Gressman, Stephen M. Shapiro, and Kenneth S. Geller. 1993. *Supreme Court Practice.* 7th ed. Washington, DC: Bureau of National Affairs.

Stetson, Dorothy. 1982. *A Woman's Issue: The Politics of Family Law Reform in England.* Westport, CT: Greenwood Press.

Stewart, David O. 1995. "Back to the Commerce Clause: The Supreme Court Has Yet to Reveal the True Significance of Lopez." *ABA Journal* 81:46–50.

Stewart, Richard B. 1975. "The Reformation of American Administrative Law." *Harvard Law Review* 88:1667–1813.

Stidham, Ronald, Robert Carp, and Donald Songer. 1996. "The Voting Behavior of President Clinton's Judicial Appointees." *Judicature* 80:16–21.

Stimson, James. 1991. *Public Opinion in America: Moods, Cycles, and Swings.* Boulder, CO: Westview Press.

Stites, Francis S. 1972. *Private Interest and Public Gain.* Amherst: University of Massachusetts Press.

Stone, Alec. 1992. *The Birth of Judicial Politics in France.* New York: Oxford University Press.

Stone, Deborah. 1989. "Causal Stories and the Formation of Policy Agendas." *Political Science Quarterly* 104:281–300.

Stychin, Carl F. 1995. *Law's Desire: Sexuality and the Limits of Justice.* New York: Routledge.

Sundquist, James. 1973. *Dynamics of the Party System.* Washington, DC: Brookings Institute.

Sunstein, Cass. 1996. "Forward: Leaving Things Undecided." *Harvard Law Review* 110:4–103.

_____. 1994. "Homosexuality and the Constitution." *Indiana Law Journal* 70:1–28.

_____. 1993. *The Partial Constitution.* Cambridge: Harvard University Press.

_____. 1984. "Naked Preferences and the Constitution." *Columbia Law Review* 84:1689–1732.

_____. 1982. "Public Values, Private Interests, and the Equal Protection Clause." *Supreme Court Review* 1982:127–66.

Swidler, Ann. 1986. "Culture in Action: Symbols and Strategies." *American Sociological Review* 51:273–86.

Symposium. 1996. "The Influence of Stare Decisis on Supreme Court Decision-making." *American Journal of Political Science* 40:971–1082.

Tanenhaus, Joseph, Marvin Schick, Matthew Muraskin, and Daniel Rosen. 1963. "The Supreme Court's Certiorari Jurisdiction: Cue Theory." In *Judicial Decision-Making*, ed. Glendon Schubert, 111–32. New York: Free Press.

Tate, Neal, and Roger Handberg. 1986. "The Decision Making of the United States Supreme Court, 1916–1985: A Three-Level Perspective." Paper, Annual Meeting of the APSA, Washington, DC.

Thernstrom, Abigail. 1987. *Whose Votes Count?* New York: Twentieth Century Fund.

Thomas, Kendall. 1993. "Corpus Juris (Hetero)Sexualis: Doctrine, Discourse, and Desire in *Bowers v. Hardwick.*" *GLQ: A Journal of Gay and Lesbian Studies* 1:33–51.

Thompson, E. P. 1975. *Whigs and Hunters: The Origin of the Black Act.* New York: Pantheon.

Thurber, James. 1991. *Divided Democracy.* Washington, DC: CQ Press.

Tocqueville, Alexis de. 1966. *Democracy in America.* Trans. George Lawrence, ed. J. P. Mayer. New York: Harper and Row.

Tomlins, Christopher L. 1985. *The State and the Unions: Labor Relations, Law, and the Organized Labor Movement in America, 1880–1960.* New York: Cambridge University Press.

Tribe, Laurence. 1987. *Constitutional Choices.* New Haven: Yale University Press.

Tribe, Laurence, and Michael Dorf. 1991. *On Reading the Constitution.* Cambridge: Harvard University Press.

Truman, David B. 1951. *The Government Process.* New York: Alfred A. Knopf.

Tushnet, Mark. 1988. *Red, White, and Blue: A Critical Analysis of Constitutional Law.* Cambridge: Harvard University Press.

_____. 1987. *The NAACP's Legal Strategy Against Segregated Education, 1925–1952.* Chapel Hill: University of North Carolina Press.

_____. 1974. " 'And Only Wealth Will Buy You Justice': Some Notes on the Supreme Court, 1972 Term." *Wisconsin Law Review* 1974:177–97.

Twiss, Benjamin R. 1942. *Lawyers and the Supreme Court: How Laissez-faire Came to the Supreme Court.* Princeton: Princeton University Press.

Uelman, Gerald F. 1987. "A Jurist to Fit Powell's Shoes." *Los Angeles Times,* November 22, pt. 2, p. 23.

Unger, Roberto M. 1986. *The Critical Legal Studies Movement.* Cambridge: Harvard University Press.

_____. 1976. *Law and Modern Society.* San Francisco: Free Press.

_____. 1975. *Knowledge and Politics*. New York: Free Press.

U.S. Census Bureau. 1996. *Statistical Abstract of the United States: 1996*. 116th ed. Washington, DC: Government Printing Office.

Vining, Joseph. 1986. *The Authoritative and the Authoritarian*. Chicago: University of Chicago Press.

Walker, Jack L. 1983. "The Origins and Maintenance of Interest Groups in America." *American Political Science Review* 77:390–406.

Warner, Michael, ed. 1993. *Fear of a Queer Planet: Queer Politics and Social Theory*. Minneapolis: University of Minnesota Press.

Warren, Charles. 1947. *The Supreme Court in United States History*. Vol. 1. Boston: Little, Brown, and Company.

_____. 1939. *A History of the American Bar*. New York: Howard Fertig.

_____. 1932. *The Supreme Court in United States History*. Vol. 2. Boston: Little Brown.

_____. 1913. "Legislative and Judicial Attacks on the Supreme Court of the United States—A History of the Twenty-Fifth Section of the Judiciary Act." *American Law Review* 47:1–34.

Wasby, Stephen L. 1984. *The Supreme Court in the Federal Judicial System*. 2d ed. New York: Holt, Rinehart and Winston.

Wattenberg, Martin P. 1990. "From a Partisan to a Candidate-Centered Electorate." In *The New American Political System,* ed. Anthony King, 139–74. Washington, DC: American Enterprise Institute.

Wechsler, Herbert. 1961. *Principles, Politics and Fundamental Law*. Chicago: University of Chicago Press.

_____. 1959. "Toward Neutral Principles of Constitutional Law." *Harvard Law Review* 73:1–35.

Wedgwood, Ruth. 1997. "Cousin Humphrey." *Constitutional Commentary* 14:247–69.

Wellington, Harry H. 1990. *Interpreting the Constitution: The Supreme Court and the Process of Adjudication*. New Haven: Yale University Press.

West, Robin. 1994. *Progressive Constitutionalism*. Durham, NC: Duke University Press.

Westin, Alan Furman. 1953. "The Supreme Court, the Populist Movement, and the Campaign of 1896." *Journal of Politics* 15:3–41.

White, G. Edward. 1997. "The 'Constitutional Revolution' as a Crisis in Adaptivity." *Hastings Law Journal* 48:867–912.

_____. 1996. "The First Amendment Comes of Age: The Emergence of Free Speech in Twentieth-Century America." *Michigan Law Review* 95:299–392.

_____. 1988. *The Marshall Court and Cultural Change, 1815–1835,* abridged ed. New York: Oxford University Press.

White, James Boyd. 1994. *When Words Lose Their Meaning: Constitutions and Reconstitutions of Language, Character, and Community*. Chicago: University of Chicago Press.

_____. 1990. *Justice as Translation*. Chicago: University of Chicago Press.

_____. 1985. *Heracles' Bow*. Madison: University of Wisconsin Press.

Whittington, Keith E. 1998. "Dismantling the Modern State? The Changing Structural Foundations of Federalism." *Hastings Constitutional Law Quarterly* 25: 104–44.

———. 1995. "Reconstructing the Federal Judiciary: The Chase Impeachment and the Constitution." *Studies in American Political Development* 9: 55–116.

Wiebe, Robert H. 1967. *The Search for Order, 1877–1920.* New York: Hill and Wang.

Williams, Patricia. 1991. *The Alchemy of Race and Rights: Diary of a Law Professor.* Cambridge: Harvard University Press.

Williams, Raymond. 1977. *Marxism and Literature.* Oxford: Oxford University Press.

Winch, Peter. 1958. *The Idea of a Social Science.* London: Routledge and Kegan Paul.

Wirt, Frederick M. 1970. *The Politics of Southern Equality: Law and Social Change in a Mississippi County.* Chicago: Aldine.

Wolfe, Christopher. 1991. *Judicial Activism.* Belmont, CA: Brooks/Cole.

———. 1986. *The Rise of Modern Judicial Review.* New York: Basic Books.

Woll, Peter. 1977. *American Bureaucracy.* 2d ed. New York: Norton.

Wood, Gordon. 1969. *The Creation of the American Republic, 1776–1787.* Chapel Hill: University of North Carolina Press.

Woodward, Bob, and Scott Armstrong. 1979. *The Brethren.* New York: Random House.

Yudof, Mark C. 1990. "Equal Protection, Class Legislation, and Sex Discrimination: One Small Cheer for Mr. Herbert Spencer's Social Statics." *Michigan Law Review* 88:1366–1408.

Zaller, John. 1992. *The Nature and Origins of Mass Opinion.* New York: Cambridge University Press.

Zemans, Frances Kahn. 1983. "Legal Mobilization: The Neglected Role of the Law in the Political System." *American Political Science Review* 77:690–703.

Zoebel, Karl M. 1959. "Division of Opinion in the Supreme Court: Reevaluating the Interest Group Perspective." *Cornell Law Review* 44:186–214.

CASES CITED

Abrams v. Johnson. 1997. 65 U.S.L.W. 4478.
Adarand Constructors, Inc. v. Pena, Inc. 1995. 115 S. Ct. 2097 or 518 U.S.
Adkins v. Children's Hospital. 1923. 261 U.S. 535.
Akron v. Akron Center for Reproductive Health. 1983. 462 U.S. 416.
Allen v. State Board of Elections. 1969. 393 U.S. 544.
Arizona v. Fulminante. 1991. 499 U.S. 279.
Arizona Governing Committee v. Norris. 1983. 463 U.S. 1073.
Ashwander v. TVA. 1936. 297 U.S. 288.
Baehr v. Lewin. 1993. 74 Hawaii 645.
Baker v. Carr. 1962. 369 U.S. 186.
Beal v. Doe. 1977. 432 U.S. 438.
Boerne v. Flores. 1997. 117 S. Ct. 2157.
Bowers v. Hardwick. 1986. 478 U.S. 186.
Bradwell v. Illinois. 1872. 83 U.S. 130.
Brown v. Board of Education of Topeka. 1954. 349 U.S. 483.
Buckley v. Valeo. 1976. 424 U.S. 1.
Burlington Industries v. Ellerth. 1997. 118 S. Ct. 2257.
Bush v. Vera. 1996. 517 U.S.
Caban v. Mohammad. 1979. 441 U.S. 380.
Califano v. Goldfarb. 1977. 430 U.S. 199.
Califano v. Webster. 1977. 430 U.S. 313.
Califano v. Westcott. 1979. 443. U.S. 76.
Capitol Square Review Board v. Pinette. 1995. 115 S. Ct. 2440.
Carey v. Population Services. 1977. 431 U.S. 678.
Carter v. Carter Coal Co. 1936. 298 U.S. 238.
Church of Lukumi Babulu Aye v. City of Hialeah. 1993. 508 U.S. 520.
City of Richmond v. J. A. Croson Co. 1989. 448 U.S. 469.
Clinton v. Jones. 1997. 117 S. Ct. 1636.
Clinton v. New York. 1998. 118 S. Ct. 2091.
Cohens v. Virginia. 1821. 6 *Wheat.* 264.
Colorado Republican Campaign Committee v. FEC. 1996. 116 S. Ct.
County Commission v. Umbehr. 1996. 116 S. Ct. 2342.

281

County of Washington, Oregon v. Gunther. 1982. 452 U.S. 161.

Craig v. Boren. 1976. 429 U.S. 190.

Cruzan v. Missouri. 1990. 497 U.S. 261.

DAETC v. FCC. 1996. 116 S. Ct. 2374.

Doe v. Bolton. 1976. 429 U.S. 190.

Dombroski v. Pfister. 1965. 380 U.S. 479.

Dothard v. Rawlinson. 1977. 433 U.S. 335.

Dred Scott v. Sanford. 1857. 19 Howard 393.

Eisen v. Carlisle & Jacquelin. 1968. 391 F. 2d 555.

Eisenstadt v. Baird. 1972. 405 U.S. 438.

Fiallo v. Bell. 1977. 430 U.S. 313.

Flast v. Cohen. 1968. 392 U.S. 83.

Florida Bar v. Went For It. 1995. 115 S. Ct. 2371.

Franklin v. Gwinnett County Schools. 1992. 112 S. Ct. 1028.

Frontiero v. Richardson. 1973. 411 U.S. 677.

44 Liquormart v. Rhode Island. 1996. 116 S. Ct. 1495.

Fullilove v. Klutznick. 1980. 440 U.S. 448.

Furman v. Georgia. 1972. 408 U.S. 238.

G.E. v. Gilbert. 1976. 429 U.S. 125.

Gentile v. State Bar of Nevada. 1991. 111 S. Ct. 2720.

Gregg v. Georgia. 1976. 428 U.S. 153.

Griggs v. Duke Power Co. 1971. 401 U.S. 424.

Griswold v. Connecticut. 1965. 381 U.S. 479.

Grove City v. Bell. 1984. 465 U.S. 555.

Harris v. Forklift Systems, Inc. 1993. 114 S. Ct. 367.

Heckler v. Matthews. 1984. 465 U.S. 728.

Hishon v. King & Spaulding. 1984. 467 U.S. 69.

Hoyt v. Florida. 1961. 368 U.S. 57.

Immigration and Naturalization Service v. Chadha. 1983. 103 S. Ct. 2764.

J.E.B. v. T.B. 1994. 114 S. Ct. 1419.

Johnson v. Transportation Agency. 1987. 480 U.S. 616.

Kirchberg v. Feenstra. 1981. 450 U.S. 455.

Kiryas Joel Village v. Grumet. 1994. 114 S. Ct. 2481.

Ladue v. Gilleo. 1994. 114 S. Ct. 2038.

Lamb's Chapel v. Center Moriches Free School District. 1993. 113 S. Ct. 2141.

Lee v. Weisman. 1992. 505 U.S. 577.

Lehr v. Robertson. 1983. 463 U.S. 248.

Lemon v. Kurtzman. 1971. 403 U.S. 602.

Lochner v. New York. 1905. 198 U.S. 45.

Los Angeles Department of Water and Power v. Manhart. 1978. 435 U.S. 702.

Maher v. Roe. 1977. 432 U.S. 464.

Marbury v. Madison. 1803. 1 Cranch (5 U.S.) 137.

McCleskey v. Kemp. 1987. 481 U.S. 279.
McCulloch v. Maryland. 1819. 4 Wheat. 315.
McGautha v. California. 1971. 402 U.S. 183.
McNamara v. San Diego County. 1988. Docket #87-5840.
Meinhold v. Department of Defense. 1993. 114 S. Ct. 374.
Meritor Savings v. Vinson. 1986. 477 U.S. 57.
Metro Broadcasting Inc. v. FCC. 1990. 492 U.S. 547.
Michael M. v. Sonoma County. 1981. 450 U.S. 464.
Miller v. Johnson. 1995. 515 U.S. 900.
Mississippi University for Women v. Hogan. 1982. 458 U.S. 718.
Mistretta v. United States. 1989. 488 U.S. 361.
Mobile v. Bolden. 1980. 446 U.S. 55.
Morrison v. Olson. 1988. 487 U.S. 654.
Nashville Gas v. Satty. 1977. 434 U.S. 136.
Nebbia v. New York. 1934. 291 U.S. 502.
New York v. United States. 1992. 505 U.S. 144.
New York Times v. United States. 1971. 403 U.S. 713.
Newport Shipbuilding v. EEOC. 1983. 462 U.S. 669.
O'Hare Trucking v. Northlake. 1996. 116 S. Ct.
Oregon v. Smith. 1990. 494 U.S. 872.
Orr v. Orr. 1979. 440 U.S. 268.
Paulussen v. Herion. 1985. 54 U.S.L.W. 4313.
Planned Parenthood v. Danforth. 1976. 428 U.S. 52.
Planned Parenthood of S.E. Pennsylvania v. Casey. 1992. 505 U.S. 833.
Plessy v. Ferguson. 1896. 163 U.S. 537.
Poelker v. Doe. 1977. 432 U.S. 519.
Price Warehouse v. Hopkins. 1988. 490 U.S. 228.
Printz v. United States. 1997. 117 S. Ct.
Quillon v. Walcott. 1978. 434 U.S. 246.
RAV v. St. Paul. 1992. 505 U.S. 377.
Reed v. Reed. 1971. 404 U.S. 71.
Regents of the University of California v. Bakke. 1978. 438 U.S. 265.
Reno v. ACLU. 1997. 117 S. Ct. 2329.
Reynolds v. Sims. 1964. 377 U.S. 533.
Richmond v. Croson. 1987. 488 U.S. 469.
Roe v. Wade. 1973. 410 U.S. 113.
Romer v. Evans. 1996. 116. S. Ct. 1620.
Rosenberger v. University of Virginia. 1995. 515 U.S. 819.
Rostker v. Goldberg. 1981. 453 U.S. 57.
Rust v. Sullivan. 1991. 111 S. Ct. 1759.
Scott v. Sanford. 1857. 19 Howard 393.
Shaw v. Reno. 1993. 509 U.S. 630.

Sherbert v. Verner. 1963. 374 U.S. 398.

South Carolina v. Katzenbach. 1966. 383 U.S. 301.

Stanley v. Illinois. 1972. 405 U.S. 645.

Stanton v. Stanton. 1975. 421 U.S. 7.

State v. Hall. 1968. 385 U.S. 98.

Steffan v. Aspin. 1993. DCCA 8 F. 3d 57.

Taylor v. Louisiana. 1975. 419 U.S. 522.

Terry v. Reno. 1997. 520 U.S. 1264.

Terry v. United States. 1997. 72 F3d 125, cert. Denied 134 L. Ed. 2d 651.

Texas v. Johnson. 1989. 491 U.S. 397.

UAW v. Johnson Controls. 1991. 111 S. Ct. 1196.

United Jewish Organizations of Williamsburgh, Inc. v. Carey. 1977. 430 U.S. 144.

United States Term Limits, Inc. v. Thornton. 1995. 514 U. S. 779.

United States v. Curtiss-Wright Export Corporation. 1936. 299 U.S. 304.

United States v. Eichman. 1990. 496 U.S. 310.

United States v. Lopez. 1995. 514 U.S. 549.

United States v. National Treasury Employees.Union. 1995. 115 S. Ct. 1003.

United States v. Nixon. 1974. 418 U.S. 418.

United States v. Robertson. 1995. 115 S. Ct. 1732.

United States v. Virginia. 1996. 116 S. Ct. 2264.

University of California v. Bakke. 1978. 438 U.S. 265.

Wards Cove Packing Co. v. Antonio. 1989. 109 S. Ct. 2115.

Washington v. Glucksberg. 1997. 117 S. Ct. 2258.

Webster v. Reproductive Health Services. 1989. 492 U.S. 490.

Weinberger v. Weisenfeld. 1975. 420 U.S. 636.

Wengler v. Druggists Mutual Insurance. 1980. 446. U.S. 142.

Wesberry v. Sanders. 1964. 376 U.S. 1.

West Coast Hotel v. Parrish. 1937. 300 U.S. 379.

Witherspoon v. Illinois. 1968. 391 U.S. 510.

Wygant v. Jackson Board of Education. 1986. 476 U.S. 267.

Zobrest v. Catalina School District. 1993. 509 U.S. 1.

CONTRIBUTORS

JOHN BRIGHAM is a professor of political science at the University of Massachusetts, Amherst. He is the author of *Constitutional Language* (1978), *The Cult of the Court* (1987), and *The Constitution of Interests* (1996). He is a Fellow of the International Institute for the Sociology of Law.

SUSAN BURGESS is associate professor of political science and director of the Center for Women's Studies at the University of Wisconsin, Milwaukee. She is the author of *Contest for Constitutional Authority: The Abortion and War Powers Debates* (1993). She is currently working on a new book, *Who Killed Politics? A Constitutional Mystery.*

KEITH J. BYBEE, assistant professor of government at Harvard University, is the author of *Mistaken Identity: The Supreme Court and the Politics of Minority Representation* (forthcoming). His current research examines the jurisprudence of affirmative action, tracing its historical linkages to legal realism and political science theories of interest-group pluralism.

CORNELL CLAYTON is an associate professor of political science at Washington State University. He is the author of *The Politics of Justice* (1992) the editor of *Government Lawyers: The Federal Legal Bureaucracy and Presidential Politics* (1995), and the coeditor (with Howard Gillman) of *Supreme Court Decision-Making: New Institutionalist Approaches* (1999). His current work focuses on the relationship between law and broader political institutions in structuring the role of the Supreme Court.

JOHN B. GATES teaches political science at the University of California, Davis. He is the author of *The Supreme Court and Partisan Realignment* (1991) and coeditor and contributor to *American Courts: A Critical Assessment* (1991). He received a Ph.D. from the University of Maryland.

HOWARD GILLMAN is an associate professor of political science at the University of Southern California. He is the author of *The Constitution Besieged: The Rise and Demise of Lochner Era Police Powers Jurisprudence* (1993), which received the C. Herman Pritchett Award for best book in public law from the Law and Courts section of the American Political Science Association. His current work focuses on the origins of modern civil liberties jurisprudence and on the influence of philosophical pragmatism on modern constitutional theory.

LESLIE F. GOLDSTEIN, Unidel Professor of Political Science and International Relations at the University of Delaware, is the author of *In Defense of the Text: Democracy and Constitutional Theory* (1992), *The Constitutional Rights of Women: Cases in Law and Social Change* (1988), and *Contemporary Cases in Women's Rights* (1994). She is currently at work on a book on sovereignty in federal unions.

MARK A. GRABER is an associate professor of government at the University of Maryland. He is the author of *Transforming Free Speech* (1991), *Rethinking Abortion* (1996), and numerous articles on constitutional law, history, theory, and politics. He is presently working on a political history of judicial review.

RONALD KAHN is the James Monroe Professor of Politics and Law and director of the Law and Society Program at Oberlin College, Oberlin, Ohio. He is the author of *The Supreme Court and Constitutional Theory, 1953–1993* (1994). He is presently working on a book on the role of social, economic, and political facts in Supreme Court decision making.

MICHAEL McCANN is professor of political science at the University of Washington. He is the author of *Taking Reform Seriously: Perspectives on Public Interest Liberalism* (1986) and *Rights at Work: Pay Equity Reform and the Politics of Legal Mobilization* (1994). He currently is working on a book about changes in legal strategies, rights claims, and group identities among unionized workers in the United States over the last half century.

KEVIN T. McGUIRE is associate professor of political science at the University of North Carolina, Chapel Hill. He is the author of *The Supreme Court Bar: Legal Elites in the Washington Community* (1993). His articles on lawyers and interest groups and on agenda setting in the U.S. Supreme Court have appeared in a variety of scholarly journals.

MARK SILVERSTEIN is professor of political science at Boston University. He is the author of *Constitutional Faiths* (1984) and *Judicious Choices* (1994), and a coauthor (with Lief Carter, Austin Sarat, and William Weaver) of *New Perspectives on American Law* (1997).

INDEX

and legal community, 8, 117, 118–27,
128–32
legitimacy, 58, 81–82, 155, 163
in literature, 63
and modernism, 151
as naked power organ, 208–10
original jurisdiction, 24, 43, 57
overturned decisions, 44, 100
and partisan change, 99–102, 105–12
and partisan conflict, 102–5
and policy, 53, 76, 98, 99, 102, 112–13,
115, 155, 156, 178–79, 187, 195(n2)
(*see also under* Judicial review)
and political context, 2–3, 4, 5, 6, 7–9,
10, 16, 18, 19, 23, 59, 64, 83, 88,
152–53, 154–55, 176, 219–20, 231
(*see also* Constitutive power; Judicial
review; Strategic interaction)
and political economy, 236, 237 (*see
also* Capitalism)
pragmatism, 151
scholars, 1, 2–3, 16, 66, 152, 235–36,
251
social and cultural context, 2, 4, 5, 7, 9,
21, 24–25, 43, 82, 88–91 (*see also*
Social facts)
staff, 115
and statutory interpretation, 178–79,
189
term, 230
See also Congress; Constitutional interpretation; New institutionalism;
Presidency
"Supreme Court and American Capitalism, The" (Lerner), 237
Sutherland, George, 74

Taft, William Howard, 19
Takings jurisprudence, 237
Taney, Roger B., 104, 236
Taney Court, 84, 236
Taranto, Richard, 121
Taylor v. Louisiana (1975), 182

Television, 170
*Tempting of America, The: The Political
Seduction of the Law* (Bork), 207
Tenth Amendment, 173, 174, 175
Term limits, 174
Terry, Randall, 111
Terry v. United States (1997), 174
Texas, 105
Texas v. Johnson (1989), 160, 169
Textualism-originalism, 154, 159
*Theory of Liberty, A: The Constitution and
Minorities* (Hirsch), 44
Thernstrom, Abigail, 225–26, 227
Thomas, Clarence, 23, 110, 111, 137,
146(n4), 158, 161, 166, 174
as conservative, 159
Thompson, E. P., 91
Thornhill v. Alabama (1940), 250
Thurmond, Strom, 157
Title 7. *See under* Civil Rights Act
Tocqueville, Alexis de, 83, 219
Tort class action, 139
"Toward Neutral Principles of Constitu-
tional Law" (Wechsler), 199, 207,
208–10
Tribe, Laurence, 141
Truman, Harry, 71
Tushnet, Mark V., 244

UAW v. Johnson Controls (1991), 179,
185
Ulmer, Sidny, 1
Unemployment benefits, 168
Unions, 72, 75, 83–84
*United Jewish Organizations of Williams-
burgh, Inc. v. Carey* (1977), 229
U.S. Sentencing Commission, 172
U.S. Term Limits, Inc. v. Thornton (1995),
174
United States v. Carolene Products (1938),
237, 247, 250
United States v. Curtiss-Wright (1936), 74,
75